© 1987 GAYLORD

Deniza D. Martin
Collection

THE LAST STUARTS

THE LAST STUARTS

British Royalty in Exile

James Lees-Milne

Charles Scribner's Sons
New York

First published in the United States by Charles Scribner's Sons 1984

Copyright © 1983 James Lees-Milne

Library of Congress Cataloging in Publication Data
Lees-Milne, James.
  The last Stuarts.

  Bibliography: p.
  Includes index.
  1. Stuart, House of.   2. Great Britain—Kings and
rulers—Biography.   3. Great Britain—Queens—Biography.
4. Great Britain—Princes and princesses—Biography.
5. Exiles—Biography.   I. Title.
DA306.S83L43 1984   941.06'092'2 [B]   83-20413
ISBN 0-684-18147-9

1 3 5 7 9 11 13 15 17 19   F/C   20 18 16 14 12 10 8 6 4 2

Printed in the United States of America.

Not all the water in the rough rude sea
Can wash the balm from an anointed king
King Richard II, III, ii

CONTENTS

ILLUSTRATIONS

ACKNOWLEDGEMENTS

I offer my humble thanks to Her Majesty the Queen for graciously permitting me to consult the detailed card index to the voluminous Stuart papers at Windsor Castle. I am much beholden to Her Majesty's Librarian, Sir Robert Mackworth-Young, and Chief Archivist, Miss Jane Langton, for their counsel and help.

To the following I am much indebted: His Grace The Duke of Beaufort for permission to have photographed and reproduced his portrait at Badminton of the young Princess Louise of Stolberg-Gedern; Lord Braye for allowing me to examine his collection of Stuart portraits and relics; the late Prince Alfons Clary for explaining to me Princess Louise's complicated family relationships and antecedents; the late Mrs Clara Louise Dentler for giving me hitherto unpublished particulars of the weddings of Prince James Edward and Prince Charles Edward; Mr Brinsley Ford for bringing to my notice Dr Moore's letter to the Duchess of Hamilton and the splendid portrait by Blanchet of the Cardinal Duke of York; and for consent to reproduce the latter the Earl of Moray, in whose possession it is; the late Donald Nicholas for allowing me access to his incomparable collection of late Stuartiana, to read some unpublished manuscripts and make use of his unrivalled knowledge of the uncrowned Stuart claimants; the Earl of Oxford and Asquith for letting me consult the papers of his ancestor, Sir John Coxe Hippisley; Mr Jock Murray-Threipland for showing me his inherited Stuart relics; and Mr Gilbert Wheat for entertaining me so hospitably in South Uist.

For various kind acts and helpful advice I am also very grateful to Monsignor John Brewer of the Ven. Collegio Inglese, Rome; Mr D. J. C. Crawley, late Minister to the Holy See; Captain and the Hon.

Mrs Humphrey Drummond of Megginch; Mr Brian Fothergill; Mr Hugh Honour; Professor J. P. Kenyon; the late Miss Georgina Masson; Miss E. D. Mercer, Head Archivist, The Greater London Council; Viscountess Mersey; Sir Oliver Millar; Mr Frank Simpson of the Paul Mellon Centre; the late Mr Henry Hornyold Strickland of Sizergh; Lieut-Colonel I. B. Cameron Taylor; the Rev. Henry Thorold; and Sir Anthony Wagner.

Finally I am specially grateful to my friends in Chatto & Windus, Norah Smallwood and Jeremy Lewis, for their unfailing co-operation and patience. Also to Mr Douglas Matthews for his professional index.

If, after the lapse of ten years since these essays on *The Last Stuarts* were written, I have omitted the names of any persons to whom I owe thanks for favours rendered, may they please forgive me.

J. L-M.
19 Lansdown Crescent,
Bath.

DRAMATIS PERSONAE

KING JAMES II Deposed 1688. Died 1701 in exile.

QUEEN MARY BEATRICE, or Mary of Modena, wife of James II and mother of James Francis Edward. Died 1718.

JAMES FRANCIS EDWARD, Prince of Wales until 1701. Thereafter King James III (known as The Old Pretender). In 1708 called himself the Chevalier of St George. In correspondence with Jacobites he bore numerous cant names. Born 1688. Died 1766.

PRINCESS CLEMENTINA (SOBIESKA), QUEEN OF JAMES III. Married 1719. Died 1735.

CHARLES EDWARD, usually called Prince Charles (The Young Pretender). After the Forty-five he adopted several different titles. On his father's death in 1766 he became King Charles III, but on the Vatican refusing to acknowledge his sovereignty he was styled Count of Albany. In correspondence he was given innumerable cant names. Born 1720. Died 1788.

HENRY BENEDICT, called Prince Henry before being made Cardinal in 1747. Thereafter known as Cardinal Duke of York, or Cardinal of York. Although after 1788 he considered himself King Henry IX he was still referred to as Cardinal of York. Born 1725. Died 1807.

PRINCESS LOUISE OF STOLBERG-GEDERN, Queen of Charles III. After her husband's death in 1788 she was often referred to as Princess Louise but usually as Countess of Albany, always signing her name 'Louise d'Albanie.' Married 1772. Died 1824.

CHARLOTTE, illegitimate daughter of Prince Charles and Clementina Walkinshaw. Created by her father in 1784 Duchess of Albany, and died 1789, aged 36.

I

FAMILY BACKGROUND

The ill-fortune which pursued the Stuarts throughout the centuries is so well-known that it hardly needs recapitulating. If we look at the lineage of the last uncrowned Stuart sovereign, Henry IX, what ancestral spectres do we encounter? His father James III, as Prince of Wales and King, in exile for seventy-eight years. His grandfather, James II, twice exiled, to die overseas. His great-grandfather, Charles I, beheaded. His great-great-great grandmother, Mary Queen of Scots, beheaded and great-great-great grandfather Darnley murdered. Mary's grandfather, James IV of Scotland, killed on Flodden Field. That king's father, James III, murdered. James II killed by accident. His father, James I, murdered. Scarcely a record to make a man with pretensions to a throne feel optimistic. The Stuarts' bad luck was indeed proverbial long before their royal line was extinct. Voltaire acknowledged that if anything could justify superstitious people believing in an unavoidable fatality it would be the continuous succession of misfortunes which for more than 300 years had dogged and, while he wrote, were dogging this dynasty. Louis XVI suspected that they were possessed of the evil eye. He was alarmed. 'The Stuarts are an unlucky family; I wish to hear no more of them,' he remarked with a shrug which, alas for him, could not shake their contagion – and they were cousins – from his shoulders. Chateaubriand recognized the effects of it. Writing after the extinction of the legitimate Stuart line in 1807 he noted that 'the fatality attached to the Stuarts dragged with them in the dust other kings, among whom was Louis XVI.' He went on to refer to the three so-called 'pretenders' – James II's son and two grandsons – who for 119 years of exile refused to renounce the shadow of the English crown. 'They had

I

intelligence and courage; what did they lack?' he asked, and answered his own question, 'The hand of God'.

That certainly was the general belief of their contemporaries. It was, too, the unshakeable belief of the 'pretenders' themselves. It was the absolute conviction of James II. The God of their fathers, the God for whom they had sacrificed the honours and the lands which by every constitutional right were theirs, was deliberately withholding from them their divine deserts. What had they done, what grave faults had they committed to merit the inexorable retribution assigned to them? That was the fearful problem which day and night tormented these wretched people, and which without remission harassed their souls until the close of their lives.

'They had intelligence.' That was only partially true. Chateaubriand was certainly careful not to include James II within the meaning of this phrase. I think he was right to omit him. For James's besetting fault was a singular lack of wisdom. Unfortunately too for his prospects James was a man of principles. On his return, when Duke of York, to the Catholic church of his fathers, which had been abandoned by Henry VIII less than one hundred years before his birth and with which probably the majority of his voiceless subjects still secretly sympathized – for the traditions of centuries die slowly – James's belief in the divine right of kings became deeply entrenched. In an address to the University of Cambridge in 1681 he declared, 'We will still believe and maintain that our Kings derive not their title from the people but from God; that to him only are they accountable; that it belongs not to subjects, either to create or censure, but to honour and obey their sovereign . . .' This strange dogma which to our incredulous minds is at worst totally unacceptable and at best slightly ridiculous, was something to be seriously reckoned with in the seventeenth century. Certainly it formed part and parcel of the Stuart philosophy so long as the first four monarchs of the dynasty were reigning in England. And it was to remain more than a figment of the philosophy of James II's rightful heirs all through the eighteenth century, down in fact to the early nineteenth century and the death of the last claimant, Henry IX.

Opposition to the divine right of kings, and so monarchical absolutism, was the very basis of Whig antagonism to the Stuart cause. The Whigs, as every schoolboy knows, won the contest.

William III, and after a decade's interval George I, were used as constitutional pawns for a different form of absolutism, namely Whig oligarchy. If the majority of the old Tory party continued to sympathize secretly with the Stuart cause so long as there remained a shred of likelihood that the Stuarts might return, belief in divine right was one cogent reason. However not all the Tories believed in it even during the reign of Queen Anne. Bolingbroke and Swift, for instance, both poured ridicule upon the doctrine. But other Tories, no less intelligent and more sound in judgment than these two unstable men of genius, did not. For example, the anonymous contemporary author of *The History of the Rebellion of 1745-6* described Jacobites as people who believed in 'the hereditary indefeasible right of the Princes; a right inalienable from their persons and families by any abuse of power or exercise of tyranny'. And as late as 1763 Boswell recorded an astonishing incident at dinner in Bennet Langton's house one evening. That pillar of Toryism Samuel Johnson, in a benign and paternal mood, apropos of nothing took his host's young niece by the hand and said to her, 'My dear, I hope you are a Jacobite.' The uncle with some warmth asked his guest what he meant by such a question. 'Why, sir,' said the doctor, 'I meant no offence to your niece; I meant her a great compliment. A Jacobite, sir, believes in the divine right of kings. He that believes in the divine right of kings believes in a divinity. A Jacobite believes in the divine right of bishops. He that believes in the divine right of bishops believes in the divine authority of the Christian religion.' I do not suppose that the doctor in giving vent to this rather debatable exegesis necessarily had his tongue in his cheek.

A concomitant of the doctrine of divine right was the traditional touching for the king's evil, or scrofula, a swelling of the throat and neck glands. This supranatural power to cure was supposedly first practised in England shortly before his death by St Edward the Confessor and traditionally reserved to his descendants. It was exercised by English medieval sovereigns in varying degrees of conviction down to and including Henry VII.

With the renewed emphasis upon the doctrine of divine right under the Stuarts belief by loyal subjects in the practise of touching was much encouraged. In 1633 a special office was inserted in the Prayer Book after the Thirty-Nine Articles. After the Restoration touching was widely regarded as a highly therapeutic treatment. Abundant cures were claimed from Charles II. The number of applicants became so large that the doctors were obliged to examine all patients beforehand to make sure that they were suffering from the evil, and not malingering. Soon the treatment was extended to all manner of sores which sometimes were so unsightly that the doctors hid them from the king's view. It is not surprising to learn that, having at one sitting in the Banqueting House stroked the faces of 600 persons with both his hands, Charles decided on future occasions merely to apply to the wounds a special gold or silver talisman, called a touch piece, which ever since Edward III's reign had been minted for distribution to the sufferers after the ceremony. Charles regarded the office of touching with much seriousness and performed it with a becoming gravity. Indeed on his walks in St James's Park sick persons would often seize the king's hand and apply it to their hideous ulcers. It is remarkable – and perhaps some affirmation of his hereditary miraculous powers – that Charles never caught a disease from these multitudinous physical contacts. He is said to have touched between 105,000 and 106,000 persons between 1660 and 1686.*

James II, who carried on the practice extensively both during and after his reign, regarded it as his singular and sacred prerogative. It is hardly surprising then that touching was spurned as gross superstition by William of Orange after his acquisition of the crown. 'May God give you better health and more sense,' he remarked caustically to one sufferer who besought him to lay hands upon his swollen glands. Queen Anne however revived it, perhaps to assert her hereditary claim to the throne, although it is highly doubtful that she believed in it. The boy Samuel Johnson was one of those who knelt before her. George I declined to practise touching, presumably for the opposite reason to Anne's, namely reliance upon his popular instead of divine right to rule. He even recommended a child sufferer from scrofula to approach the Old Pretender. The child did so and was promptly cured. The service of touching was henceforth omitted from Georgian prayer books. James Edward Stuart was seen to touch at Glamis Castle in 1715 and again at Lucca in 1722 with singular devotion and earnestness. Charles Edward, who was the least devout

* John Evelyn gives a graphic account of Charles II touching on 6 July 1660.

of the later Stuarts, touched a child in Edinburgh in 1745 saying, 'I touch, but God heals,' and again at Albano in 1786. The Cardinal King Henry touched frequently and had numerous touch pieces minted.*

This seeming digression into the dogma of the divine right of kings and its chief manifestation in the gift of touching for the evil has an extremely important bearing upon our understanding of the Stuarts' monarchical principles and the Jacobite creed. The Stuarts' irrefragable claim through the grace of God to the throne of England, Scotland, Ireland and indeed France, and their supernatural powers of healing were the absolute belief of James II, as they had been of his elder brother, and were to be of his posterity in the legitimate succession. The remainder of James's life after 1688 and the whole of those of his son and two grandsons were thrown into utter confusion by the nation's disavowal of their divine sovereign rights, coupled with their jealous retention of divine curative power. That their subjects chose to repudiate this claim and power, the dispossessed Stuarts regarded as a sort of blasphemy on the part of mankind. It accounted for the tragic disillusion of their several existences.

If the victorious Whigs would not have James II they certainly would not have his son and heir on his father's terms. This they made abundantly clear from the start, indeed one may say before the start. For although the Prince of Wales's birth took place on 10 June 1688, strong opposition to it was manifested several months before it happened. The warming pan canard is an extraordinary instance of predetermination not to believe in an event which was undeniable.†

It may be true that there is seldom smoke without fire; but it is not true that there is always fire with smoke. There were reasonable grounds for questioning whether Queen Mary Beatrice of England could again be pregnant after an interval of six years, during which time she had been in wretchedly poor health. For the Queen, having had since her marriage in 1673 four children who died in infancy and two miscarriages – the last in 1682 – had by 1688 been written off by

---

* As recently as 1901 a handkerchief stained with the Cardinal King's blood was believed in Ireland to be capable of curing scrofula.

† It was of course only one of several infamies invented by the Whigs. Others were that the Catholics had started the Fire of London in 1666, and that Charles II had been married to Lucy Walters. The Titus Oates Plot and the Rye House Plot were both engineered by the Whigs.

the English as incapable of motherhood. And, it must be admitted, James's chances of becoming a father again were considered unlikely. The gossips whispered that this philanderer of over fifty years of age was riddled with the pox. The Comte de Gramont hinted as much in his memoirs; and anonymous tracts of a scurrilous kind proclaimed it out loud. One of them sought to prove that James's incapacity to reproduce was 'owing to the infirmity of the male agent, the disease supposed having a natural designation against the generative faculties . . . the above said is yet more corroborated, his not having for these many years past any [children] by his Misses, who are more apt than the Queen, and with whom t'is more probable he has a greater Gust.'

Evidently the King had no such misgivings. In August of 1687 he made a special pilgrimage to St Winifred's holy well in North Wales to importune the saint (a curious choice considering how this virgin had met martyrdom rather than submit to carnal intercourse) to present him and his wife with an heir. In November he accompanied the Queen to Bath where she splashed about in the efficacious waters while musicians played to her from the wings. The King's determination to beget a son, by hook or by crook as it were, was interpreted by malicious persons as suspicious.

At all events, as early as 5 December 1687 the ambassadors at the court of St James's were reporting in dispatches home that the Queen was pregnant. Lord Ailesbury in close attendance upon the royal family, affirmed that there were no doubts whatever that she was. On the 15th Evelyn noted in his diary that prayers were being said in the London churches for a happy outcome of her Majesty's pregnancy. On 1 January 1688 Lord Clarendon, James's brother-in-law, recorded in his diary that the Queen was quick, and on the 15th of the same month that a thanksgiving service was held in St James's church, Piccadilly. On 14 March the Princess Anne, the King's daughter, with her habitual bitchiness towards the stepmother who had always been kind to her, wrote complaining to her sister the Princess of Orange that Mary Beatrice while undressing had refused to let her feel her big belly. 'Quite the contrary, whenever one talks of her being with child she looks as if she were afraid one would touch her. And whenever I happen to be in the room as she has been undressing she has always gone into the next room to put on her smock.' Hardly surprising! In actual fact the Queen had been obliged to throw a glove at her stepdaughter for her impertinence, an incident which Anne was not going to forgive in a hurry. 'Her being so positive it will be a son,' Anne went on, 'and the principles of that religion being such that they will stick at nothing, be it never so wicked, if it will promote their interest, give some cause to fear there may be foul play intended.' In other words that a supposititious birth may be imposed by the Papists upon the nation.

James getting to hear of these ugly slanders, regaled them in his guileless way to Anne, little guessing that his beloved daughter was herself spreading, if she was not inventing them. At first he treated them as a bad joke. At Easter, and again in May, Mary Beatrice fell very ill. Then a month later she found herself in labour before she expected it. She happened to be in London. The royal apartments in Whitehall were for some reason out of commission, it having been anticipated that the birth would take place at Windsor. Hastily a room in St James's Palace was chosen, oddly enough a small room, no preparations having been made in advance. One hour and three quarters before the birth a warming pan was slipped into the beautiful canopied bed. Speedily the Privy Council was summoned, and as many as could get to the palace gathered to witness the birth. According to the barbarous custom of the time they crowded and jostled to get as close a view of the proceedings as possible. Professor Kenyon calculates that twenty-nine people, fifteen women and fourteen men, Protestant and Catholic alike, were cooped in a small bedroom in which, although it was midsummer a coal fire was kept burning, for nearly an hour. The Queen's labour pains were terrible, not to mention her discomfort through lack of air. But her chief concern was one of modesty. She begged the King to hide her face with his head and periwig even though much of her person had to be exposed to public gaze. The foetid atmosphere and smell in the room were overpowering. It is thought that the windows were purposely kept shut for mistaken health notions. Before midday on Trinity Sunday, 10 June, the Prince of Wales was born. The child was immediately rushed by a nurse to an adjacent room where it was washed and robed. When the King was notified that the baby was a boy he was so transported with joy that he hugged to his bosom the Modenese agent, Gaspard Rizzini, who happened to be present. By the time Lord Clarendon reached the palace, which was after dinner, 'I found the King shaving . . . He said the Queen was so quick in her labour, and he had so much company, that he had not time to dress himself till now. He bid me go and see the prince.'

James's joy was short-lived. The Ambassador from the Holy Roman Emperor had in April written to his master giving his opinion that the birth of a Prince of Wales would, in the present mood of England, be fatal to the King. And so it proved. But for a few weeks the father and mother gave vent to jubilation. The Prince and Princess of Orange were notified. They ordered prayers to be said for the Prince of Wales in Holland. They sent Count Zuylesteyn to convey their congratulations. After delivering them the emissary promptly met the seven rebellious Whig lords who were in process of framing a message to William to come over in person and seize the throne. Meanwhile Anne, who had not been present at the birth because she was taking the waters in Bath, was busily writing to Mary her disbelief in the child's parentage. Bishop Burnet, who was then at the Hague, added his voice to Anne's protestations which, because of his absence abroad, he was in no position whatever to corroborate.

By the end of June the seven lords' letter of invitation had been dispatched to William. The Prince on receiving it began drafting a declaration to the English people, giving the supposititious birth as his chief reason for invading their country. Never can so blatantly hypocritical a reason have been offered in excuse for so callous an injury. When it finally dawned upon the slow-witted King that the genuineness of his son's birth was seriously questioned by reputable people he was appalled. On the political situation becoming critical in October he desperately called a Privy Council. Those who had witnessed the Queen's pregnancy and those who had attended the birth in that crowded chamber in June were commanded to give evidence on oath as to the truth. By November their signed depositions were made public. The necessity for these measures was deeply wounding to James's sense of honour, and humiliating to his pride of parenthood. The conclusion of the evidence was a complete denial of the fabrication. Mrs Dawson the chief midwife who with her own hands delivered the child, although a Protestant and pumped by spies and bribed to perjure herself, asserted categorically that the birth was genuine. She had seen the fire in the only warming pan which had been put in the bed nearly two hours before the birth. One female witness had seen the child attached to the umbilical cord. Other witnesses had seen the milk running from the Queen's breasts. The Duke of Berwick, a man of incontestable honour and a signatory, swore till his dying day that the birth was genuine. As for the derisory charge that a newly-born baby not the Queen's had been smuggled into the bed in a warming pan, Swift disposed of it in a very convincing manner. 'The warming pan is no feasible project, unless you break the back of the child to put it in; moreover as this is supposed to be a tender infant, just reeking and wet from it's mother's womb, in that tender state, it would either have cried out in the passage or have been stiff and dead, and in the variety of motions of tossing it up and down, it would have been a perfect jelly,' – which the Prince, although born blue in the face, never was.

Nevertheless the unanimity of the witnesses' denial was interpreted by James's enemies as another Papist plot. Tracts containing the most preposterous charges continued to be published until Queen Anne's reign. No stories were too fanciful or incredible in the persistent attempt to damage the Jacobite cause.

The perfectly legitimate offspring of the royal union was baptized according to the full rites of the Catholic Church openly and brazenly. In no circumstances whatever would his parents compromise one jot or tittle of what they deemed to be orthodox procedure in order to assuage the susceptibilities of others – in this case the tender conscience of their Protestant subjects – and incidentally to keep their throne. At the christening ceremony Pope Innocent XI, who had in his worldly wisdom counselled James II not to impose Catholicism upon a reluctant nation, was persuaded to be represented as a sponsor, and the Dowager Queen Catherine to be a godmother in person. The baby prince was given the names James after his father, Francis after his grandfather the Duke of Modena and St Francis Xavier, and Edward after the Black Prince and the Confessor. Within a week the minute fist of this sickly infant, whose face was a mass of pimples, had been kissed unenthusiastically by the mayor and corporation of the City of London. For the prognostications of those hardy advocates of the warming pan canard that, whether the child was or was not supposititious, then it must by the nature of things – his mother's leukemia, his father's pox – be doomed to an early grave, seemed destined to be fulfilled. James Francis Edward, already created Prince of Wales, was on the point of death, not apparently from hereditary causes but from colic induced by the crass stupidity of the royal doctors. They insisted, according to a report of the Tuscan envoy, Terreiri, upon feeding him with a nauseating gruel, a sort of paste compound of barley flower and oatmeal, sugared currants and canary wine. On this concoction proving unpalatable they prescribed 'Dr Goddard's drops', which were composed of God knows what in addition to a distillation of hartshorn, the skull of a person hanged, dried viper and raw silk. So strong were the drops that 'if one falls on a piece of cloth it burns a hole through in half an hour.' Alarming symptoms were the consequence, vomiting, diarrhoea and general debility, to the amazement of the assembled physicians.

The King to his credit saw at once that all the child needed was, not surprisingly, ordinary woman's breast milk. He took matters into his own hands. He dismissed the profession and, contrary to their advice, quickly procured a wet nurse, thus saving the infant's life and giving rise to innumerable charges that this woman was the child's real mother by every sort of father except the King.

Hardly had these measures been taken before William of Orange's invasion fleet reached Torbay and James's Dutch son-in-law was marching towards London. Arrangements were hastily made for the Queen and her infant son to escape to France. In drenching rain they left St James's Palace and were driven to Gravesend whence they sailed, storm-tossed to Calais. It is miraculous that the child on reaching the château of Saint-Germain-en-Laye (put at the disposal of the English royal family by Louis XIV) was, at the age of six months, alive at all. He did not in fact grow up a healthy boy. Nor was he ever to be a healthy adult in spite of living to an advanced age.

On 11 December James slipped out of the back door of the Palace on the tracks of Mary Beatrice and the Prince. During his passage down the Thames occurred the dramatic incident beloved by every historian. With solemn deliberation the King dropped the Great Seal of England into the river. The action was intended to signify that no one on earth had power to divest him of his divine authority. But the quirks of fate are unpredictable. The seal was, by an extraordinary chance, retrieved by some fishermen who to their surprise caught it in their net.

For nearly thirteen years the exiled monarch lived with his small family and an ever-increasing number of Jacobite dependents in strict retirement at Saint-Germain-en-Laye, a small town twelve miles to the west of Paris and within easy reach of Versailles. Apart from the abortive Irish campaign of 1689–90 to regain his lost kingdoms, a campaign which James, prematurely broken and senile, felt honour-bound to undertake, he never left the gloomy castle perched above a wide sweep of the Seine. As the years closed upon him he subsided into a state of contented spirituality, spending hours of the day and night on his knees, and finally collapsing at Mass in the castle chapel.

The moment the last breath was out of James II's body on 16 September 1701, Louis XIV had the Prince of Wales proclaimed King of England, Scotland and Ireland (but not, it is interesting to note, France) at the gates of Saint-Germain. The herald, as though to make sure that the whole of Europe must understand the import of his message, delivered it in Latin, French and English. Louis had promised the dead King, his cousin, that he would make the proclamation in defiance of the terms of the Treaty of Ryswick (1697) in which he had been compelled against his will to acknowledge William as King of England and Anne as his successor. Saint-Simon was not alone in stressing that the precipitate words caused more prejudice in Great Britain against the Stuarts than all the past abortive efforts by James II to regain his throne by means of the sword – the invasion of Ireland, the defeat of the Boyne and the rout of the French and Jacobite fleet off Cape La Hogue. The seeming treachery of Louis to William and the interference of a foreign autocrat in English domestic affairs merely stiffened English resistance and rallied the Protestants in support of the Prince of Orange's asserted rights. An attempt by some Jacobite mock-pursuivants in London to proclaim the Stuart prince incensed the populace far less – it merely pelted them with rotten eggs – than the French monarch's presumptuous declaration. Parliament at Westminster was provoked to bring in a Bill of Attainder against Prince James Edward and to pass the Act of Settlement of 1701 whereby the Electress Sophia should succeed to the throne after the death of Anne. By 1701 James Edward Stuart's chances of ever being recalled to England by his own subjects seemed remote. He was just thirteen years of age.

Until he reached his majority in 1706 the young prince continued to live in the gloomy household of Saint-Germain under his mother's jealous supervision and the strict tutelage of a series of Jacobite Governors, for the most part worthy and educated but, as is the nature of old exiled noblemen, inward-looking and feeding on past memories. No individual, who was not a royal relation or a Governor, was allowed to address a word to him. His only communication with the outside world was through the court of Versailles, with whom his mother constantly exchanged visits. And God knows that court's connection with the outside world was remote enough. The single companion of his childhood, his younger sister, the pretty and beloved little Princess Louise Marie, died in 1712 of smallpox. No wonder that 'the blackbird', as they toasted him at St Germain on account of his dark eyes and swarthy complexion, grew up to be a solemn and melancholy youth.

Although the prince's abortive expedition to the Firth of Forth in 1708 – he was prevented from landing by adverse winds and the timidity of the French admiral – alienated whatever sympathy his half-sister Queen Anne may secretly have cherished for his ultimate succession in spite of the Act of Settlement, at least it brought about his break with Saint-Germain,* the bickering, spying, and intriguing Jacobite courtiers, and the Jesuit-dominated Queen Mother, Mary Beatrice. At the age of twenty James Edward was his own master. Although congenitally pacific the young prince wisely volunteered to enlist in the army of his well-wisher, Louis XIV, and fought gallantly against the English at the Battles of Oudenarde (1708) and Malplaquet (1709). The consequence of these two French defeats was that Louis was put under strong pressure by England to expel James Edward from French territory. He became a wanderer and lived a hand to mouth existence for short periods in hiding at Montpellier, Toulouse and Bordeaux before being received in 1712 out of pity by the reigning Prince of Lorraine, rubicund, stout, amiable Prince Leopold, who gave him a residence at the château of Bar-le-Duc. It

---

* His mother, Queen Mary Beatrice, went on living at the Château of Saint-Germain-en-Laye until her death in 1718.

was from this gay and attractive little city that he left for the ill-fated expedition of 1715.

The accession of George I as King of England on 1 August 1714, the very day that Queen Anne expired, happened so clandestinely, so smoothly, so suddenly that time passed before the Jacobites realised the full horror of it. In fact once again the Stuarts' luck was out. Had the Chevalier* been nearer at hand than Lorraine, events might have been quite different. The Duke of Hamilton, one of the most far-seeing and reliable of the Scottish Jacobites had evolved a scheme for the Chevalier to come to Scotland, there to await Anne's death, and thence to descend upon England immediately, Scotland being deemed closer to London than Hanover. But this scheme was thwarted by the Duke's death in a duel. Had the Duke of Ormonde†, the recognized Jacobite leader in London whose influence with the army he commanded was immense, not lacked resolution, and had he been more heroic, had the Tories with their overwhelming majority the previous year only revoked the Act of Settlement when they had the chance, and had only a few other trifling accidents occurred, the Chevalier's chances might have prevailed. As it was the few active Tory peers, overcome by surprise at the turn of events, either escaped pell-mell abroad or were put in the Tower. Rebellion fizzled out before it took fire.

The moment the news of his sister's death reached him at Bar-le-Duc, the Chevalier rushed incognito to Paris to see Louis XIV. But on being informed that the King could do nothing to help him he returned disconsolately to Lorraine. All he then did was to issue a manifesto protesting against the Elector of Hanover's usurpation while describing himself as 'the only born Englishman now left of the royal family'. The response of the English government to this gesture was to put £100,000 upon his head, and of the exultant Whigs to issue a mock-manifesto. The skit purported to be 'sent by post from Pombières the 29th day of August 1714 being the 14th year since the

---

* The Chevalier of St George was the title by which Prince James Edward proclaimed his arrival in the Firth of Forth in the Expedition of 1708. It was thus that he was referred to by many adherents in Great Britain.
† The Jacobite 2nd Duke of Ormonde proved a broken reed on successive occasions. Affable, respected and popular though he was, he wanted the qualities of leadership.

first thoughts of our heart ascended into our head'. It went on to proclaim that 'the present King was born in Germany and is unacquainted with the laws and customs of these Kingdoms. Whereas we ourselves was born (once, if not twice) in our own country and continued there until our age of eight months or thereabouts by which we became early acquainted with the Genius of the people and the customs of the Country . . .' The surest way to kill your enemy's pretensions is not by indignation or retaliation, but by ridicule.

The Chevalier's half-brother, the Duke of Berwick,* had also counselled him before Anne's death to cross boldly to London, throw himself upon her sisterly mercy, insinuate himself into her affections and by a process of charm-shock prevail upon her to announce to Parliament that he was her heir. Now had only James Edward been Charles Edward when he was twenty-five this quixotic method would have been readily undertaken. Moreover it might have worked. But James Edward was not abounding in charm, and was besides a cautious man. Had he been prevailed upon to undertake so hazardous a move he would undoubtedly have blundered. Yet Berwick was an eminently practical fellow. In giving this particular piece of advice he was allowing himself to be misled or deceived by Lord Oxford, Anne's Lord High Treasurer, with whom he was then intriguing for a Stuart succession, and showed a lack of his customary good sense. He showed still less in advising his half-brother to change his religion. He was constantly advising him to take one step or another, to marry a relation of the Emperor, to improve his handwriting – 'a strange scrawl' the Chevalier admitted – or to be more demonstrative in his friendships: 'Methinks that you should caress people, and not always speak of duty.' He evidently considered it a brotherly privilege to be outspoken. He was indeed a blunt man, caring little whether or not he caused offence. 'A great dry devil of an Englishman who always goes his own way,' is how the Queen of Spain once described him.

In his boyhood James looked up to Berwick as a hero. From 1712 until the break in their friendship in 1715 the brothers carried on a confidential correspondence. Sometimes they wrote to each other in English, sometimes in French. 'I beg your Majesty's pardon for

---

* Illegitimate son of James II by Arabella Churchill.

having writt part of this letter in french,' Berwick said on the 19th of March 1713, 'but I did not perceive it till half was writt, and reading your letter which is in french made me mistake.' His influence became more and more pronounced. Although Catholic in upbringing and by profession, Berwick was a free-thinker in religion and a liberal in politics. He held no brief for the Tory party, although he was the Chevalier's principle link with them. He disliked his brother's Catholic entourage and the Secretary of State, Lord Middleton, in particular. It was largely owing to Berwick's pressure and that of the Protestant advisers that the Chevalier dismissed Middleton in December. This was a mistake. Middleton was in fact a Compounder, and his judgments were never extreme. With him Sir David Nairne resigned as Under-secretary of State. Thus the Chevalier lost two of his most level-headed servants just at the time when they were most needed.

The 1715 invasion was as much the contrivance of Berwick as of anyone else. And it was unfortunate for the Chevalier that his half-brother fell so completely under the spell of the least responsible, most devious, most brilliant Tory of the age, Henry St John, Viscount Bolingbroke. In March 1715 Bolingbroke, having been dismissed from office by George I, was obliged to flee from England at a moment's notice. After attending a performance at Drury Lane theatre he made a lightning dash to the coast disguised in a black wig and with blackened eyebrows. In April he turned up in Paris where he straightway assured Lord Stair, the British Ambassador to France, of his loyalty to George I. Nevertheless he struck up an immediate friendship with Berwick who, realizing that here at hand was the cleverest, God-given instrument any man could desire, introduced him without loss of time to the Chevalier in Bar. James Edward was likewise attracted, only to a lesser degree, by Bolingbroke's charm and ability, and although suspicious of his motives from the first, willingly accepted his offers of service. In July he made him his Secretary of State and created him an Earl.

Never were two collaborators more different in temperament than Bolingbroke and the Chevalier. The one was brilliant, scoffing, cynical and unscrupulous. The other humdrum, serious, straightforward and honourable. For a while the Chevalier was dazzled by the meteor which had so unexpectedly crossed his vision. The two men in uneasy partnership concocted plans for the 1715 invasion, while Berwick having effected their introduction, withdrew from the fray. This was a disastrous sequel. Berwick's common sense, powers of mediation and military genius were exactly what was most needed by his half-brother. The Chevalier rather naturally had assumed that Berwick, now acknowledged to be one of the greatest generals of the age, would be the commander-in-chief of his expedition. But Berwick excused himself on the plausible grounds that since 1703 he had been a naturalized Frenchman and could not serve his brother without the Regent, Philip of Orleans' consent, which was not forthcoming. He reminded the Chevalier that for this same reason he had been unable to join the 1708 expedition. Indignantly the Chevalier riposted that in 1708 Berwick was absent in Spain on military duties, whereas now he was free. As his sovereign, James commanded his service. Berwick resolutely refused to obey. Whereupon the Chevalier lost his temper, and for the first time in his life gave vent to base sentiments to, of all people, Bolingbroke. On 24 November he remarked in a letter, 'I shall write to him [Berwick] no more, and must suffer the humiliation of courting a disobedient subject and a bastard too.' It was a caddish remark, quite uncharacteristic of its author. We need not be surprised that for years the brothers were not on speaking terms.

There is reason for supposing that the Chevalier had always been a trifle resentful of Berwick's fraternal manner of speaking and a little suspicious of his superior wisdom. He warned Secretary Dicconson never to show any of his letters to Berwick. He was more at ease with Berwick's son, the Duke of Liria, who became a great favourite. Liria, who was eight years his junior and did not presume on their blood relationship, was besides a most lovable man. He became a naturalized Spaniard and married a Spanish duchess in her own right. Liria had no hesitation in joining his uncle in the 1715 expedition. But he did not possess his father's qualities of leadership. Throughout the Fifteen the Chevalier conspicuously lacked a general of ability. The major cause of the expedition's failure can be attributed to Berwick's unfortunate defection.

Until he actually set sail for Scotland the Chevalier leaned more upon Bolingbroke than any other adherent. Cyphered letters of appeal for advice from the former and of advice given by the latter flew post haste between Bar-le-Duc and Paris. 'Your Majesty must

16

link unto your own cause that of the Church of England, of the Tory party, and of your sister's memory,' Bolingbroke wrote on 24 October. 'Others may perhaps represent things to you as they want them, but I shall, as long as I have the honour to serve you, represent them as they are.' It is worthy of note that he never made a condition of his help that James Edward should change his religion, although he was later to complain that the prince was entirely governed by priests. If this had been his opinion in 1715 then he might have pointed it out to his master. He did not do so. Plans for the rising of the ill-fated Fifteen were rendered more complicated by the entry into the Jacobite scene of another highly controversial figure, John Erskine, the 6th, 11th or 23rd Earl of Mar (the genealogists do not seem to be sure which), and more difficult of fulfilment because Mar was in Scotland at the time.

'Bobbing John' as he was called by his enemies – and they were legion – had been Secretary of State for Scotland under Queen Anne. He was short of stature and a trifle deformed. The Master of Sinclair called him the son of 'a notorious whore whose figure did not give her merits enough to gaine by her trade, so that he profited nothing of her but the hump he has got on his back, and her dissolute, malicious, medling spirite.'* In 1713 he advocated repeal of the Union. On the accession of George I he was, not surprisingly, snubbed by the new monarch who turned his back on him at a levée. In pique Mar resolved to opt for the Stuart cause. His motives have been variously interpreted, but a study of his correspondence and an assessment of his ultimate misfortunes through Jacobite involvement must leave a conviction in the mind of impartial critics that they were on the whole genuine. Devious he undoubtedly was, and at intervals when his services to the Chevalier were shelved, he displayed questionable methods of obtaining redress for himself, his family and his estates. As far as his personal interests were concerned he was finally unsuccessful for he was to die in exile, impecunious, stateless, rejected by his legitimate sovereign and reviled by the majority of Jacobites. His was an unenviable lot.

From Scotland then Mar corresponded with James Edward and Bolingbroke. To the first his letters are couched in an off-hand style,

---

* The 'notorious whore' was Lady Mary Maule, a daughter of the 2nd Earl of Panmure.

which can be taken as honest John stuff, or double dealing. I prefer to take the charitable view because a sincere devotion to the Chevalier is detectable in those letters which were to continue long after the Fifteen had failed. At all events the Chevalier came to repose unquestioning confidence in Mar, which transcended his confidence in either Berwick or Bolingbroke while they were in favour, and lasted far longer. Unfortunately, whatever conflicting views may be held as to Mar's character, only one can be reached as to his capacities for organization. He was an incorrigible muddler.

On 27 August 1715 Mar, having left London in dudgeon, summoned Huntley, Tullibardine, Nithsdale, Panmure and some other prominent chiefs of clans to an ostensible 'hunting match' at Braemar. Emboldened by the successful celebrations and inebriated by days of loyal oaths and toasts Mar on the 6th of September, after making an eloquent and stirring speech, recklessly raised the Stuart standard on behalf of the Chevalier, who in fact had not been consulted, and proclaimed him James VIII of Scotland and III of England. He then extolled the virtues of the young king in a somewhat hysterical fashion, holding before the chiefs a portrait of their royal master which he 'kissed frequentlie with the appearance of more than ordinarie affection.' The impropriety of the action was evident. He was, it must in fairness be conceded, unaware that five days previously Louis XIV, the Chevalier's guardian, most consistent European champion and purveyor of pensions in spite of the terms of the Utrecht Treaty (1713) which had been forced upon him, had died. He was succeeded in the government of France by the ambitious, cautious, cunning and lecherous Regent Philip of Orleans,* moved by no romantic obligation to espouse his cousin's cause which he saw as hopeless in face of the stringent clauses in the Treaty of Utrecht, binding him not to do so. He instantly resolved not to finance and equip an invasion force.

No leader with fewer qualifications could have arisen on his own authority than Mar. It was a disastrous self-elevation. The success of the rebellion depended, apart from leadership, upon funds and arms.

* The Duc d'Orleans was as unprincipled in his private as in his public life. His lechery was unrestrained and cynical. To his mother who protested against his promiscuity with all available women no matter how beautiful or hideous, he replied, 'Bah! maman, dans la nuit tous les chats sont gris.'

These were in process of being amassed in both Scotland and England, but they had not yet been assembled. Moreover the Braemar proclamation should have been followed by simultaneous risings in both countries. Bolingbroke had the intelligence to realize this. As it was the Duke of Ormonde had failed to raise the pre-arranged rebellion in the west country, and fled instead to France. One sentence of a letter from Bolingbroke to Mar dated 20 September in answer to Mar's request that the Chevalier ought at once to join him in Scotland, makes any further opinion of the writer on Mar's egregious folly redundant. 'I must therefore be of opinion that a more fatal conjunction can never happen and that the attempt can probably end in nothing but the ruin of our cause for ever.' Three days later the Chevalier wrote dolefully to Bolingbroke that every post was bringing bad news, 't'is all rowing against the tide.' Nevertheless he was determined to embark before the tide became more adverse. Not a propitious launching upon a perilous venture; nor a happy augury of future relations between sovereign and Secretary of State.

On 29 October a supper party was taking place at the Château de Commercy in Lorraine at which the Chevalier was present. To the disappointment of the assembled guests he retired early with a fit of the ague. His host, the Prince de Vaudémont, made excuses for him. But instead of going to bed the invalid, having changed clothes with one of his entourage, galloped off to Paris. Lord Stair's spies soon got wind of his flight and instantly set off in pursuit. Stair coolly planned to have him assassinated on the road. James Edward was only saved from death by the postmistress of Nonancourt, where he had stopped to bait his horses, who overheard the plot. In pity for the poor young gentleman she directed him down side lanes. By this means he avoided falling into an ambush. He reached Paris in safety, masquerading as an abbé in a violet cassock. Berwick would not credit the story that Stair had contrived any such plot on the curious grounds of his being a gentleman. But there is evidence that one Kelly, an Irishman, was hired by the ambassador to murder the Chevalier in Bar. James hereafter always went in fear of assassination, and not without reason.

On 8 November the Chevalier, now disguised as a servant, reached St Malo, where he was joined by Ormonde. Delayed by contrary winds they deemed it wiser not to loiter longer in this seaport, and rode to Dunkirk where they picked up 200,000 crowns sent by Philip V of Spain. The money was put on board a shallop which, having set sail, was promptly shipwrecked. The hoard was salvaged by English sailors. For over a month the party skulking in Dunkirk received conflicting directions from Berwick and Bolingbroke as to where they were to sail. First it was to be the west of England, then the west of Scotland. Finally, Ormonde embarked for the west of England. He landed at Plymouth but finding no support forthcoming, returned to France. Not for the first or last time he achieved nothing. The Duke's secretary, by name Maclean, had in fact betrayed the intended rising to the Whigs in advance of Ormonde's expedition which was duly awaited. On 16 December the Chevalier, now dressed as a common sailor (the different disguises had been recommended by Bolingbroke), set sail in a ship of 200 tons. Having eluded the English fleet he landed on the 22nd of December at Peterhead, then a dismal little fishing harbour on the extreme eastern point of the Buchan coast of Scotland, with five or six companions. He was carried ashore on the shoulders of a Captain Park. One of his companions, Lieutenant Cameron instantly rode to Perth to spread the glad tidings of the Chevalier's arrival. At Peterhead James Edward was greeted with two pieces of news. The first was that his army was not composed of 10,000 men, as he had been led to expect, but a mere 3,000. The second that the battles of Sheriffmuir and Preston had taken place the previous month.

In fact both encounters occurred within two days of each other, and both were disastrous for the Jacobite cause. Sheriffmuir was a drawn battle in which the slaughter of both sides was terrific. 2,000 raw Highlanders and an equal number of Marlborough's veterans clashed together in a typhoon of metal. On the bleak moors, encircled by distant rolling hills, there was no shelter beyond a few scattered groves, belts of stunted fire trees and the long coarse grasses swept by the November wind. Locked together, whole companies of English and Scots destroyed each other practically to a man within minutes. Mar, who should easily have carried the day, withdrew unaccountably to Perth, thus missing the opportunity of advancing through Stirling to the English border. His excuse was that he was not ready for a further engagement and was hourly expecting the arrival of the Chevalier with money and ammunition. While Sheriffmuir was being waged a gallant little Border army under Lords Derwentwater, Nithsdale and Kenmure, joined by General Forster's Northumberland rebels were marching into Lancashire. At Preston Forster ignominiously capitulated, and all the Jacobite leaders were captured. On reaching London they were paraded round the city by a jubilant mob carrying a warming pan at their head. Within months Derwentwater and Kenmure were executed. Nithsdale and the undeserving Forster escaped. The story of Nithsdale's get-away from the Tower of London is one of the most heroic Jacobite sagas. The dogged Lady Nithsdale, having pleaded to no avail with George I for her husband's life to the extent of being dragged on her knees across the audience chamber at Whitehall before she could be released from his coat tails, took matters into her own hands. She got permission for a last interview with her husband in his cell where, having changed clothes with him, she pushed him through the door to liberty. The aged Kenmure gallantly pleaded guilty and made no effort to save his life. Lord Derwentwater's end was poignant. This brave, constant, loving and lovable young man was offered his life if he would consent to abandon the Catholic Church. He stoutly replied that 'had he a thousand lives he would sooner part with them than renounce his Faith.' His tribute on the scaffold to the Chevalier was more than a mere gesture of loyalty. It was an expression of faith in his master's excellent qualities. Derwentwater referred to James Edward as 'him I had an inclination to serve from my infancy, and was moved thereto by a natural love I had to his person, knowing him to be capable of making his people happy'. His untimely death caused the Chevalier intense grief and weighed heavily upon his conscience. A generation later Lord Derwentwater's brother and heir was to suffer the same penalty for his participation in the Forty-five.

In an indiscreet, if understandable, aside Mar was overheard to say before the Chevalier's actual landing on Scottish soil that he now wished he would not come at all. His arrival was in fact too late. In other words either Mar had anticipated the rebellion too soon or the Chevalier's advisers across the channel had deferred it too long. Both parties were in fact to blame. In addition the Stuart ill luck had ordained that when the Chevalier did come, it was with insufficient money. Meanwhile the young prince, rather ill, very cold, disappointed by the bad news which was pouring in from all sides, but still full of courage and resolution, decided to move straight away from the inhospitable harbour of Peterhead. He passed through Aberdeen incognito. On 4 January 1716 he arrived at the Lord Marischal's house at Fetteresso near Stonehaven, where for a few days he waited for Mar and further information as to what he ought to do next.

From Fetteresso the Chevalier wrote his first letter since landing in Scotland. It was addressed to Lord Huntley, desiring him to capture Inverness and so secure the north. Lord Huntley did nothing except exclaim, 'Now there's no help for it, we must all ruin with him: would to God he had come sooner.' This discouraging echo of Mar's remark expressed the opinion shared by the majority of the Scottish Jacobites, and there is every reason to presume by the prince himself in spite of the brave show he was endeavouring to put up. Unfortunately he was not one of those people who find it easy to act a convincing part when a situation is near desperate. He looked and was profoundly disappointed. And his illness throughout the campaign was aggravated by the bitter northern weather to which he was unaccustomed. Worst of all he had no reliable counsellor to turn to for advice. At the gates of Fetteresso he was proclaimed king. To a small gathering of clergymen and magistrates he was obliged to make a short speech which aroused little enthusiasm.

After a severe attack of ague the Chevalier continued his southward march to Lord Panmure's house at Brechin, whence he wrote an urgent letter to the Pope begging to be sent without further delay the remainder of the money promised him from that quarter. From Brechin he struck south-west, halting en route at Glamis. He made a public entry on horseback into Dundee, and rested at Fingask Castle. At Scone he took up residence in the palace. Plans were set on foot for his coronation. They were not made brighter by the erroneous news that French ships conveying many officers and much gold had been lost on a sandbank off the coast of Fife. It was reported that on 19 January Lord Huntley had submitted himself to the Government's mercy, and that terrible reprisals were being taken by the Hanoverians in consequence of the Preston fiasco. The Chevalier wrote self-pityingly, 'For myself it is no new thing to be unfortunate.' Towards the end of January Perth was made the Jacobite headquarters and fortified by Mar. The Chevalier reviewed his troops, but did not mix with the soldiers. It was remarked that he was never once seen to smile. An anonymous eye-witness recorded that 'his speech was grave, and not very expressive of his thoughts, nor overmuch to the purpose.' He was in truth lacking in confidence and excessively shy when out of his element. He did not make a good impression upon his Scottish subjects who, not themselves the most light-hearted race, nevertheless found their new sovereign lugubrious. 'Some said the circumstances he found us in dejected him; I am sure the figure he made dejected us; and had he sent us but five thousand men of good troops, and never himself come among us, we had done other things than we have now done.'

The Duke of Argyll reinforced by English and Dutch troops advanced towards Perth. Whereupon Mar organized a retreat to Dundee. The Chevalier shed tears on evacuating Perth, only consenting to leave because he would not expose his brave men to inevitable defeat. From Montrose he despatched one final desperate bid to the French Regent for further help and arms, still sincerely meaning to hold out if it were remotely possible. But no relief was forthcoming. From Montrose the Chevalier did a thing which typifies his merciful disposition and also indicates his unsuitability to the profession of a warrior. He sent money to the general of the Hanoverian army which had defeated him, entreating him to distribute it among the inhabitants of those villages he had been forced by his officers to lay waste. At first he had refused to sign the officers' order and only consented when convinced of the disagreeable necessity. He was haunted by guilt for what he did. His conduct towards the enemy throughout the farcical campaign compares favourably with that of the English General Cadogan, after it. For although Cadogan's reprisals nowhere nearly reached the horror of Butcher Cumberland's after the Forty-five, he destroyed wholesale the dwellings of those Scots implicated in the rebellion. Apart from the unfortunate peers captured at Preston human lives were not sacrificed in mass by the English victors. Within eighteen months an Act of Pardon was passed, and only the clan Macgregor was outlawed for a hundred years.

On 15 February the Chevalier hurriedly embarked with Mar on board the *Marie Thérèse*, a French vessel of ninety tons, without informing the clans. They were by no means mollified on receiving their King's 'letter of Adieux to the Scotch' with its implication that he was deserting them for their own good. Nor was General Gordon of Auchintoul flattered by receipt of the Prince's full authority as Commander-in-Chief of non-existent forces to negotiate with the enemy on his behalf. The Highlanders did not at all appreciate what Sinclair termed his decision 'to leave his poor subjects the freedom of making terms for themselves'. After six days the *Marie Thérèse* anchored at Waldam near Gravelines. The Chevalier's first act on landing in France was to send two ships to help as many as possible of his Scotch adherents to escape abroad. He then proceeded to Paris where his situation was hardly happier than it had been in Montrose. He was deeply humiliated by his enforced return and the Regent's refusal to see him. He was left wretched by the plight of those Scottish people who had served and suffered for him. 'It is crushing to me,' he wrote to his friend the Duke of Lorraine, 'who would have thought myself to some degree content if I were alone in my misfortune but the death and misfortunes of others of which I am the innocent cause pierces my heart.'

The Chevalier's prospects in Scotland had from the moment of his landing been untenable. The prevailing opinion of contemporaries was that Mar had deliberately tricked him into coming over. Sinclair insinuated it, Bolingbroke – for what his opinion is worth – blazoned it abroad, and Berwick definitely affirmed it while attributing the failure of the actual campaign to Mar's hesitancy. He also blamed the Chevalier for leaving Scotland too precipitately without actually impugning his half-brother's courage. But Berwick likewise admitted that the lack of French arms made the failure inevitable from the start. For this reason Mar's hesitancy – and he was certainly not a general endowed with the gift of improvisation – may be partly excused.

In Paris the Chevalier discovered that Bolingbroke had in his cups betrayed his plans of campaign to one of his mistresses, who in turn had informed the government in Whitehall. In a letter of 5 March 1716, Mar wrote to General Gordon about Bolingbroke's disgraceful conduct. 'Some attribute it to negligence and others to a much worse reason . . . it is hard to think that negligence alone could have been the only reason.' The Chevalier was convinced it was not. On the same day he dismissed Bolingbroke from the Secretaryship of State while reviling him for his treachery in not forwarding information to him in Scotland, and for withholding money and ammunition. Bolingbroke may have had a case in protesting that several of his letters to Scotland were intercepted, but he could not clear himself of the baser charge of betrayal, the very charge which he had intemperately levelled at Mar. He is self-accused by his own correspondence. And nothing he subsequently wrote in his famous published *Letter to Sir William Windham*, a most disingenuous document intended to justify his loyalty to the Tory party, exculpates him from shameless opportunism. He claimed that he only engaged in the Chevalier's service in the Tory interest, and accepted the seals of office with reluctance. He finally condemned his own conduct with these words: 'the consideration of his [James's] keeping measures with him, joined to that of having once openly declared for him, would have created a point of honor, by which I should have been tied down, not only from ever engaging against him, but also from making my peace at home.'

Before the year 1716 was out Bolingbroke asked Stair to tender his services once again to George I. Not unnaturally they were rejected. Unfortunately Berwick, still blinded by the brilliance of his friend's intellect, rebuked the Chevalier for his unjust dismissal of Bolingbroke in what he called 'the most disgraceful manner'. He was underestimating the sense of honour in the one and the total lack of it in the other. Bolingbroke knew how to turn the tables against so simple a man as his erstwhile sovereign. He had the audacity to counter-accuse him of treachery. He proclaimed that the Chevalier on his return to France received him 'with open arms . . .' when all the time he intended to throw him over. 'No Italian ever embraced the man he was going to stab with greater shew of affection and confidence,' he wrote of their last interview. He gave vent to vitriolic criticism of the prince's blind subservience to the Church of Rome and reliance upon his stupid entourage, especially Ormonde, which completely unfitted him to govern a kingdom. 'The Pretender,' he wrote offensively, 'with all the false charity and real malice of one who sets up for devotion, attributes all his misfortunes to my negligence.' If indeed he did, can he have been entirely mistaken?

Having broken irrevocably with Bolingbroke the Chevalier, whose need for a prop and stay was absolute, transferred all his confidence to the man whose ill-considered action in Scotland had contributed to the failure of the Fifteen, but whose agreeable companionship in Scotland and in the confined cabins of the *Marie Thérèse* he had come to value. Mar was above all a positive character, and it was forcefulness which James Edward respected and needed to bolster his own indecisiveness. Mar was never behind hand with advice, and advice was what the prince craved. But unlike Bolingbroke whose brilliant mind flashed forth phrases that barely concealed mockery of the prince's slower understanding, Mar's superior intelligence did not make his master feel a fool. Although his opinions were forthright, and at times almost impertinent, they were couched in a paternal, near-affectionate manner which the younger man could not resent. The trouble was that James Edward tended to be exclusive with his favourites, monogamous in his friendships. The result was that he aroused intense jealousy and resentment of the reigning confidant among the rest of his entourage – the court of an exiled monarch is a closed, inward-looking society – who busily sowed in their master's mind seeds of suspicion. These suspicions ultimately grew to disillusion with the favourite's counsel, and even to conviction of his unworthiness. James Edward's relations with his favourites followed a familiar Stuart pattern. The course of Mar's fate was no exception to that of most Stuart protégés. It was made the more inevitable in that from the first he was intensely disliked by all the Jacobite leaders.

But in the spring of 1716 Mar's favour with the Chevalier was at its zenith. Having been created a duke he accepted on the 6th of April the Secretaryship of State, which he was to hold for three years.

The immediate question after the setback of the Fifteen was where was James Edward to go. As early as February of 1716 the prince had begged the King of Spain for asylum and pecuniary help. Neither one nor the other was forthcoming. Venice and the Papal States were at first ruled out because refuge in these territories would prejudice him in the eyes of his Protestant supporters in the British Isles. Switzerland, Flanders and even Sweden were considered. Since the Regent was now urging him without delay to leave France, where he had been obliged to land on the retreat from Scotland, he made off early in March for Lorraine. But even his old friend the Duke, whose wife was a daughter of the French Regent, dared not keep him in the Duchy. With reluctance and sadness the Duke was obliged to get rid of 'ce pauvre petit roi'.* It seemed therefore that no alternative to the Papal States presented itself. So on the invitation of the Albani Pope Clement XI, the poor little King set off on the 14th for Avignon. He arrived on 2 April and settled in the Hôtel de Serre where he was joined by Lord Mar and, to his embarrassment, by five hundred escaped Jacobites, who somehow had to be housed and fed.

The ensuing three years were about the most wretched of James Edward's existence. He was unwanted, under threat of assassination by agents of King George I, driven from his adopted country, a nomad, over-staffed and exceedingly poor. He had not yet reached the stage when he was to reconcile himself to permanent exile. He still felt impelled to strive to regain that crown which since the Fifteen seemed more elusive than ever before. The immediate years ahead of him were to be spent in futile intrigues with sympathisers in England for another invasion. Help from France, notwithstanding the Regent's overt reconciliation with George I, was not entirely ruled out. Help from Russia, then casting an acquisitive eye upon Hanover, was entertained. Help from Sweden was very nearly concluded when the sudden death in battle of King Charles XII (who had been at enmity with George I) put a term to hopes from that quarter. Meanwhile an ultimatum from Great Britain induced the Regent to threaten the Prince with expulsion from Avignon by force, although it was papal territory.

Pope Clement XI, always a steadfast supporter of the Stuart cause, finally offered the Prince and his court an asylum in Rome. Gratefully the young wanderer accepted. He had suffered a serious operation for fistula of the anus in the autumn of 1716, and until February 1717 was not fit to travel. On the 6th he left Avignon in a post-chaise, the citizens gathering to speed him on his journey for they had been charmed by his gentle manners and piety. He and his party ascended the Mont Cenis and crossed the Alps in appalling weather. Because he was not yet able to sit astride a horse he was carried in a chair while his coach, having been taken to pieces, was laden on mules. By the end of February he reached the royal castle of Moncalieri in Pied-

* He was thus described by the Marquis de Dangeau (1638–1720) in writing to the Duke. On refusing Queen Anne's request in December 1713 that he should get rid of the prince, the Duke described him as 'the most amiable of the human race, who only wants to be seen to be admired, and known to be almost adored.' (Dangeau, *Journal*)

mont where he stayed with his cousin Anne Marie, Duchess of Savoy. At Piacenza he was entertained by the Duke of Parma. At the beginning of March he was at Modena in the palace of his great-uncle, Duke Rinaldo d'Este. Here he fell deeply in love with the Duke's eldest daughter, Benedetta, who, he wrote to his mother, closely resembled her. It was a case of love at first sight, and James Edward asked the Duke of Modena for her hand. Rinaldo, fearful of offending George I, demurred and adopted an attitude of wait and see.

By way of Bologna and Imola James Edward reached Pesaro on 20 March. For two months he stayed in this small city set in a dead flat landscape which extended to the Adriatic. A palace infested with fleas and bugs, was put at his disposal by the Vice-Legate, Cardinal Davia. To add to these discomforts he was love-sick. His torments were not mitigated by the equivocal letters he received from his great-uncle Rinaldo. From Pesaro by way of Loreto in the Marche he arrived in Rome towards the end of May. Even now his peregrinations were not at an end. Although the kindly Pope Clement was at this time the only head of state prepared to give the Prince active succour, even he was obliged to heed the growing might of the Triple Alliance of England, France and Holland, formed to ensure the Hanoverian succession and to prevent the possible union of the crowns of France and Spain in the event of the sick Louis XV not surviving infancy. Having been deprived of large sections of the Papal dominions under the terms of the Peace of Utrecht, Pope Clement had to watch every step with caution in order to avoid their further diminution. As a temporary measure he arranged for James Edward to stay in the Palazzo Gualterio until a more permanent refuge could be arranged for him.

On 28 May the Prince wrote from Rome to Mar: 'I think my being here a dream, and I wish it were one, but alas, it is not.' He passed his time in sight-seeing. His observations were typical of the incurious tourist. 'St Peter's church passed all our expectations, and the statues of the Capital are exceeding fine . . . and indeed in less than a month more I can never see at leisure all that is to be seen.' A month more was just about what he did have. His aesthetic appreciation was never very keen. He soon became bored by painting and sculpture, agreeing with one of his suite who complained that the ancient statues of Rome were no better than old stones in his native Herefordshire. Music too at this time had little appeal for him.

Then Pope Clement XI proposed to the Stuart Prince that he should take up residence in the papal city of Urbino. The Chevalier of St George gratefully assented. Promptly Clement sent two decorators with a quantity of furniture to prepare the Gonzaga palace. Once a decision to move was made the Chevalier like all Stuarts, packed up and took to the road with great suddenness. At midnight on 4 July he and his large retinue drove out of Rome. Their first stop was at Caprarola. Their second at Soriano. On the 8th they were at Foligno. On a Sunday morning the procession of carriages wound slowly up the hill on which is perched the little city of Urbino, dominated by the dome and brick campanile of the cathedral and the pink and brown bulk of the ducal palace. The Chevalier was met at the great door of the palace in the piazza by an assembly of local nobles. At first the Chevalier was enchanted by what is, all things considered, perhaps the most magical, and most beautiful Renaissance palace in all Italy. But it was not on account of the incomparable setting overlooking the olive-draped hills of the Marche, or the poetry of Federico Montefeltro's architectural masterpiece that the English prince was pleased. He pronounced it the most 'convenient' of all the Italian palaces he had so far inhabited. Convenience is, one would suppose, the one quality which the Palazzo Ducale at Urbino conspicuously lacks. For the labyrinth of vast rooms, interminable passages, lofty vaulted ceilings, bare walls, brown polished tiled floors and the paucity of fireplaces (those that do exist being monuments of Renaissance carving) make it one of the chilliest winter residences imaginable, a fact the Chevalier was no doubt to discover another six months hence. But on his arrival at Urbino this July morning everything seemed bathed in sunshine. Soon indeed he was to complain of isolation from the great world of events, and intense loneliness. The society of a handful of dispirited and pessimistic Jacobite followers did little to dispel his natural gloom. The Chevalier found fault with the walks and drives limited by the steep hill on which the palace was set. In fine weather his sole outdoor recreation was to visit the Cappuccini monastery in the valley where he coursed hares with his 'two clever little Danish doggies' in the monks' orchard. On wet days he was reduced to playing battledore and shuttlecock in the empty galleries of the palace. He complained too of – what seems surprising – the lack of decent wine to drink.

As the autumn wore on the Chevalier wrote interminable letters to the distant friends and supporters from his desk either in the ravishing little cabinet wainscoted with *quattrocento* intarsia of perspective views and *trompe l'oeil* musical instruments, or from the open loggia between the slender pink towers with dunce cap turrets. High on his precipice of brick he would gaze between the turned balusters of the parapet across the rolling foreground, dotted with cypresses and mantled with groves of olives, through which the ribbon of a road twists out of view and twirls back again until lost in infinity. He would scan the bare scoriated hills in the middle distance behind which Modena and the object of his affection lay on the far side of the Apennines. The retreat was all too beautiful and melancholy for a youth of twenty-eight, the life too uneventful and empty. The days were punctuated by social gatherings which he attended with reluctance. Of an evening he would play a round or two of ombre with the ladies of Urbino, and when the dancing began he retired. Even the *Feats of Hercules* which were repeatedly performed for his delight during the carnival of 1718, soon palled. At first he was enchanted by the troop of performing acrobats who turned themselves into a pyramid of six, seven, eight tiers standing on the shoulders of those below, a single boy at the top finally turning a somersault. The Chevalier presented them with a silver bowl, which they promptly sold.

He was popular in Urbino. His court brought an interest to the duchy and it brought trade. The local nobility were gratified by having in their midst a king who happened to be young and who invariably conducted himself in a becoming manner, and was attentive to their customs. Like all Italians they approved of the rigid ceremonial which he observed. It was at times carried to absurd lengths, a word I use advisedly. For the English king would, on feast days, drive from the palace to the cathedral in a coach and six, escorted by his courtiers on horseback and attended by liveried postillions. The actual distance from the one door to the other was scarcely that from the back of the state coach to the leader of the six horses when harnessed, and could be covered on foot within less than a minute.

The great matter of moment at Urbino was the prince's marriage.

The Jacobites were eager for it. They considered it high time that a Stuart heir was produced. Only a year ago the Chevalier had expressed a disinclination to matrimony, and his mother Queen Mary Beatrice had felt obliged to make her son realise its absolute necessity. She wrote him a strong letter to that effect. Then he met and fell in love with his cousin Benedetta d'Este. Alas, any hopes he may still have harboured in her direction were dashed by a final, categorical snub from Modena. At all events this sad episode made him see the desirability of taking to himself a wife. Henceforth the long winter evenings at Urbino were largely occupied in discussing what suitable European princesses were available. Mary Beatrice wrote insisting that the bride for her son must be a Catholic. His closest advisers on the other hand disagreed, and counselled a Protestant princess. Discord between mother and son was the consequence.

Indeed ever since Prince James Edward came of age the difference of their respective attitudes to religion made it impossible for the two to live together in amity. Mary Beatrice, a pious and an undeniably good woman, was a bigoted Catholic. James Edward was not. On this account alone, even if the old Queen's health had allowed her to travel, the son, once settled in Urbino, did not invite her to join him. The last time he had taken his farewell of her was in 1712. Even in correspondence they continued to dispute, and towards the end of Mary Beatrice's life relations between the two reached a crisis. The prince abruptly dismissed her Almoner and Confessor, Father Lewis Innes, upon whose spiritual and temporal advice she had grown totally to rely. The reasons the prince gave were that Father Lewis made mischief between the Catholic and Protestant followers and between his mother and himself by his intransigent Catholic bias. His letter (dated the 28th February 1718 to the Abbé Gaillard, conveying the dismissal) reveals that members of the Church of England would have nothing to fear had they accepted the Chevalier as their legitimate sovereign. 'Alas!' it ran,

'all Catholics are not saints, and there are only too many among them who have still more ambition than true zeal. With such people the solid foundations of religion are little regarded; and when they think of the situation in which it has pleased Providence to put me, of the necessity under which I lie of giving them preference in posts, honours, etc., and of the little part they themselves will have in business, this great resemblance to the primitive church is unbearable to those who lack its true spirit . . . Who does not know the prudence and even charity with which the Protestants here behave towards the Catholics? Who does not know that there is no longer any question of my personal religion? . . . I am a Catholic, but I am a King, and subjects of whatever religion they may be, have an equal right to be protected. I am a King, but as the Pope himself told me, I am not an Apostle. I am not bound to convert my people otherwise than by my example, nor to show apparent partiality to Catholics, which would only serve to injure them later.'

These wise and cautious sentiments show better than any deductions historians care to make from his character to what degree he was prepared to relax the rigidity of his parents' political convictions without in any sense compromising his own religious beliefs. No one can ever deny that his faith was to remain steadfast. In fact his father's death-bed exhortation was always ringing in his ears: 'Never put the crown of England in competition with your eternal salvation.' And when in the spring of 1714 the Abbé Gaultier had written on behalf of Louis XIV's minister, de Torcy, now tired of Stuart dependence upon French hospitality, actually propounding the ultimatum – 'either you disguise your religion absolutely or change it entirely, to adopt that established by the laws of your country' – the Prince was horrified by its brutal cynicism.

When the news reached Urbino that Mary Beatrice had died at Saint-Germain the following May, having sent a message to her son of total forgiveness over the Father Lewis affair and the assurance that her love for him was in no way diminished, the Chevalier was so overcome by grief and remorse that he became seriously ill. Meanwhile schemes for the Prince's marriage went on being hatched at Urbino. Letters flew around the continent to different diplomats and agents who were asked for and sent their opinions on marriageable princesses in those countries to which they were accredited. Prince Louis of Baden had a daughter of thirteen, 'of the size we generally find in seven or at most eight.' She was 'little to a degree that it is not reasonable nor scarce natural for any man to think of her'. Her claims were dismissed. So too were those of Peter the Great's younger daughter. The fastidious Chevalier, on learning that the Czar habitually ate meat with his fingers, used no handkerchief and blew his nose into his hand, did not fancy her. Besides this child was only twelve. A Princess of Fürstenberg had a red nose and pustules, and was therefore scratched off the list. Her younger sister was 'a little lank about the hips'. Another candidate was the Princess of Hesse, but she had bad teeth and bad breath, defects about which the Chevalier felt strongly. He wrote to the Duke of Ormonde approving another princess, 'provided there is no stinking breath in the case, of which I desire you will previously enquire,' and yet another, 'provided she be not horrible'. He was fairly particular. He was assured that German ladies did not expect constancy, which however the Chevalier, being a pious and naturally monogamous man, was prepared to concede.

Meanwhile Charles Wogan, a dashing young Catholic Irishman of twenty-one, was at the Chevalier's instigation actually combing the petty German courts for a suitable wife. Wogan had taken part in the Battle of Preston in 1715 as a boy, and had been captured. He made a dramatic escape from Newgate prison to France. He immediately attached himself to Lord Dillon's private regiment and while stationed at Sélestat in Lorraine attracted the Chevalier's notice. The prince was fascinated by the young man's enthusiasm and craving for adventure. After having seen and reported on a number of further possible brides Wogan finally came upon the family of Prince James Sobieski at Ohlau in Poland. This Sobieski was the son of King John III of Poland, the famous conqueror of the Turks at the gates of Vienna in 1683. He and his family were under the suzerainty of the Emperor Charles VI, then in alliance with George I who was supporting his claims to the throne of Sicily. In January 1718 Wogan wrote to James Edward such ecstatic reports of the beauty and virtues of the eldest daughter Clementina, that the Chevalier sent James Murray, as representing his Protestant supporters, to make a formal request for her hand.*

* James Murray (1690–1770), 2nd son of 5th Viscount Stormont. As Secretary to Bolingbroke he became privy to all arrangements for the abortive Fifteen. As a young man he was bumptious and unpopular with the older Jacobites; but in his maturity became trustworthy and trusted. In 1721 he was created Earl of Dunbar by the Chevalier. He spent his last years with his widowed sister, Lady Inverness, in Avignon.

Miss Peggy Miller, in *A Wife for the Pretender*, has recounted in full detail the romantic story of the little princess's journey from Ohlau, her arrest by the Emperor's orders, incarceration at Innsbruck, her abduction by Wogan and eventual arrival in the Papal States. On 2 September the Chevalier and Clementina met at Montefiascone, a small town at the foot of the Apennines and a little to the south of Lake Bolsena. Without further ado they were married in an upstairs chapel of the cathedral.

Clementina Sobieska was just seventeen. She already spoke Polish, German, French, Italian and English with ease. In other respects she was insufficiently educated, and her mind was as empty as a sparrow's. At this age she was still a sweet-tempered child, inclined to be wilful. She was undoubtedly pretty and delicate with, according to Wogan's description of her, light brown hair and black eyes. Her complexion was fair and her features were lively. Hers were the sort of looks which do not long survive adolescence. She brought her husband a large dowry – Prince James Sobieski was by no means poor – of 25 million francs and the famous Sobieski treasures. They included the gold shield given by the grateful Emperor Leopold I to Clementina's grandfather King John, and the historic trophy of victory over the Turks which had been converted into a state bed. The bed's hangings were made from the curtain embroidered with gems which had traditionally draped the standard of the Prophet. The framework of the bed was inlaid with silver. What eventually happened to these particular treasures I have failed to ascertain.

The newly wed couple turned leisurely for Rome. Here they were acknowledged by Pope Clement XI as reigning sovereigns, given a papal guard of troops who accompanied them wherever they went, and treated with every honour. The Pope settled upon them a generous pension. He had already put at the Chevalier's disposal, before his marriage, the Palazzo Muti which stands at the north end of the Piazza Santi Apostoli. As things turned out the assignment of the Palazzo Muti to the Stuart family was extended for at least seventy years. Thither the bridal cortège proceeded.

The Palazzo Muti was to be the Roman home until their deaths of both the uncrowned King and Queen of England. It is not among the most distinguished of Rome's palaces. As baroque palaces go it is small and unpretentious. The main façade of three bays, pedimented windows and a porch with balcony, is plain but dignified. In spite of the palace forming one side of a lively *piazza*, with the colonnaded church of the Apostles to the east and Bernini's Palazzo Odescalchi to the west, there is an air of melancholy about it. The façade proclaims, as an aged human face the soul behind it, the sad, unfulfilled destiny of the Stuart occupants over many decades. On the first mezzanine of the modest staircase a fanciful recess of columns with *trompe l'oeil* suspended curtains, fashioned in stone, may date from the Stuart tenure. The barrel vaulted ceiling of the large *salotto* on the *piano nobile* retains in the coves some stucco caryatids and roundels which James Edward and Clementina's eyes must often have rested upon. At the rear of the palace and approached down a dark passage is the tiny chapel of La Madonna dell'Archetto added in 1690. At the Chevalier's special request it was kept open all night for the benefit of devout wayfarers, and guarded by a papal sentry.

For a summer residence Pope Clement put at the King and Queen of England's disposal the Palazzo Savelli at Albano. Round the lake of this name numerous Roman families had villas in which to retreat during the hot season. Again the Palazzo Savelli is not one of the most distinguished of them. Today it is the Palazzo Municipale, or town hall, in the very middle of modern Albano, whereas in the eighteenth century it lay on the outskirts of the town, and had open views of the Mediterranean from the bedroom windows. It is of two storeys, low and long, the walls washed yellow, and with four very wide arcades on the ground floor of the entrance side. The Albani family arms — three mounts and a star — are carved on the keystone of each arcade. A large staircase with vase-shaped balusters and wide, shallow treads, rises in a return flight under a high vaulted ceiling. A bridge corridor, or *cavalcavia* once connected the villa to a separate house in the via del Plebiscito where the royal household was lodged. Both buildings were redecorated and enlarged for the king by Pope Benedict XIV. The Chevalier loved this unassuming retreat and would pass many a *villeggiatura* at Albano walking in the olive groves and hunting in the chestnut forests which formerly sloped westwards towards the sea and eastwards to the lake.

It is questionable whether the union of the solemn, morose and reserved man of thirty-one with the winning but flighty little girl, her head filled with romantic notions of what a queen's status ought to be, was much of a success at the outset. It ended in disaster both for the King's personal happiness and the Stuart cause. Their life together soon became turbulent and wretched. The Chevalier, although a dutiful husband, can never have been a passionate lover. He comes within the estimable and unappealing category of husband represented in English literature by Mr Kennedy in *Phineas Finn* and Mr Casaubon in *Middlemarch*. Charles Wogan who was totally loyal described him at this time as 'a prince whom a continuous chain of misfortunes and reversals since birth had already made over-pensive and over-serious and who, consequently, was not always inclined to savour jokes or give himself up to gaiety.' It was hardly the spirit calculated to relish the schoolgirl pranks and titterings of an infant wife. Clementina's childlike charm quickly evaporated with her childish dreams. She grew resentful and quick-tempered. She became suspicious, and her youthful piety turned to an almost fanatical prudery and bigotry. It is true that she managed to give birth a little over a year after marriage to a son, the future Prince Charles, and five years later, in 1725, to a second son, Prince Henry.

In 1722 Colonel John Hay* was already worried by the domestic disharmony within the Palazzo Muti. John Hay was the Chevalier's most trusted friend, and moreover popular with all the Jacobites who came in contact with him. His sister Margaret was the first wife of Lord Mar and his wife Marjorie was the sister of James Murray.

What greatly disturbed the Hays was the fact that they should be the involuntary cause of strife between their king and queen. It was very ridiculous and would have been totally unimportant, were it not that the king's enemies rejoiced over the scandal and thus were able to do his reputation harm. The young Prince Charles's governess, Mrs Sheldon, was really at the root of the trouble. She was an ardent papist, like the Queen, whereas the Hays were then Protestants, as was Marjorie Hay's devoted brother, James Murray. Mrs Sheldon, who soon gained an absolute ascendancy over the young queen, worked upon her royal mistress to express disapproval of the Protes-

* The second son of the 7th Earl of Kinnoul, Hay had fought at the battles of Perth and Sheriffmuir. He escaped from the Orkneys to France and Avignon where he joined the Chevalier's service, and on Lord Mar's dismissal succeeded as virtual though not actual Secretary of State, the office to which he was formally appointed in 1724. Hay had been created Earl of Inverness in 1718, but did not use the title before his dismissal.

tant Murray's appointment as Prince Charles's governor, whereas only the under-governors were Catholics. Worse still, Mrs Sheldon managed to persuade Clementina into believing that Mrs Hay was having an affair with the Chevalier. In actual fact Clementina could not do without Mrs Hay's services, although she deeply resented her presence. In 1719 she complained that Mrs Hay was too intrusive. In 1721 and 1722 she declared that she was entirely dependent upon her. In 1723 she asked for her removal. In 1725 she clamoured for her attendance at her second confinement. Sick of these weathercock moods her husband did what he ought to have done long before. He sacked Mrs Sheldon.

There was no foundation whatever to Clementina's charges against the virtuous Mrs Hay. A strongly worded yet respectful letter written to the Queen by Colonel Hay in September 1722 testifies as much. He even offered, such was his loyalty, to send away his wife notwithstanding her innocence, if it would conduce to the Queen's peace of mind. But Clementina had got the bit between her teeth and was determined upon trouble. On 15 November 1725 she had herself driven to the convent, in the narrow via Vittoria, of the Ursuline sisters whom she entreated to give her asylum.* These foolish virgins readily swallowed the stories of her ill-treatment which the hysterical queen poured into their ears. In vain her husband wrote her a stern but dignified letter:

'I know but too well that we have often experienced anxieties and difficulties, but these I should always have endured with greater equanimity, had I not observed them to be occasioned less by the vivacity of your disposition, than by your over-readiness to listen to petty complaints and insinuations, and to fancy yourself hurt in the persons of those who retailed them; and you cannot but recollect with what patience I have for two years submitted to your sullen humours, and how, when you scarcely would speak to me or look at me, I had recourse only to silence.'†

* Lying to the east of the Corso. The Convent (now the Academy of Santa Cecilia) was founded by Duchess Laura of Modena, mother of Queen Mary Beatrice. On the frescoed walls of the refectory are preserved grisaille medallion portraits of the two royal ladies. Princess Clementina first lodged here on her arrival in Rome in 1719 before she met the Chevalier on his return from Spain in search of help.
† 9th November 1725. Rawlinson MSS, D909.5. Bodleian Library.

For a year and a half Clementina remained incarcerated by her own will behind the high, rather forbidding, ochre-washed convent walls where, in a corner of the chapel, the prieu-dieu at which she knelt in solitary hours of self-martyrdom is still preserved. She resolutely declined to return to her husband and two children – of whom Prince Henry was only eight months old when she left him – until James Edward consented to dismiss both Hays. This he was obliged sorrowfully to do on the 3rd of April 1727. Colonel and Mrs Hay, as they were always addressed in Rome, although actually Earl and Countess of Inverness, retired to Avignon. This marital trouble had cost the Chevalier the best and most reliable of his servants and forfeited him his pensions from both the Pope and the King of Spain, so great was their disapproval of his reported ill-treatment of Clementina. Benedict XIII, unlike his predecessors, was no particular friend of the Stuarts. He sent a bishop to the Palazzo Muti to inform James Edward that His Holiness would not tolerate his adultery with Lady Inverness. In a spirited manner the King retorted that had he taken the Pope's charge seriously the bishop would have 'run the risk of leaving the house by the window instead of the staircase'. A sequel to the whole distressing story is that Clementina in 1730 begged Lord Inverness most penitently to return – he naturally refused – and left him and Lady Inverness tokens of esteem in her will. There is final irony in the fact that in later years Lord and Lady Inverness were converts to the Catholic Church.*

On quitting the Ursuline convent in the via Vittoria Clementina instead of returning straight to the Palazzo Muti went to live in a villa outside Bologna where she had her two sons brought to her. She also, to the extreme annoyance of her husband, had the mischievous Mrs Sheldon taken out of her convent in Rome in order to rejoin her service.

The death in June 1727 of George I stirred once again the half-hearted hopes of the Chevalier that the throne of England might be offered to him. Needless to say the Whigs saw to it that no *démarche* from England came James's way; and George II succeeded his father without the smallest protest.

Aimless and restless, as is the nature of expatriate kings, and

---

* Lord Inverness died at Avignon in 1740. His widow lingered on until 1760.

temporarily wifeless, James Edward moved to Avignon and then Lorraine. But the ruler, Duke Leopold, who was his old friend, begged him to depart, and the Pope, fearful of what the British fleet in the Mediterranean might not do in a show of strength, recalled him to Rome.

The Chevalier's reasons for renewed hope were not entirely unwarranted, because during the 1720s Jacobitism in Britain was rampant. It was chiefly brought about by popular Tory discontent with the Whigs. The corrupt oligarchic government under Sir Robert Walpole was so firmly entrenched that the opposition were driven to the opinion that only violent measures could ever dislodge it. Now the mass of the squires and the yeomanry as well as the Church were not flourishing. Banks were failing, agriculture was in decline, the European alliances were considered an unnecessary drain on the national resources Hanover – a third-rate continental power – was regarded as a millstone round John Bull's neck, and the Hanoverian kings George I and II were cordially despised for being the uncouth foreigners they were. In Scotland the transportation of 1,000 Stuart supporters after the Fifteen was still bitterly resented. Scottish youths openly wore white roses in their bonnets. At Winchester school the sons of the aristocracy were divided about equally into Jacobites and 'Georgites', and so strong was party feeling that the twain refused to mix at work or play.

The strength of Jacobite sympathy at home explains why throughout the 1720s and early 1730s James Edward assumed a key role in European power politics. He may have been an exile, dependent upon the shifting whims of continental princes for his very subsistence; but he was not a mere pawn in their hands. It was in their interest and England's to reckon with him. The extent of Jacobite sympathy at home also explains why the English government found it necessary to establish in Rome, and indeed wherever the exiled Stuarts might be residing, a network spy system. Rome became a hotbed of intrigue. Informers were everywhere, and often quite unsuspected individuals apparently friendly to the Stuart court were in the pay of the English government. One of these was Cardinal Alessandro Albani, who supplied information to London over a period of sixty years until his death in 1779. This cardinal was a nephew of Pope Clement XI (the staunchest Stuart supporter of all the successive pontiffs), a brother of Cardinal Annibale who was the Chevalier's close friend, and an uncle of Cardinal Gianfrancesco who was to become an intimate of James Edward's son, Prince Henry. Cardinal Alessandro was on socially good terms with the Chevalier. He was a man of much charm and kindliness. He was enormously rich, mundane, a woman lover and one of the great art collectors of all times. He built and furnished the villa Albani outside Rome and was the friend and patron of Winckelmann. It is a mystery why this wealthy art collector and prince of the Roman Church should have constituted himself protector of the Protestant English visitors to Rome and have carried on a lifetime vendetta against the family of the Catholic Stuarts, for gain.

The equivocal prince of the Church was also the inseparable friend and accomplice of one of the most notorious figures of the age, Baron Philip von Stosch. Von Stosch had been born in Brandenburg of an impoverished noble family. For thirty-five years he was paid by the British government to send them despatches under the pseudonym of John Walton, a commission first undertaken in 1722. He knew little English and his French was faulty. But he had a superb memory and the mind of a computer. He was constantly in debt and his private life was scandalous. Once during the Roman carnival he was watching from a window the annual procession down the Corso. A certain carriage containing a mother, her daughter and two sons passed by. Von Stosch turned to a companion beside him and confided that on different occasions over the years he had slept with each of the carriage's occupants. Yet he was well read and highly cultivated. Above all he too was a discriminating collector. His interest in works of art first brought him into touch and then collaboration with Cardinal Alessandro Albani.

Von Stosch lived, apart from spying, on dealing in antiques. He was not above faking, or purloining them. There is a story of a small party of connoisseurs including Stosch, being conducted round Versailles by a royal custodian. On leaving a room of the palace the custodian noticed that a famous gem, which the visitors had just been admiring, was missing. With commendable presence of mind the custodian turned to Stosch. 'Sir,' he addressed him, 'I know all the party except you, and besides that I fear for your health. You seem to have a very yellow complexion which denotes repletion. I think that a little dose of emetic taken on the spot is absolutely necessary for you.' Whereupon the custodian insisted upon administering it. In due course the gem which Stosch had, while being cross-examined, swallowed, was retrieved. This deplorable character and his collaborator the Cardinal maintained a regular correspondence with Sir Horace Mann, the English envoy in Florence. Mann kept a microscopic watch on every movement of the royal family in Bologna and the north of Italy between the years 1740 and 1786. He reported practically every detail of what they said and did, not only to Albani and Stosch, but to his old crony Horace Walpole as well. Von Stosch's death in 1757 released a spate of letters between the two Horaces on how they might procure the best of the baron's cameos, medals, rings and intaglios, the last of which alone numbered 800.

It is hardly surprising that the Chevalier, who was well aware of the existence of spies, without always knowing precisely who the individuals were, cultivated caution and extreme discretion, which he imposed upon his household. The necessary safeguards account for the codes in which all letters from himself and his servants had to be written, the substitution of counterfeit for real names, and the use of numerals and cyphers which make reading of the Stuart papers a laborious and confusing exercise. It is no wonder too that the Chevalier was never sure that those people who protested they were his friends were not acting all the time against him. He was constantly unlucky in his casual encounters. For example, in 1731 he gave a warm welcome in Rome to his half-sister, Catherine Duchess of Buckingham – the illegitimate daughter of James II by Catherine Sedley – who on her return to London promptly divulged his confidences to Sir Robert Walpole. The silly woman excused her treachery with the plea that she believed Walpole could be won over to the Stuart cause. The prevalence of the spies and the flow and repetition of their tittle-tattle were the source of a mass of information about Stuart movements, of which a great deal was wholly inaccurate or spurious.

On finding that George I's death did not precipitate an open invitation to a return to England and that his own peregrinations round Provence and Lorraine caused embarrassment to their respective governments, the Chevalier fell in with Pope Benedict XIII's command and recrossed the Alps. In January 1728 he was reunited in Bologna with his wife, with whom he had lately been corresponding on affectionate terms. Loving little letters from Clementina, beginning 'Caro mio' and making kittenish advances towards a reconciliation, had encouraged the husband to expect a reformed character. He was to be disillusioned. True, Clementina agreed to send Mrs Sheldon back to a convent. But she continued to act like a spoilt, fretful child. She refused to lead the normal social life which her position demanded, and devoted herself to ceaseless prayer. She developed a spiritual passion for the new Pope Clement XII (1730 –40). By accompanying him publicly in his state coach she started the tongues of the salacious Romans wagging furiously. Her exaggerated piety turned to religious mania. Later on she would never go out of the Palazzo Muti except to church. She shut herself up for days on end in a darkened room. She fasted so long that she developed scurvy. Horace Mann suggested that her motives were to ensure early canonization after a death deliberately brought about. It is only fair to record that her good works and relief of suffering made her beloved by the poor of Rome who claimed that after her death miracles were performed through her intercession. Shallow, ambitious, disappointed and neurotic, 'she had been in love with a dream which had proved illusory.'

In 1735 Queen Clementina faded away – tuberculosis was the ostensible cause – in the Palazzo Muti. Her wasted body having been embalmed, it was dressed in a robe of royal purple lined with ermine and gold. It was borne on a catafalque to the church of the Santi Apostoli in the piazza a few paces from the palace. After the funeral obsequies it wended its silent way in procession to St Peter's for burial. James Murray, now Lord Dunbar, wrote of his master: 'I thought he would have fainted when he left the Queen's room; the princes are almost sick with weeping and want of sleep, and on all sides there is nothing but lamentation.' The Queen's heart was enclosed in an urn of *verde antique* and set on the side of a pier in the right aisle of the Apostoli church. A marble putto with apple cheeks and peach-like chin plays with her crown under a sunbeam, while another holds aloft the flaming heart. An epitaph on a red marble slab briefly records the deceased's merits. To the foot of this memorial the Chevalier would wander from his palace in the years to come and pray there by the hour. In St Peter's a more splendid monument to her memory was erected ten years later. It is to be seen over the doorway to the lift, which now wafts millions of visitors to the roof and dome of the basilica. A sarcophagus draped with a gold-fringed shroud of variegated marbles manifests the baroque artifice of the architect Filippo Barigioni, and sculptor Pietro Bracci. Bracci's white-clad figure of Virtue supports a framed portrait in mosaic, taken from an oil painting by Ignazio Stern, of the Queen as she was in her early thirties. All traces of that feline prettiness have gone. The face portrayed is that of an ordinary, flabby, middle-aged lady of no particular distinction or charm.

Clementina's death affected the Chevalier grievously. When dead she became an object, winning the love and sympathy which he had tried but failed to render her when alive. The fact that she had been her own worst enemy and had caused him much embarrassment and pain was forgotten now by the husband who was a fundamentally generous and well-disposed man, but deficient in self-confidence and reserves of understanding. He blamed himself that her life had been a failure and a bitterness to them both. He doubtless suspected that had he been more demonstrative and uxorious his silly but intensely feminine child-wife might have developed into a normal and rational adult, although never more than a mediocre one. Yet he was constitutionally incapable of giving her what she needed. He knew himself to be to blame, and he suffered agonies of remorse which only true penitence could mitigate. Only through unremitting prayer might God be induced to translate into the everlasting bliss of a heavenly state this union which on earth had so signally lacked it.

Henceforth James Edward led a retired life. He appeared less and less in public, preferring Albano to Rome, for in the country he could avoid public ceremonies, and entertain a few close friends at a time. When in Rome he went as often as he could to the opera, where he would dine quietly in his box. This particular form of entertainment called for the minimum social contacts. His old ambitions and the opinions of the external world left him cold. His religious exercises were intensified. They alone brought him consolation. He passively accepted adversity. He gave up. Indifference to fate hastened a physical deterioration. By 1735 he was no longer the same man whom the Duke of Marlborough's grandson, Robert Spencer,* had once met face to face, 'taking the air in the stately gardens of the Villa Ludovisi', with his young consort. That was in 1721. The 'Pretender' was easily distinguished by his star and garter as well as by 'his air of greatness', which affected Mr Spencer with 'a strange convulsion in body and mind such as I never was sensible of before'. The King fixed his eyes on the young man and acknowledged his salute. He was then 'a well-sized, clean-limbed man', by which Spencer meant spare with upright figure. A few hours later Spencer again came upon the royal party strolling down another alley of the gardens. This time he was presented. The Chevalier was gracious, and Clementina invited him to a concert in the Palazzo Muti. Young Spencer went and listened to the best music in Rome. He watched the Chevalier drink English beer which he had specially shipped to Leghorn, and eat roast beef and Devonshire pie. The King of England was pathetically at pains to stress his Englishness. Yet he would take a glass of champagne 'very heartily'. He lamented the misfortunes of his subjects at home groaning under a load of debts. He said to Spencer, 'Some may imagine these calamities are not displeasing to me, because they may in some measure turn to my advantage. I renounce all such unworthy thoughts.' Spencer was agreeably taken with Clementina who spoke 'the prettiest English I ever heard. She is of middling stature, well shaped, and has lovely features – wit, vivacity and mildness of temper are painted in her looks.' Alas, for these fugitive graces!

In the winter of 1739–40 the Président de Brosses recorded that the Chevalier was tall and still thin, and resembled his father in looks. 'There is no lack of dignity in his manner. I have never seen any Prince hold a large court with so much grace and majesty . . . he speaks little but always with gentleness and kindness.' De Brosses likewise accepted the hospitality of the Chevalier's table. 'The dinners are not amusing – but if by chance they become so, the King appears well pleased . . . When he comes to table his two sons, before sitting down, kneel and ask his blessing . . .' Every day his table was laid for ten or a dozen persons who might call and dine with him. Etiquette dictated that guests at table should not drink before the King drank, and he

---

* Born in 1701. On the death of his father in 1722 he became the 4th Earl of Sunderland, and died unmarried in 1729. He was succeeded by his brother Charles who, on the death of his aunt in 1733, became the 3rd Duke of Marlborough.

drank but little. The meals cannot have been very hilarious. De Brosses referred to 'the sad and simple look' of his host's face, a description confirmed in less flattering terms by the poet Thomas Gray who saw him in Rome, also in 1740. He wrote brutally that he had 'extremely the looks and air of an idiot particularly when he laughs or prays . . . the first he does not often, the latter continually.' It was de Brosses too who remarked that he was 'devout to excess'. But what the Whigs – and Gray was one – liked to write about 'old Mr Misfortunate' was invariably uncharitable and usually exaggerated. They said of him, 'If you tell him it is a fine day he weeps and says he was unfortunate from his mother's womb.' In most senses he was.

II

SACRED AND PROFANE

However unsatisfactory a helpmate to the Chevalier the Princess Clementina proved to be, at least she managed to produce for him two sons. In this respect she fulfilled her principal purpose admirably.

Charles Edward Louis Philip John Casimir Silvester Severino Maria Stuart was born in the Palazzo Muti a little after nightfall on 31 December 1720. Dozens of Roman princes and princesses, cardinals and members of the English nobility in Rome at the time were summoned to attend the birth. The infant prince, usually referred to on the Continent as Edward, but in Britain as Charles, was instantly created Prince of Wales by his jubilant father. The dying Pope Clement XI gave him royal recognition and called at the Palazzo Muti to pronounce a special blessing and deliver swaddling clothes for the child's christening.

Responsibility for the young Prince's education having been entrusted to the Protestant John Murray (in 1721 created Earl of Dunbar) he delegated the task of teaching the Prince to a series of under-governors or tutors, including old Sir Thomas Sheridan,* the Abbé Legoux and the Chevalier de Ramsay, all of whom were papists. Legoux who came from the University of Paris undertook Charles's religious instruction. He was not very successful. Nevertheless he delighted the Prince with his jokes and even raised an occasional smile from the Chevalier. Andrew Michael Ramsay, the son of a baker in Ayr and a convert, had attracted the Chevalier's notice by his friendship with Fénélon, whose life he published in

---

* Sir Thomas Sheridan (d. 1746) doted on his charge, Prince Charles. His mother Hélène was the eldest (and illegitimate) daughter of James II and Anne Hyde. So he was a half-nephew of the Chevalier, although many years his senior.

46

1723. It cannot be said that the army of tutors yielded very startling results, and doubtless they all would have concurred that their material was from the outset intractable. It is true that the pupil became trilingual in English, Italian and French in so far as he spoke these languages fluently. His pronunciation of English however was noticeably foreign. And he had a trick of ending every sentence in Italian with 'Ha capi!' which was only matched by his kinsman George III's 'What! what!' His spelling in all three languages remained atrocious throughout his life. In fact Prince Charles was unlearned and ill-read. He was totally unversed in the classics. Literature generally meant little to him although after the Forty-five while in Paris he asked a friend to send him *Tom Jones* and *Joseph Andrews*, as well as Richardson's novels to relieve the extreme tedium of his existence. Dr William King, Principal of St Mary Hall, Oxford, a scholar with Jacobite leanings, to whom I shall refer later, at once recognized his shortcomings on the occasion when he met the Prince. 'In polite company he would not pass for a genteel man,' he wrote. Yet 'he hath a quick apprehension.' Dr King was shocked to discover that he was totally unacquainted with the history and constitution of England, in which he ought to have been instructed before all else, since he expected to become the nation's accepted sovereign. Altogether the doctor formed a very poor opinion of the Prince's mental equipment.

On the other hand, like his younger brother Henry, Prince Charles was genuinely fond of music of a simple melodious sort, and in his old age revelled in sentimental Jacobite songs, of which *Lochaber no more* unfailingly reduced him to tears. Certainly at an early age his engaging manners and naturally lively intelligence impressed visitors. In 1727 his cousin the Duke of Liria* pronounced him to be 'the most ideal prince he had ever seen, a marvel of beauty, dexterity, grace, and almost supernatural address.' At that date the object of his admiration was but seven years old.

The Prince was clearly no highbrow. The things of the mind made little appeal. Sport and games meant a great deal. Lord Elcho remembered watching both princes when boys taking exercise in the

---

* The eldest son of the Duke of Berwick (natural son of James II), created by Philip V Duke of Liria and a Grandee and married to Donna Catarina de Veraguas, the richest heiress in Spain. Ancestor of the Dukes of Alba and Berwick.

Borghese gardens. The elder brother diverted himself with killing blackbirds and thrushes and playing 'goff'. In the twilight when the birds were roosting he would shoot bats. He was then a normal, healthy – I was going to say, English boy, were it not for his predominantly foreign ancestry and continental upbringing. Nevertheless Prince Charles was, in many respects, surprisingly and intensely English. He was a compound of English virtues and vices. He was adventuresome and brave. He longed to prove his mettle. Irritated by his father's too passive concern for his lost throne, the Prince felt impelled to win it back. Unlike James Edward he endeavoured to do so with all his might and when he failed, he refused to treat with his failure. When barely fourteen he seized the opportunity of accompanying his cousin, the Duke of Liria, on an expedition to Naples to conquer that kingdom for the Duke of Parma. He was appointed by Don Carlos of Spain General of Artillery, and at the siege of Gaeta refused to take shelter as an onlooker. He took some part in the fighting, and displayed distinct courage. 'I wish to God,' Liria wrote to his brother the Duke of Fitz-James, 'that some of the greatest sticklers in England against the family of the Stuarts had been eyewitnesses of this prince's resolution during the siege, and I am firmly persuaded that they would soon change their way of thinking.'

Already in these early days he was what is called a manly youth. On his return to Rome he was lionised by society. The nature he inherited from his mother was frank and engaging, and like hers it was superficial. Unfortunately he also inherited her unstable temperament. It was a great pity that from tenderest youth he was spoilt by a father who doted on him and a court which flattered him. People found it difficult to resist the Prince of Wales's beguiling ways, whereas his brother Henry's sobriety was by contrast far less winning. Carluccio to his father and Carlusu to his mother was a pretty boy with a clear complexion. His upright figure was slender and steely and his sloping shoulders carried a proud head. His face was oval with a high, noble brow and a long pointed chin. His eyes were alert and merry. There has always been dispute as to their colour. Andrew Lang declared that they were brown and not blue. Some portraits depict them as topaz; others, notably the handsome pastel of him as a young man at Drumlanrig, and the tragic one of the old roué by Battoni (of which several versions exist) depict them as pale sea blue.* His hair, judging from the quantities of fragments piously cherished by Jacobite families and the long plaited tress in the Inverness Museum, curled naturally and was very fair, sometimes almost yellow, with pale brown streaks. His eyebrows and lashes were chestnut.

In 1737 Prince James Sobieski died and left his two Stuart grandsons money and part of the fabulous Sobieski collection of jewels. With a selection of these adornments upon a crimson velvet coat trimmed with lace, a canary waistcoat, white silk pleated shirt with tight stock round the throat, deep blue Garter sash across the left shoulder and diamond star pinned on the breast, the boy prince made a brave show at balls and masquerades. The same year he was deemed old enough to be sent on a tour of Italian cities. He was warmly received in Tuscany and Venetia, the two powers which still openly espoused the Stuart cause. In Venice a jealous watch was kept on his movements by the English Ambassador who recounted them in detail to the home government.

Four years later Horace Mann reported from Tuscany that the Prince made a visit to France where he was paid considerable attention and given presents by Cardinal Pierre Guérin de Tencin, shortly to become Louis XV's Minister of State. This is not improbable for several reasons. Tencin owed his cardinalate to the Chevalier. He was high in the favour of Pope Benedict XIV (1740–58) who was an intimate friend of the Chevalier. Pope and King were constantly exchanging visits and courtesies like two old cronies; and the Pope, when presented with choice delicacies, such as venison or sturgeon, would often dispatch part of them with his compliments to the Palazzo Muti. Furthermore, France was seriously at variance with England then supporting Maria Theresa's claims to the Holy Roman Empire. Indeed it was because the War of the Austrian Succession (1740–48) involved Hanover, threatened by Prussia, that the Forty-five took place when it did. Tencin protested his readiness to lend support to the Stuarts in order to divert George II from active participation on the Continent in Austria's interests. This readiness

---

* Miss Henrietta Tayler always maintained that they were hazel. This is very probable, because hazel eyes are notably chameleonic.

was turned to action by Tencin's indignation at George's victory over France at the Battle of Dettingen in 1743.

Prince Charles was as unlike Prince Henry Stuart as chalk is unlike cheese. Whereas the elder brother was basically frivolous yet positive, the younger was serious and passive. Whereas the one was a mercurial the other was a balanced man. Charles from his hopeful youth till his disillusioned old age fought steadfastly against his fate (and lost), whereas Henry came to terms with his destiny at an early age. In consequence his long life was no failure. Apart from a concatenation of family wrangles which persistently dogged and puzzled him, and a few exceedingly lean years brought about by international events, he was fortunate in his career and more successful than his natural endowments might be supposed to merit.

Henry Benedict Thomas Edward Clement Francis Xavier (five more names were given him) was four and a quarter years younger than Charles Edward. He was born on 6 March 1725 in the cheerless Palazzo Muti to the sounds of cannon fire from the Castle of St Angelo. All appropriate arrangements for his advent had been taken well in advance. Soon after his birth the infant prince was baptized in the palace by Pope Benedict XIII in person, and created by his father Duke of York, the title by which he was recognized by all true Jacobites. There was heartfelt rejoicing among the faithful courtiers that a second string to Stuart pretensions had thus been assured, and the King was extremely satisfied. Whatever were the true feelings of the Queen over this pledge of submission to her conjugal duties, have to be surmised. The spoilt, querulous little woman left her husband and the baby prince eight months later, and bolted herself behind the convent doors of the Ursuline sisters.

How far Clementina's extraordinary behaviour affected her second son's character it is hard to say. At the time of her flight he must have been too young to be aware of her absence. It is more likely that Prince Charles suffered immediately from the deprivation of his mother's attentions. For when she returned to their home he was seven years old and Prince Henry merely two. Charles was devoted to his mother and in his boyhood may have borne King James a grudge for what he was persuaded to believe was his cruel treatment of her, a grudge which he fanned into open hostility as soon as his father directed criticism upon his own not dissimilar follies. One thing is certain. Both brothers inherited from their mother her wilfulness and petulance. As a child however Henry was, according to report, generally bright, cheerful and normal. A contemporary described him as 'merry, spirited, with martial instincts', which instincts evaporated as he approached manhood. A traveller to Rome reported that he was 'more beautiful and dignified than could be imagined'. Certainly portraits of him in his tender years testify as much. That by Antonio David in the National Portrait Gallery is of a very pretty child with wide, sparkling hazel eyes. The cheeks are full and the chin is long and pointed in the true Stuart style. He already holds himself with princely aplomb. Other boyhood portraits of him, by Nattier at Stoneyhurst and by L. G. Blanchet at Holyrood Palace, suggest that his features were more regular than Prince Charles's and his countenance more smiling. The sunny disposition was to disappear behind a sombre cast before he grew much older. His father was intensely proud of him. He wrote in 1729, 'I am really in love with the little duke, for he is the finest child that can be seen.' Henry's baby looks, unlike his brother's which were fair, turned dark and swarthy. His figure was short and compact although his build was delicate. He was called by the Italians 'il ducchino di Yorck'. He was as a boy full of fun and fire. He loved dancing and hunting, but above all things music. He played the violin competently and sang Italian airs in an engaging treble. The Président de Brosses related how one evening he came into the Palazzo Muti when both princes were nearing the end of Corelli's Eighth Concerto, *La Notte di Natale*. In the most natural and charming manner they insisted upon repeating the performance from the very beginning for their guest's delight. In the family circle Henry was made to converse in English, which he never mastered very well, Italian being his first and French his second language.

In 1740 the Président de Brosses recorded that of the two princes, then aged twenty and fifteen, 'the elder is more worth while and has a sweeter disposition. He has a large heart and is full of courage.' Nevertheless de Brosses was quick to observe, 'both are of mediocre intelligence and less developed than princes of their age ought to be.' We get another glimpse of them in 1741 through the eyes of Lady Mary Wortley Montagu. She wrote that the royal family were living very splendidly. She saw the two boys at a masque richly adorned with jewels. Her opinion was the reverse of de Brosses's. 'The eldest seems thoughtless enough . . . The youngest is very well made, dances finely, and has an ingenious countenance.' They certainly made a handsome pair as their portraits testify.

The careless rapture of childhood did not last very long. Either the sadness of his parents' life together and his mother's premature death, or the state of Jacobite affairs generally – in 1733 the invitation to stand as candidate for the Polish throne was considered but turned down by the parents on his behalf – changed Prince Henry's temperament to an unnatural solemnity. In 1742 when he was seventeen the Protestant governor Lord Dunbar was much concerned about him. He compiled a long report, extensively quoted in biographies of the prince, upon his pupil's mode of life which strikes us as neurotic, to put it mildly. The Prince was called, according to custom, at a quarter to six each morning. Before getting up he spent a quarter of an hour praying in bed. At six o'clock he rose, washed his face and hands and put on his shoes and buckles. After this he prayed for one hour in his closet and bedroom loudly enough for his attendants to hear through the closed door. He spent no more than seven to ten minutes breakfasting. At half past seven his confessor, Father Ildefonso arrived and stayed up to one hour with him. After which the prince danced and fenced, but only for a few minutes, in order to hurry off to chapel. On Sundays and holy days he might hear as many as three or even four Masses. When the last Mass was over he remained in the chapel praying until dinner time. Having dined he would wait, watch in hand, until the minute arrived which he had allotted himself to embark upon a further three quarters of an hour's prayer in the chapel. Thereafter he went out of doors, usually to some church where he might pray for another half hour. At four o'clock he came home and spent always an hour and a half in chapel, reciting his rosary in great agitation, 'with a blackness about the eyes, his head quite fatigued and his hands hot'. The tutor continued:

'It is observable that the Duke is the whole day in constant inquietude for fear of not having time for all he ought to do and very often has his watch in his hand on that account. His temper and inclination is so far changed that to propose to carry him of an evening as next Sunday to an assembly, in place of doing him a pleasure it gives him pain and he seems to have no pleasure in anything.'

No wonder. If this behaviour of a youth of seventeen does not betoken religious mania I do not know what does. It was his Sobieska mother and Stuart grandfather's pietism all over again. Lord Dunbar justly remarked,

'It deserves serious attention that he undergoes much greater application of mind [he might have written *soul*] than his delicate health can bear, yet there is little of it directed towards forming his judgment or adorning his mind with knowledge of things suitable to his station . . . During the rest of the day he never reads a word on any subject nor could he probably do it, so that were not the course he is in noxious to his health, as it certainly is, he would arrive at the age of twenty-two without having cultivated his understanding . . .'

It is extraordinary that the governor – admittedly he was a Protestant and the tutors were Catholics – had no authority to put an end to this deleterious mode of life of a pupil in his charge, and that the doting father was apparently unaware of what was happening under his roof. The plots and intrigues for a Stuart restoration which were rife this year and the complicated arrangements being made for Prince Charles's visits to the several Italian cities should not have deprived him of the little time needed to devote to his younger son's upbringing. Odder still seems the governor's additional anxiety expressed in these words: 'When he is not employed as above he is always singing, which I am far from thinking indifferent in regard to his breast.' One would suppose that unless Prince Henry's singing was confined to hymns such a relaxation would be considered salutary. Lord Dunbar begged the King to determine what should be done and feared that if the Prince were deprived of what amounted to his only pleasure, namely almost ceaseless prayer, 'it will have a very violent effect upon him.' The extraordinary régime which the royal adolescent had chosen suggests that he was labouring under a tormenting sense of guilt, the cause of which can be anybody's guess. He was behaving at the beginning of his life just as James II behaved at the end of his.

We do not know if the Chevalier was moved by the governor's remonstrances to take action. In any case Prince Henry's over-indulgence in religious exercises with its accompanying neglect of his education was shortly to be interrupted by developments on the political scene.

The trouble was that the Chevalier, always a fond parent, spoilt both his sons while they were children in allowing them to go their several ways without hindrance. It no more occurred to him to put a stop to Prince Charles's endless shooting of song birds in the Borghese gardens when he should have been doing his lessons, than to check Prince Henry's exaggerated devotions. Yet throughout the two boys' adolescence the father's letters show him to have become a tremendous fusser over their bodily and spiritual welfare. In other words his anxieties were misdirected. For he would beg the boys to avoid draughts and the risks of infection. He would continually exhort them to prudence, restraint and holiness. Clearly the stream of his letters of advice to Prince Charles, whom he insisted upon treating like a child long after he was grown up, were very irksome to that young man. The Chevalier who was not insensitive, probably came to realize this fact. He wrote to his elder son when he was overseas, on the 25th of July 1746, 'Though I have never missed a week writing to you, yet a number of my letters have to be sure miscarried one way or another, and it matters little whether you ever see most of them, since I could say little to you from hence of any importance.' Sad words indeed. They provoked a casual response such as only a callous child makes to a doting parent. Prince Charles replied, 'I must own my fault but I have not as yet read all ye old letters that I received in one bundle upon my arrival in this country [Scotland] my only excuse is I really did not imagine their [sic] was anything in them that needed be answered immediately.'

The Chevalier's relations with both sons, once they were grown up, were never entirely happy. He was very reluctant to allow Prince Charles to depart from Rome in 1744 on what proved to be the abortive expedition of the Forty-five; and more reluctant still to let Prince Henry, who was only twenty, follow his brother to Paris the next year. From the outset the King was doubtful about the wisdom, even the desirability of the expedition. He was not too confident of his elder son's ability to carry it through, and very mistrustful of

54

French offers of assistance. Was the whole thing worth while? Were they not a contented enough family living in the Pope's dominions, and being granted the privileges without the responsibilities of sovereignty? As far as his own interests were concerned, he was perfectly satisfied with the *status quo*. Besides James Edward was a natural realist, and pessimist. Whereas King James II had believed in his muddle-headed way that things were bound to come right for his family in the end, the Chevalier was under few illusions, and in his heart of hearts no longer particularly wanted things to come right. He was not at all sure that regaining an earthly crown was worth the risk of losing a heavenly one. Prince Charles was quite certain it was. 'I go, sire, in search of three crowns,' he informed his father on the eve of his departure, 'which I doubt not but to have the honour and happiness of laying at your Majesty's feet. If I fail in the attempt, your next sight of me shall be the coffin.' He was given to melodramatic statements. 'Heaven forbid,' the King exclaimed, 'that all the crowns of the world shall rob me of my son!' These were wasted words. The Prince was but twenty-four and burning with the lust of adventure. 'In my brother Henry,' he said, 'you will find no small comfort and a son certainly better than I am.' The King embraced him and said, 'Be careful of yourself, my dear Prince, for my sake and, I hope, for the sake of millions.' Although he was to live another twenty-two years he never set eyes on Prince Charles again.

Elaborate plans were concocted by which the Prince might leave Rome without the spies suspecting any untoward movement. They were even kept from Prince Henry with whom in these days the Prince of Wales was on the best of terms, lest his distress at parting from the elder brother he idolized should give rise to suspicions. Only Sir Thomas Sheridan the tutor, Francis Stafford one of the royal equerries, and François Vivier, Prince Charles's French valet, were made privy to them. The day fixed for the departure was 9 January 1744. At 3 o'clock in the morning the Prince rose. Having sent word to Henry to follow at his leisure he set out with Sir Thomas from the Palazzo Muti on the pretext – kept up with the brother but not with the tutor – of a shooting expedition to Cisterna in the Latium plain. Stafford was sent ahead to arrange for the gates at the Porta San Giovanni to be opened. Once beyond the gates Prince Charles got out of the carriage in which they had crossed the city. So that everyone might hear, he announced to Sir Thomas that he preferred to ride to Cisterna by way of Albano on the spare horse which Stafford had led ahead of the carriage. 'Let us see,' he cried out, 'who will arrive first.' Sir Thomas pretended to argue with his royal charge that the King would be angry because the Albano road was so muddy in winter as to be almost impassable. But after scolding the Prince Sir Thomas let him have his way, and proceeded without him. Prince Henry followed the tutor in a second carriage. Prince Charles however, having sent Stafford off to Albano, turned his horse's head in the opposite direction and galloped round the walls of Rome. He hastily changed his wig and put on a large courier's cap drawn down so as to obscure his features. Having met François and a servant by prearrangement he made off along the via Aurelia northwards. Long after the shooting party reached Cisterna the subterfuge was maintained. News from Stafford kept arriving by different messengers announcing that the Prince had fallen from his horse and was slightly indisposed at Albano, and indicating his arrival within a day or two. In actual fact Charles, accompanied only by François and the servant rested the first night in the Villa Farnese at Caprarola. Thence he rode at great speed to Massa. On the fourth night he reached Genoa where he was joined by Sir John Graeme.* For five whole days he had subsisted on eggs and had not undressed at nights. François afterwards attested that they were nearly worn out by the speed at which he made them travel. The Prince wrote home, 'If I had been [obliged] to go much further I should have had to get them tyd behind the chase with my portmantle, for they were quite *rendu*.'

By now the truth of the Prince's flight had leaked, and the spies in Rome had alerted the English representatives in Tuscany and Liguria. Horace Mann was vociferous in telling his correspondents every movement of what he called 'the Pretender's boy'. At Savona the fugitives halted until a *speronara*, a small coasting vessel propelled by oars and lateen sails, could be hired. In this rapid vessel they put in at

---

* Sir John Graeme (d. 1773) was appointed Secretary of State to the Chevalier on the dismissal of John Hay (Lord Inverness) in 1727. Between 1745 and 1747 he was attached to Prince Charles's household in Paris. He fell into disgrace with the Chevalier who held him partly responsible for his elder son's disorderly conduct. Later he was forgiven and received back in the Palazzo Muti. In 1760 he was created Earl of Alford.

Monaco, and then proceeded to Antibes, pursued by an English boat whose captain's suspicions had been aroused. From Antibes the small party went overland to Avignon where they stayed with the Duke of Ormonde. In February they reached Paris.

In Paris Prince Charles met with the first series of frustrations that were to render his hopes of success nugatory. In March a French squadron under Admiral Roquefeuil set sail for England from Dunkirk with 7,000 soldiers commanded by Marshal Saxe on board. Anxiously Prince Charles waited at Gravelines. Alas, the Stuart ill-luck intervened. The usual severe storm blew and the fleet was dispersed. After this crushing disaster the Stuarts were never again to enlist from the French more than sympathy and token help in sporadic handfuls of troops and munitions. Prince Charles was obliged to retire to Paris where for fifteen intermittent months he waited, incognito, impecunious. He paid one visit in the winter to the château de Fitz-James on the Paris–Calais road which belonged to his cousin the Bishop of Soissons, a son of the Duke of Berwick.

The Jacobite advisers in Paris were at loggerheads which, on hearing about, the Chevalier strongly deprecated, to little avail. He deprecated no less strongly the stories which reached him of the Prince's dissipations in the French capital. For truth to tell the Rev. George Kelly, until lately the Duke of Ormonde's secretary who was sent to join Charles in Paris, was leading his charge into every kind of mischief.* King James wrote his son some very aggrieved letters which were not received in the spirit of contrition they demanded. The Prince was surly. 'I know for certain that some people have said I have nobody about me at all that is discreet,' he replied, and insinuated that his father's informers were malicious liars. Repeatedly he maintained that Kelly was the most virtuous of men. The Jacobite Buck Club in Edinburgh sent the Prince word that unless he could come over with at least 6,000 troops, with adequate arms and money, he had better keep away altogether. But this admonition was

---

* William MacGregor of Balhaldy in a letter to James Edgar, 31 May 1747, referred to Kelly as one 'who now succeeds by the influence the first [Thomas Sheridan] had, is a monster of quite a different turn; trick, falsehood, deceit and imposition, joined to the qualities that make up a sycophant . . . are the rules of his policy.' He was sent back to France by the Prince after Prestonpans. Kelly was a non-Juring parson of Irish extraction.

contradicted by John Murray of Broughton, who crossed to Paris expressly to convey different advice. At a clandestine meeting by night with the Prince behind the stables of the Louvre he falsely withheld the true state of affairs in Scotland, averring that the chiefs had plenty of arms. Since 1738 Murray had been the official channel through which Secretary Edgar, on behalf of the Chevalier, communicated with the Highland chiefs. The authority he wielded was consequently one of great importance, and the Stuart Court in Rome was almost entirely dependent upon his interpretation of Scottish opinion. His advice was heeded. But how often his advice was honourably given is still open to question. Lord Elcho maintained that his personal finances were so embarrassed that it was in his own interests to persuade the Prince to come to Scotland contrary to the chiefs' warning that he should not.* It was only on his return to Scotland that Murray was shamed into writing the truth to the Prince warning him that the chiefs were reluctant to receive him. By the time the bearer of his letter arrived in Paris the Prince had already set sail. He never received the letter.†

The defeat by the French of the English under Cumberland at Fontenoy on 11 May had encouraged the Prince to take the plunge. It was now or never. The decision to sail was his alone, and no one else's. It was made in the face of his well-wishers' attempts at discussion. The Prince however kept his own plan secret from the large body of his advisers in Paris – and, of course, from his father to whom he piously wrote on 19 April 1745, 'My want of experience is what I two [sic] much know and would fain get as soon as possible.' With the aid of Aeneas Macdonald, the Prince's banker in Paris, he succeeded in borrowing 180,000 livres from Waters, the Chevalier's banker. Towards the end of May he moved to the Château de Navarre near Évreux, the seat of an uncle by marriage on his mother's side, the Duc de Bouillon.

On 5 of July Prince Charles embarked from Belle Isle in the *Du Teillay* with a small band of trusted companions, known as the Seven Men of Moidart. They were a mixed bag, men of different ages,

---

* Elcho, a contemporary, was practically brought up as a child with Prince Charles. Having been his intimate friend he turned violently against him after the Forty-Five.
† When the rebellion was over Murray was captured and interrogated. He turned King's evidence and implicated several Jacobites.

nationality and principles. Old Sir Thomas Sheridan his doting tutor, Captain John O'Sullivan, the only trained soldier of the lot, attractive but unreliable, and the egregious George Kelly were Irish. The Marquess of Tullibardine (described as 'tottering with age and infirmities and supported by an attendant on each side') and Aeneas Macdonald were Scots. Francis Strickland was English. Eight servants accompanied them. They were, in the Lewis Carroll language of a Scot who met them in the Highlands, as 'Allagrugouss fellows as ever I saw.' The *Du Teillay* was escorted by another French ship the *Elizabeth* bearing provisions and arms. The little fleet was met in the Channel by an English man-of-war, the *Lion* which engaged them. The *Elizabeth* was so badly mauled that she was obliged to hobble back to Brest. The *Du Teillay* with sails pierced by cannon shot, managed to escape. After eighteen days at sea the ship stood off Barra, one of the southernmost islands of the Outer Hebrides. Aeneas and Kelly were despatched in a rowing boat to find out the lie of the land, but returned with the information that MacNeil of Barra was away. On the 23rd the *Du Teillay* anchored off a silvery sandy bay on the north-west coast of Eriskay. Here the Prince first set foot on Scottish soil. By a strange chance ever since his landing the fleshy pink *Convolvulus major*, known as Prince Charlie's Flower, of which a seed is said to have been brought from France in his pocket, has flourished on Eriskay island and nowhere else in Scotland.

The night was spent in a cottage with a fire in the middle of the floor and a hole in the roof. The peat smoke was so choking that the Prince had several times to go out during the night for air. Next morning he sent across the Sound a summons to Macdonald of Clanranald on South Uist. Clanranald returned a not very civil message by his brother, Macdonald of Boisdale, advising him to go home. To which the caustic reply was, 'I have come home.' Undiscouraged by the rebuff the Prince crossed to the mainland of Scotland, and on the 25th anchored in Loch nan Uamh off Arisaig. Arisaig was also Clanranald country. Aeneas immediately landed in search of his brother, Donald Macdonald of Kinlochmoidart. On learning of the Prince's arrival Kinlochmoidart and several Macdonalds boarded the ship and tried to dissuade him from disembarking. Even old Sheridan joined in the clamour that he should now see sense and return to France. But the Prince was adamant.

There then took place the first of many scenes at which the Prince's charisma was called upon to work wonders. The cautious clansmen who assembled to meet him were bitterly disappointed that he had come without money, without troops, and with only 1,000 muskets and 1,800 broadswords. His arrival, they protested, was most ill-considered. It was preposterous. They were unanimous in begging him to go away. Yet the Prince's naiveté, enthusiasm and charm were too much for their resistance. Piteously he appealed to their loyalty, earnestly declaring that he was come to relieve their sufferings under the Hanoverian yoke. At the end of a moving impromptu speech he turned to young Ranald, Clanranald's son, and with outstretched arms asked, 'Will *you* not assist me?' 'I will, I will,' was the immediate reply, 'though no other man in the Highlands should draw a sword, I am ready to die for you.' Whereupon all the Macdonalds followed suit. Highlanders are an emotional and quixotic people. Appeals to their loyalty and romantic sentiment seldom fail to evoke a quick response.

When Kinlochmoidart at his trial the following year was asked why he had joined the Prince his reply was, 'Lord, man! What could I do when the young lad came to my house?' He was executed for this touching admission. Cameron of Lochiel, the most respected chief in the Highlands, succumbed in like manner to the Prince's desperate approach. Indeed it was irresistible. One witness warned a friend, who was still wavering on the brink, against 'ye Bonny Prince . . . who if he once sets eyes on you will make you do whatever he pleases, therefore do not see him.'

The Prince disembarked, dismissed the *Du Teillay* and took up quarters in Borrodale House. Until this moment Charles was still dressed as a divinity student of the Scots College in Paris, going by the name of Douglas, and was so believed to be by the crew.* Henceforth he discarded all disguise and put on Highland dress. He instantly began drilling the clansmen who were electrified by his spell, 'and would never leave him calling themselves his Guard of Safety'.

But the situation was precarious. The refusals of the MacLeod of MacLeod and Macdonald of Sleat to join him were a serious setback because their combined influence in Skye was paramount. These

---

* After 1749 nearly all his letters to his father were signed John Douglas.

chiefs had not set eyes upon him and their refusals had been conveyed by messenger. The Prince in between his drilling despatched pitiful letters to the Jacobite agent in Paris, beseeching help and funds from the French Government.

On 11 August the Prince sailed out of the Sound of Arisaig, past the sinister rocky headland of Arnish, into Loch Moidart with its remote and densely wooded shore. In Kinlochmoidart House (later burnt by Cumberland) which stood at the end of a straight avenue of beech and ash, he was joined by Murray of Broughton, who there and then became his secretary. On 19 August the Prince, having marched over the hills to Glenaladale sailed up the straight narrow Loch Shiel between sharp pointed hills folded one over another like the flaps of envelopes, to Glenfinnan at its head. Here he jumped ashore upon the shingle of little brown pebbles flecked with what seem diamonds glistening in the summer sunshine. In this still, silent, most melanchony spot, where the loch abruptly ends and the ravens croak high overhead, he spent the night in a small barn. The following day the Prince and his little band waited anxiously for the clansmen to join them. At last preceded by the strains of the pibroch echoing down the separate glens came in long, thin files more Macdonald, Cameron and Keppoch men. The cavalcade of Lochiel's men was accompanied by Jenny Cameron, a widow over forty years old, 'dressed in a sea-green riding habit', wearing a velvet cap with a scarlet feather, and holding a drawn sword in her right hand. When the army had swelled to a decent size the Prince addressed them in a stirring speech; and Tullibardine, who now resumed his attainted title as Duke of Atholl, unfurled a standard of red silk with a white centre.

The army marched eastwards. At Kinlochiel they learned that in the absence of George II in Hanover the Regency in London had proclaimed a reward of £30,000 for the Prince's head. The Prince wanted to issue a counter-proclamation putting £30 on George's head, declaring that it was not worth more. But he was persuaded to raise it to £30,000 likewise. At Fassfern on Loch Eil the white shrub rose, *alba maxima*, now called the Jacobite rose, was in bloom. Each man picked one and put it in his bonnet. At Moy on the 24th news came that Sir John Cope, the Hanoverian general was marching from Stirling to Fort Augustus. At Invergarry Castle (also to be burnt by Cumberland) a document was signed on 26 August by the chiefs, pledging themselves not to lay down arms without the consent of all. At Aberchalder the army was swelled by more Macdonalds and Grants. For the first time the Prince donned the tartan trews, a pair of which can be seen today in the Fort William Museum, the tight legs turned over the feet in the manner of socks in one attachment. At Aberchalder the Prince practised with the claymore and spent all his time among the common soldiers, with whom he was already immensely popular. He addressed them by their christian names and dispensed money to those who seemed in need. He marched by their side and the hardiest complained that his pace was too fast for them. Prince and men marched southwards from Aberchalder over the Corrieyairack Pass to Garveymore, where they were informed that Cope, whom the Prince had hoped to meet, had instead turned north towards Inverness. The Prince was anxious to pursue him but was dissuaded because his men were too exhausted. So they continued leisurely to Dalwhinny, sleeping the night of the 29th in the heather. He wrote to his father, 'I keep my health better in these wild mountains than I used to in the Campagna Felice, and sleep sounder lying on the ground, than I used to do in the Palaces of Rome.' Strong, confident, purposeful and beloved, he was as happy as a sandboy.

And so Prince Charles Stuart was launched upon his famous expedition known as the Forty-five. His ensuing hopes and disappointments, adventures and misadventures, euphoric triumphs and appalling hardships are legendary. The proclamation at Perth of his father as King James VIII of Scotland, the occupation of Edinburgh, victory at Prestonpans, the march into England as far south as Derby mark the upward grade. Then comes descent in the retreat to Scotland, the disastrous defeat of the Highland troops by the Duke of Cumberland at Culloden Moor on 16 April 1746, followed by five and a half months of escape, with a price on his head, across the wildest parts of Scotland, his rescue by Flora Macdonald in the disguise of a spinning-maid, Betty Burke, and their sail by night from Benbecula to Skye. These historic events are so well known and have been so often related that even an abbreviated recital of them in these pages would be supererogatory.

When at last Prince Henry discovered that his brother had slipped away to win his spurs on British soil he was overcome by the grief of separation. In February he wrote to Prince Charles that he had been 'upon thorns' until he learnt of his safe arrival at Antibes. He also bitterly resented not being allowed to share in the perilous adventure. His father insisted that the younger son should stay at home. This he was obliged against his will to do for a year and a half. Let us hope that the interval was spent less at prayer and rather more at books of a profaner sort than formerly.

Henry was certainly not yet the dedicated lover of peace of his later years. For he itched to be off and join his brother's campaign. The Chevalier eventually had to give way, and on 29 August 1745 Henry was allowed to leave Rome. He was accompanied by Sir John Graeme, who had joined Prince Charles in the course of his flight. His departure had also to be carried out in secret so that the spies should not get to hear of it. News was released that the Prince was ill with smallpox which accounted for his temporary absence from Roman society. He rode by way of Poggibonsi — whence he wrote to his father that the postmaster remarked upon his resemblance to Charles, a thing which had not previously occurred to him — Pisa, Genoa and Savona. At Savona he hired a boat to Antibes. The route was the one taken by his brother. At Avignon he fell ill of a fever and was obliged to rest there for two months. He proceeded to Paris and as soon as possible made for the French court, then at Fontainebleau, bearing his father's written recommendations to Louis XV. Having announced his arrival at the château he was kept waiting in a small room for several hours. The King after receiving a servant's message, forgot all about his visitor. On being reminded he sent for the Prince whom he treated with scant courtesy. The Prince beseeched the King to lend his brother more support. The appeal met with frigid in-difference. Those in attendance on the King at the time remarked upon his young cousin's dignity and composure. Henry was not a royal Stuart for nothing.

The Duke of York was eventually posted to Dunkirk where he was given nominal command of the small French expeditionary force previously agreed upon between Louis and the Jacobite court. It was meant to set sail for Scotland when Prince Charles's affairs in that country should warrant the risk of embarkation. Prince Charles's affairs however were not deemed to warrant it by the actual com-manders, who naturally enough were Frenchmen. Prince Henry was thus kept hanging about the north coast of France all through the winter of 1745 to 1746 until in fact intelligence of the defeat at Culloden reached him. Whereupon the expeditionary force was disbanded with indecent haste. The winter months were an agony to Prince Henry. The virtual commander of the troops was the veteran Marshal Duc de Richelieu, a great-nephew of the Cardinal of that name. His life was one series of debauches and scandals. He lusted after women day and night. He had mistresses galore and was even to marry – not for the first time – at the age of eighty-four. He was not only vicious but contemptuous of anyone who was virtuous. Henry's piety and natural prudery revolted against the Duke's behaviour and blasphemies. They were intensified by the Duke's undisguised pleasure in shocking this boy of twenty. 'You may perhaps gain the kingdom of heaven by your prayers, but never the kingdom of Britain,' he jeered at him. The more the Duke swore the more the Prince looked disapproving. Finally Henry totally withdrew into his shell. The Marquis d'Argenson, Minister of Foreign Affairs, so wise according to Voltaire that he was worthy of being Secretary of State in the republic of Plato, was no less a man of the world than the Duke; and he too laughed at what in truth must have seemed to him sanctimoniousness. The young Englishmen, he wrote, 'never passes before a crucifix or an altar without genuflecting like a sacristan'. The French people were contemptuous of such 'absurd prejudices'. D'Argenson who knew and admired Prince Charles was nonplussed by the younger brother's seeming indifference to pleasure. He totally misconstrued his character, in pronouncing him 'thoroughly Italian, sly, deceitful, superstitious, miserly, loving his ease and above all jealous and hating his brother.' The last observation was palpably false since Henry still idolized and hero-worshipped Prince Charles. Finally d'Argenson and Richelieu blamed Henry for indecisions at Dunkirk which prevented the French fleet from sailing. Hardly in the circumstances a fair indictment. The foreign youth of twenty in his turn blamed the Duke for inertia in never once attempting to leave the harbour, and for having no will to do so from the beginning. His accusation is more likely to be the true one.

In April 1746 Culloden came and went. The French expeditionary force dissolved, and the Duc de Richelieu was able to return to the laxity and licence of Paris. Prince Henry was left to worry over the unknown hazards which his beloved brother was running in the wilds of an alien land and to brood over the inadequate qualities of which the French Marshal and Foreign Minister accused him. It was to his credit that he did not give way to self-questioning and self-recrimination for long, and that he refused to return to Rome. How could he go back to the ease and comforts of home while his brother was skulking in utmost danger of his life? It was no good his father bombarding him with letters beginning, 'My dearest Harry,' reiterating what a mistake Charles's expedition had been, and fore-telling disaster before it had actually come about. Although Culloden was fought and lost on 16 April the Chevalier had written on 29 March, 'By all I can remark I am affray'd all is lost in Scotland, and really all things considered it is a great wonder that it did not happen sooner than that it should be the case now.' King James's jeremiads were vexatious, to say the least. All they did was to confirm his younger son's resolve to stay away. Although Prince Henry must have known that a martial career was not for him, he at once obtained Louis XV's consent to accompany the Comte de Clermont's expedition to Flanders where the Maréchal de Saxe was conducting a campaign against the English under Cumberland. He was deter-mined to show the world that he too was possessed of guts. After the siege of Antwerp which ensued d'Argenson was forced to admit that 'he behaved with a valour which was at once natural and hereditary.' He cleared himself from the ugly imputations which the French minister had been levelling against him.

The siege of Antwerp was the first and last military engagement in which the pacific Duke of York took part. When it was over he retired to his cousin the Duc de Bouillon's château de Navarre near Évreux.* From there he made frantic efforts to get the French government to send ships to Scotland for Prince Charles's relief. In these efforts he was successful and at the beginning of October had the happiness of welcoming his brother to Paris in a tumult of joy, tears and rapture. Prince Charles, shortly after midnight of 19 September had embarked at Borradale on the west coast of Scotland with a small party on the French ship *L'Heureux*. After seeing everyone aboard he

* A sister of Clementina Sobieska, mother of Prince Charles and Prince Henry, married Charles Godefroy de Latour d'Auvergne, ruling Duc de Bouillon. Prince Charles was lent a little château by his cousin in the valley of the Semois in 1755–6.

was the last to spring on deck. There he sat alone in the dark fixedly watching the coast recede, without uttering a word.

It must not be supposed that the Prince was unaware of or indifferent to the terrible distress which the failure of the expedition had brought to the Highland clans. The very morning of sailing he wrote on board by lamplight a letter to Cluny the Chief of the clan Macpherson, ordering him to disburse various sums of money to his needy clansmen. He likewise sent to Sir Stuart Threipland another letter begging the recipient to distribute money to deserving followers. Both these undertakings were honoured and accounts of the expenditure sent to the Chevalier in Rome to defray.

It is as difficult not to be as moved by the Prince's adventures leading up to and following upon his defeat at Culloden as was James Boswell on listening to their recital during his visit in 1773 with Dr Johnson to Skye. 'As he [Mr Donald M'Queen, their host] narrated the particulars of that ill-advised, but brave attempt, I could not refrain from tears.' The poignancy of the aftermath lies in the abrupt change of character which the reverses of the Forty-five brought about in the Prince. From the moment he sailed out of Loch nan Uamh the Bonnie Prince Charlie of Scottish romance ceased to exist. Donald Nicholas has succinctly summed up the *volte-face* in the following epitaph: 'It was the end of Charles's youth, the end of all his dreams, and from henceforth he lived only in the past.' The man lived another forty-two years, or rather dragged out an existence over which, did the sequel not have a far-reaching effect upon the fate of his luckless dynasty, it would be better to draw a veil. Little that is edifying marks his character henceforth. An absolute degradation of the spirit was the consequence of the poor Prince's misfortunes and failure. Nevertheless it is true to say that the legend of the messianic prince is still one of the cherished components of Highland nationalism. Although every Highlander is well aware that their Prince Jekyll turned – after he left them – into Prince Hyde, they venerate the former, in spite of the trail of misery which his defeat brought upon the clans. There is scarcely a great family in Scotland (even of Whig descent) that does not boast some relic of the Bonny Prince. Wherever he carried with him a personal belonging, a cup, a spoon, a snuffbox, he would readily hand it to his host or hostess on parting. And besides he had an engaging habit of absent-mindedly leaving his watches under his pillow. It would be a bold Sassenach who in 1983 ventured to cast aspersions upon his conduct during the eighteen months when he was sanctifying Scottish soil with his presence.

And wherein lies the peculiar charm which Prince Charles lavished upon the Highlanders at the time of the Forty-five? It is difficult to lay one's finger precisely upon it. He was of course only twenty-five. He was tall, as his surviving coats, trews and waistcoats testify. He was healthy. He was extremely personable, if not strictly beautiful. He had sad eyes and a seductive mouth. But his pale features had defects. His forehead sloped back from his brows and his long chin, as we have already remarked, disappeared into a sort of button. The nape of his neck was bull-like.* It was his free and easy manner which was so captivating. He was debonair. Always smartly but heedlessly dressed (except of course when he was on the run) he had an endearing trick of snatching off his bag wig and with a shake of his curls, thrusting it into his pocket. He introduced a panache which was foreign, not to say exotic, into Scotland. His accent too was pleasingly unfamiliar and made amusing by his slangy expressions. He could adapt himself effortlessly to both exalted and humble, being in fact happier in the company of the latter. And withal there was an unmistakable greatness in his demeanour, which, no matter what his disguise, could not be dissembled.

There was in short a glamour, almost a mystique about his personality which was not simply engendered by the aura surrounding his royal birth and the extraordinary circumstance of his landing in Scotland unarmed and unsupported to recover the land of his forefathers. After all, his kingly father had made a similar ill-fated attempt in the Fifteen without winning for himself the adoration of his own and future generations. The old Chevalier's undoubted heroism did not render him the idol of posterity. No, Prince Charles possessed some special qualities hard for us to define. They were sufficiently rare to move old Lord Balmerino on the scaffold to

---

* These defects are noticeable in the two likenesses of him taken at this climacteric of his career. They happen to be the two portraits by which the Prince himself set most store. They are the pastel by Maurice Quentin de la Tour, which was exhibited in the Paris Salon of 1747 and the bust by J. B. Lemoyne. In a letter of 1752 to the banker Waters the Prince asks him to take special care of them. The 'marble busto' was his particular favourite.

declaim to the crowds drawn to enjoy the spectacle of his execution these memorable words:

'I am at a loss when I come to speak of the Prince; I am not a fit hand to draw his character. I shall leave that to others. But I must beg leave to tell you the incomparable sweetness of his nature, his affability, his compassion, his justice, his temperance [meaning equability], his patience, and his courage are virtues, seldom to be found in one person. In short he wants no qualifications requisite to make a great man.'

These phrases were the assessment of an aristocrat on the brink of death. Those from the mouth of Jenny, an uneducated abigail, translated into verse by John Byrom, are less particular but no less convincing:

> If you but saw him once . . .
>   Do see him once! What harm is there in seeing?
> If after that there be not an agreeing,
> Then call me twenty rebel sluts if you
> When you have seen him, be'ant a rebel too!

Possibly the most tragic instance of the Stuart ill luck is the exception which Prince Charles makes to the old adage that those whom the gods love, die young.

On 29 September *L'Heureux* berthed at Morlaix. The Prince proceeded at once to Paris where he was acclaimed a hero both by populace and society. The château de St Antoine was put at his disposal by Louis XV. For several days he was obliged to remain indoors until he could be fitted with a new wardrobe. He had arrived literally in rags. And they were

'looked upon as so many reliques, there were a great many disputes and quarrels about them, not only among the King's [James III's] subjects, but the French, especially the Ladys . . . one had his bonnet, one his coat another the old Shoose and Stokens another his pipe, etc., but there were still some dissatisfied, there was nothing left but the wig; which was a most abominable one, but a Lady discovered it was not given away, but thrown aside, & she wou'd have it. She was told it wou'd infect her, yt was full of vermine, as really it was.'

Once re-accoutred the Prince presented himself at court in some style. He arrived splendidly dressed in a coat of rose coloured velvet embroidered with silver and lined with silver tissue. His waistcoat was of rich gold brocade with a spangled fringe set in scallops. The cockade in his hat was studded with diamonds. The popular and social idol was indignant that Louis XV would not receive him as Prince of Wales, but only *incognito*, for the French king was at this juncture very fearful of offending the English government. Louis soon became highly embarrassed by the Prince's establishment in the capital. On the one hand his ministers looked upon Charles's presence as sure cause of European friction; on the other his own family, notably the Queen and the Dauphin, were adoring and spoiling their cousin without restraint. For a time the Prince kept his head and his own counsel. He could not prevent himself being adored, but he did not yet feel like being fêted. 'How can you imagine yt I can enjoy any pleasure,' he wrote to his father, 'when I have constantly before my eyes, the cruelty with wch my poor freinds are traited in England.'

During the excitement of the brothers' reunion, to which Henry had so desperately looked forward, the younger did not omit to impart the glad tidings to the Chevalier. Apparently Charles did not at first recognize Henry who in his absence had changed from boyhood to manhood, whereas Henry recognized Charles instantly. In spite of the adventures he had experienced the Prince of Wales had for some unaccountable reason 'grown broader and fatter'. The two at once set up house together at Clichy. But alas! the mutual joy of the reunion was short-lived. Henry was shocked by the raffish company Charles kept and the dissipations into which he plunged headlong. Charles for his part was bored by his younger brother's uncontained disapproval and sermonizing. Two of his associates upon whom the Duke looked particularly askance were the Princesse de Guémené and their mother's cousin, the Princesse de Talmond.

Was the latter Charles's mistress? It was supposed so by all and sundry. That gossip the Marquis d'Argenson – Louis XV's Secretary of State for Foreign Affairs, 1744–7 – maintained that in Paris the

Prince spent all his time making love and gambling. This may or may not have been true. He also affirmed that Madame de Guémené 'almost' ravished him by force, which implies that she did not quite. For as well as being in the eyes of Parisian ladies a romantic hero he was physically very attractive to them. Marie de Talmond was certainly in love with him. She wore a bracelet with a portrait of the Prince on one side and Jesus Christ on the other. When asked what the two had in common she quoted the passage in Scripture, 'My kingdom is not of this world'. She was a Pole, the daughter of Count Jablonowski, a relation of Queen Marie Leczinska of France and married to the influential French Prince de Talmond. She also happened to be ten years older than Prince Charles who referred to her as 'la Grandemain' (*sic*), an unusual term to be applied by a lover to his mistress even in jest. Marie delighted in meddling in politics and may have encouraged his unaccommodating attitude towards Louis XV because of her close intimacy with and sympathy for the ill-used Queen. She had beauty, wit and vivacity. Yet Horace Walpole, who usually evoked some response from ladies of spirit whom he met for the first time, considered her empty-headed. He told Thomas Gray that he was taken to see her in the Luxembourg Palace, 'sitting on a small bed hung with saints and Sobieskis, in a corner of one of those vast chambers, by two blinking tapers. I stumbled over a cat, a footstool, and a chamber-pot in my journey to her presence. She could not find a syllable to say to me, and the visit ended with her begging a lap-dog.' He had for once drawn a complete blank.

Prince Charles's relations with the Princesse de Talmond were, if not passionate, then tempestuous. One senses that the lady did not receive from him all that she thought her due. At any rate soon after his expulsion from Paris in December 1748 the affair petered out. Another whose relations with him were calmer and happier was Mlle. Luci de Ferrand des Marres, an extremely intelligent woman who was probably a lesbian.* Mlle. de Ferrand, although constitutionally delicate, became his tireless slave until her untimely death in 1752. She did his shopping, acted as his amanuensis, chose his books and directed his reading of romances. The Prince made shameless use

---

* She lived with Mme de Vassé at the Convent of St Joseph in Paris. The Abbé Condillac dedicated 'Le Traité des Sensations' (1749–51) to her.

of her attentions, and because she made no demands upon him, esteemed her in return.

Indeed it is open to question how fond of women Prince Charles really was. There is no doubt whatever that women were mad about him. The Marquis d'Éguilles remarked in 1746, 'It is not as though he is flirtatious or even particularly attentive to women. On the contrary he is neither.' Lord Elcho, who had been his playmate when both were boys and knew him fairly intimately, albeit his later criticisms of the Prince were infused with malice, thought that he was positively indifferent to the opposite sex. Elcho noted in 1745 that towards the Edinburgh ladies of fashion 'his behaviour . . . was very cool: he had not been much used to Women's company, and was always embarrassed while he was with them.' It did not apparently occur to Elcho that on the eve of a battle which might determine his whole future the Prince would have little inclination to gallantry. For when asked at the great ball at Holyrood Palace why he remained moodily alone, not participating in the dances, he beckoned to a gigantic Highlander who was standing sentinel at a doorway. Charles, stroking the man's beard and toying with his bristly cheeks, exclaimed, 'These are the beauties to whom I must now make love, and for a few thousands of whom I would fain dispense with all yonder fair damsels.' The gesture by no means implies that he was homosexual. It is true that during the Forty-Five reports from his enemies that he was, were rife. The *Glasgow Courant* boldly stated that 'Charles loved the men better than the women.' One story went about that he liked to travel in a carriage dressed as a woman; another that his affection for the close companion of his escape in the Highlands, John O'Sullivan, was unnatural. But we know that he enjoyed disguises. In later years he used to mingle incognito with unsuspecting English travellers on the continent and, wearing a false nose or beard, eavesdrop their conversations about himself. As for O'Sullivan, the Prince before Culloden shocked the prudish citizens of Perth with his unseemly horseplay in pulling the Irishman out of bed — surely a harmless, boyish prank.*

---

* O'Sullivan's *Journal of the 1745 Campaign* gives the following account of the companions' enforced separation on South Uist in June 1746 when the Prince's prospects of escape to France were at their lowest and he had to be on his own. 'The Prince's parting from Sullivan was like tearing the heart from the body . . . [He] burst

As the months dragged by in Paris Prince Charles's indignation with the French government mounted to frenzy. His attitude towards the court was offhand, when not downright rude. He refused Louis's tactful offer of a residence in Fribourg where he would be out of the way. He refused the offer of a pension. He bitterly reproached the King for his lack of support during the Forty-Five, and demanded an army for another invasion. The request was at once turned down. His tactics were very childish. He wrote to his father on 6 November, 'I find it, and am absolutely convinced of it, that ye only way of delying [sic] with this Government, is to give as short and smart answers as one can, at ye same time paying them in their own Coin by loding them with sivilities and compliments, setting apart business, for that kind of' vermin the more you give them, the more thel take . . .' But the vermin did not, as vermin are notoriously disinclined to do, interpret the Prince's undiluted insults as civilities. He even made a rapid journey to Spain; and the Spanish court was no more disposed to give him help than the French.

It was not long before the Duke of York began to think that he could be of little service to the Prince of Wales or the Jacobite cause by remaining in the neighbourhood of Paris, which anyway was disagreeable to him. Indeed it seems that Henry soon shared his father's conviction that for the present at any rate further attempts at a restoration were useless. On the other hand so much as a hint of throwing up the sponge now or in the future put Prince Charles into paroxysms of indignation.

The elder brother's conduct was certainly irrational, but then he had experienced an ordeal calculated to break most men, an ordeal for which possibly the Duke failed to make sufficient allowance. Like ex-prisoners of war, the Prince could not immediately readapt himself to conventional ways of civilized living. Unfortunately he was never thoroughly to do so again. The Duc de Luynes made an interesting distinction between the brothers whom he met at Fontainebleau, interesting because he reversed what we suppose the

---

out a crying to quit the Prince . . . The Prince embrasses him, and holds him in his arms for a quarter of an hour. All the sailors cry and roar, and looks upon the Prince as lost.' O'Sullivan was twenty years older than the Prince, and acted as a kind of guardian and mentor during the Forty-Five.

character of each to have been. He wrote, 'The Prince is serious enough: his brother the Duke of York has an entirely different character: he talks too much, he laughs too readily, he appears alert and loves music passionately.' And he added, 'He is much smaller than his brother, and his face is less distinguished'. In high society the Prince was still weighed down by his recent disappointments; the Duke was merely ill at ease. He probably talked and laughed too much from nerves, and tried too hard. No doubt when chatter gave place to music he felt happier.

The Chevalier's letters to Henry urging him to return grew more persistent. Displeasure with each other's company turned to violent squabbles between the brothers. They were together less and less. Yet the elder accepted an invitation to dine with the younger on 29 April 1747. He duly went to the Duke's lodgings to find that Henry was not there. He had fled without a word of warning. He merely left a letter to be delivered to Charles three days after his departure. What was the reason for this seemingly unkind and discourteous behaviour? A sudden impulse to get away from the fraternal bickering which considerably upset him? Or the receipt of a hint from his father of the honours which were in store for him in Rome, if he hastened back, and a desire to avoid unpleasant arguments with Charles which a pre-announcement of these prospects would inevitably involve? At all events he returned to his father.

Henry had barely been back in Rome a month before the Pope offered him the Cardinal's hat. Prospero Lambertini, Benedict XIV (1740–58), was a close friend and fervent supporter of James III. It is hardly credible that the two old cronies had not discussed the offer while Prince Henry was still in France or that the father had not let his son know what was in the wind. From Benedict's correspondence with Cardinal Pierre Guérin de Tencin we gather that Henry while in Paris spoke of his determination to be made a cardinal one day, and that at the beginning of June James was urging the Pope to make him one. The Chevalier was in agonies of apprehension lest the elder son should get to hear of the scheme before the King of France's consent could be obtained. This consent was essential because of the Stuart family's dependence upon Louis XV for financial support in one form or another. To flout that King's disapproval would mean James forfeiting his pension. And that could not be faced. When Louis was asked he readily approved that Prince Henry should be raised to the purple.

It seems to us an extraordinary office to befall an untried youth of only twenty-two who was not even in holy orders. As things turned out the decision was in all respects a suitable one, for both Benedict and James had ample evidence of the young man's religious convictions and devoutness. It was, moreover, not until Pius IX's reign in the following century that men were prohibited from being made cardinals before they were priests. Benedict called a consistory and in informing the Sacred College of his intentions reminded them of previous juvenile creations. There was no murmur of dissent. On 30 June Prince Henry received the tonsure from the Pope's own hands in his private chapel in the Vatican. On 3 July the Prince proceeded in state to St Peter's where he was given the hat of a cardinal deacon, the lowest of the three degrees of cardinal – again from Benedict at the Sistine chapel altar.

The titular church allotted to him was Carlo Rainaldi's beautiful Baroque Santa Maria in Campitelli below the Capitoline Hill. The Cardinal Duke of York became greatly attached to this church which he embellished and in which he endowed prayers for the conversion of England to be said at noon every Saturday. With the cardinalate went various minor orders, a sub-diaconate and a diaconate. The youthful cardinal was obliged by the Pope to spend more than a year's intensive course of theological studies under three directors, including Father Ildefonso, chosen for him by the Holy Father himself. When these preparations were deemed complete he received priestly ordination in public on 1st September 1748.

Henry went about his studies with commendable regularity and zeal. The Pope was delighted with his conduct, pronouncing him incredibly industrious as well as intelligent. The young pupil's grasp of Latin was highly satisfactory. When the first year's crash course was over the budding cardinal still spent five evenings every week at his books, devoting only two to *conversazioni* in his apartments. This was just as it should be. In the autumn of 1748 he was perfection in Benedict's eyes. The Pope wrote that he was an angel in human form and the paragon of Rome. 'This holy young man' he called him. And so he seemed to be. That year Horace Mann wrote, 'The Cardinal is all devotion. He fasts and prays as much as his mother used to do, and they say, has ruined his constitution already.' In other words he was practically back to the régime of 1742 which had so worried his tutor Lord Dunbar.

The Cardinal Duke's advance in ecclesiastical preferments and honours was, throughout his long life, as regular as clockwork. It is true that he was royal, and that his father was very importunate in making demands in his favour. But he was also eminently presentable. In 1751 he was to be nominated Arch-Priest and Prefect of the Vatican Basilica in succession to Cardinal Annibale Albani, a close friend of the Chevalier and the staunch ally of the Stuarts. With the office went the specific function of performing in the Pope's absence several sacerdotal duties in St Peter's, and the enjoyment of an apartment in the Piazza della Sagrestia. In 1758 Benedict appointed him *Camerlengo*, or Chamberlain, of the papal court. In this office – the last he was to receive from Pope Benedict XIV – he administered the properties and revenues of the Holy See, and had to organize the conclaves which elected new popes. On 19 November of the same year he was consecrated by Pope Clement XIII in the church of the Santi Apostoli Archbishop of Corinth *in partibus infidelium*. The occasion was marked by great ceremonial splendour. The Cardinal Duke was obliged to resign this titular archbishopric on his translation in 1761 to the see of Tusculum (Frascati). Already at the age of thirty-six he was one of six cardinal bishops who constituted the highest degree of the Sacred College. He was enthroned in the cathedral of Cato's ancient city on the Alban Hills on 13 July; and was to remain Frascati's bishop and faithful pastor for forty-six years. Two years later he was made Vice-Chancellor of the Holy Roman Church. With this office went a residence in Bramante's huge and famous Palazzo Cancelleria in the heart of Rome. Finally in 1803, upon the death of his intimate friend Cardinal Gianfranceso Albani he became the senior member of the cardinalate and so, automatically, Dean of the Sacred College.

We must now return to 1747 and to Prince Charles, who was residing in Paris with Sir John Graeme, then master of the household and in disgrace with the Chevalier for being yet another courtier leading his son and heir astray. The Prince was about to receive from his father the oft-quoted letter of 13 June beginning, 'I do not know whether you will be surprised, my dearest Carluccio, when I tell you that your brother will be made a cardinal the first days of next month.' It must be admitted that the King's announcement was phrased with some cunning. 'Naturally speaking, you should have been consulted about a resolution of that kind before it had been executed,' he went on.

'But as the Duke and I were unalterably determined on the matter, and as we foresaw you might probably not approve of it, we thought it might be showing you more regard, and that it would be even more agreeable to you, that the thing should be done before your answer should come here, and to have it in your power to say it was done without your knowledge and approbation.'

We may detect in the father's circumlocutions both fear of his son's reaction and a sense of guilt. The phrase, 'but as the Duke and I were unalterably determined on the matter,' was a confession that father and younger brother had been scheming behind the Prince's back. The letter was calculated to arouse deep indignation in the recipient. And it did.

On receipt of the news the Prince was appalled, and incensed. He replied on 10 July: 'had I got a Dager throw my heart it would not have been mor sensible to me than at ye Contents of yr first.' As he viewed the situation, his brother's acceptance of the hat seriously jeopardized all future chances of the Stuarts winning back the throne of England from its strongly entrenched Protestant occupant; and also snapped the second string to the Stuart bow, so to speak, in that, failing any heirs from his own loins, none might be expected from those of a prince of the Church. From now on the Prince broke with his father to whom he rarely wrote letters and nearly eighteen years were to elapse before he communicated with Henry. His father's protestation that 'in your behaviour towards your brother there is something so incomprehensible and so contrary to your natural temper and to that spirit of justice and mildness which gained you so much honour in Scotland, that I really know no more what to make or think of you . . .' did nothing to mitigate his anger. Prince Charles would not allow Henry's health to be drunk at his table or his name to be mentioned in his presence.

It was not only 'dearest Carluccio' who was upset. His attendants were equally annoyed. Father Myles MacDonnell had the temerity to write from Paris to the King that 'your Majesty's subjects here are agreeing in nothing so unanimously as in thinking it a mortal deadly stroke to the Cause.' Whereas in Scotland, he added, 'all the old bugbears of Popery, bigotry, etc. will be renewed with (I am afraid) too much success.'

Prince Charles's resentment against his brother persisted until, after his father's death, it suited him, as a supplicant to the Pope for recognition of his kingly prerogatives, to come to terms with the influential Cardinal. But in 1754 he wrote of the Cardinal Duke, 'He has always acted, as far as in his power, against my interest,' and saw in his brother's close relations with the Pope intrigues directed against himself. These imputations and suspicions were totally unwarrantable. It was of course irksome that while he was living in great financial straits in a hostile country, working as he firmly believed like a beaver to retrieve the family rights, his younger brother, having washed his hands of the supreme cause, was luxuriating in power and affluence in the service of the one institution, namely the Catholic Church, which was the chief obstacle to his chances of success. He knew full well that both his father and brother had given up the fight, and had reconciled themselves to defeat.

Had Charles only realized it the Cardinal Duke bore no resentment towards him in spite of his manifold follies, but continued to love him and promote his interests whenever opportunity arose. He happened to be extremely jealous of his father's and subsequently his brother's rights to the English throne, as we shall see. As an instance of his goodness of heart and generosity he readily agreed in 1751 that the Chevalier should bequeath to Prince Charles all the French rents inherited from their Sobieski grandfather in 1737 which by rights were to come to him on the Chevalier's death; and furthermore he gratuitously offered to make over at once, subject to his father's life interest those which he was already enjoying. Incidentally the large sums of money owing to the Chevalier by Poland were never received by the grandsons, the Republic conveniently freezing them the moment James died.

At first the Chevalier derived consolation for the elder son's peccadilloes in the successful and blameless life of the younger. But although the Chevalier and the Cardinal Duke saw eye to eye on matters pertaining to their faith, their day to day relations were not always harmonious. If dearest Carluccio was a constant source of anxiety, and often intense misery, to the father, dearest Harry could be tiresome. Charles, in spite of his vices which to the religious James were anathema, was probably the favourite son in that undeserving way (so incomprehensible to the virtuous and deserving) which prodigal children have with weak parents. Because of his absence — and Princes Charles's cruelty in refusing ever to see his father after 1744 was inexcusable — his memory as the handsome and dashing hero never grew dim. It may at first seem strange that James came to look upon the straightlipped Henry's private life a little askance. But he did so with some reason.

When Prince Henry's theological studies were over and he had received his ordination he found himself a person of authority. The young Cardinal no longer relished being treated like a schoolboy in the Palazzo Muti, where he still resided and took over the management of the household. He was not content to sit at home evening after evening reading to his father the Life of St Augustine by the light of a single candle — for the Chevalier was parsimonious. He made his own friends and he liked to entertain them in splendour and refulgence. He particularly relished the society of musicians. He not only organized sung Masses and oratorios in Santa Maria in Campitelli, where he appointed Baldassare Galuppi choir master, but gave musical parties and weekly receptions in his apartments in the Palazzo Muti, which became extremely popular. He even entertained Galuppi at his table. The Chevalier was scandalized by this condescension. A composer of opera with titles like *Didone Abbandonata* and *Il Vilano Geloso*, who played the violin for a living was, kept at a proper distance, one thing: a guest on equal terms with a prince of the blood royal was quite another. And this particular musician's father had been a barber in Burano! The Chevalier accused the Cardinal of keeping low company. The Cardinal took offence. When father and son were alone at meals the latter sulked, and refused to utter.

Further trouble ensued in 1749 when the Cardinal suddenly dismissed his English *maestro di camera*, Monsignor Leigh or Lee, and appointed in his place a personable young Genoese priest, Padre Lercari. The Chevalier was greatly put out. He set much store in employing as many of his own countrymen, (and whenever possible, Protestants which in the Cardinal's case was of course out of the question) at his court. For some reason which is not explained but can be guessed, he took a personal dislike to Padre Lercari, whose influence upon his son he deplored. He blamed the Cardinal's confessor, Padre Ildefonso for consenting to the dismissal of Monsignor Leigh and condoning his replacement by the Italian, and forbade the confessor entry to the palace. Whereupon the Cardinal, losing control of his temper flounced off to Nocera with Lercari. James appealed to the Pope. Benedict was bewildered by the father and son's hysteria and merely remarked to his correspondent Cardinal de Tencin that the young Cardinal of York was too much under the influence of certain clerics though these were worthy men. In *Memoirs of the Reign of George II* Horace Walpole mentions the affair in these terms:

'The Cardinal of York, whose devotion preserved him from disobedience to his father as little as his princely character had preserved him from devotion, had entirely abandoned himself to the government of an abbé, who soon grew displeasing to the Old Pretender. Commands, remonstrances, requests, had no effect on the obstinacy of the young Cardinal. The father, whose genius never veered towards compliance, insisted on the dismissal of the abbé. Instead of parting with his favourite the young Cardinal with his minion left Rome abruptly, and with little regard to the dignity of his purple.'

Walpole's is the first direct written reference to the Cardinal's infatuation for a young man. This particular infatuation was the cause of considerable embarrassment both to the father and the Pope. The Chevalier, who after every domestic tiff suffered from grievous remorse, as well as indigestion, invariably gave way and craved his son's forgiveness. Cardinal and 'minion' returned to the English court, then at Albano. Not a word passed between father and son about the incident.

In January of 1751 the Cardinal was taken very ill. At first the Pope attributed the illness to over-attendance of Masses at Christmas time. This may well have been the case in that thereby the Cardinal exposed himself to infection, for he had developed smallpox. So great was the Pope's regard for his protégé still that he rashly visited the sickbed. The Cardinal recovered, but suffered from prolonged after-effects. In his convalesence he was wracked by scruples which Benedict assured him, 'torment the body just as much as the soul'. He sent for his confessor twice and sometimes thrice a day, until the poor man could no longer bear to listen to the scruples that came pouring from the penitent's lips and the entreaties for absolution.

In 1752 the Chevalier resumed his querulous remonstrances against the friendship with Lercari and the Abbé's residence in the Palazzo Muti. This time he forbade correspondence between Lercari and Ildefonso whom he again accused of responsibility for the appointment of the young priest as his son's chamberlain. The King called once more upon the Pope's intervention, and Lercari was dismissed by papal decree. The Cardinal fretted, made himself ill again, and again left Rome in high dudgeon. The Pope commanded the fugitive Cardinal to return from Bologna, where he made a show of intending to remain for good. He told him bluntly that he was an undutiful son to the best of fathers. Henry wrote the Chevalier a contrite letter. He was of course instantly forgiven, and welcomed back to hearth and home.

By now the affair was known all over Rome. It was gossiped about in drawing rooms and cafés. It assumed the proportions of comedy. Numerous people intervened. On insisting upon Lercari's dismissal from his son's establishment the Chevalier had forbidden Lercari's return to Rome in any capacity whatever. This was arrogating to himself ecclesiastical jurisdiction which he did not possess. Besides Lercari had an uncle who was a cardinal of influence and resented the *de jure* King of England's interference. He complained to the Pope about the unjustifiable persecution of his nephew by this foreigner. Pope Benedict, more bewildered than ever, found the row singular because 'on neither side is there any question of venial sin'. Henry explained to His Holiness that unless he was caressing his father he was accused by him of ingratitude. When he did caress him he was accused of dissimulation. It was impossible to do the right thing by him. The Pope tried to persuade James to be less demonstrative of affection towards his son and less interfering in his affairs. Sons, he said, can never love their fathers as much as fathers love their sons. Besides, boys grow up and will not tolerate their every action being

determined by a parent, however devoted. He could not quite
understand why James had taken so violently against Lercari, a
seemingly harmless young man. All the answer he received was the
distraught old man's threat to shut himself up in a monastery. Henry
declared that his father was driving him to the same distraction into
which he drove his poor mother. This remark was considered by the
Pope and the King to be cruel as well as in extremely poor taste.
Benedict was obliged to reprove him. Henry was treating his doting
father with contempt and insult. Then the Chevalier, heedless of the
Pope's advice, unwisely nominated a substitute *maestro di camera*
for his son. Henry would have nothing to do with him. The man, he
said, was old, hideous, and he stank atrociously in hot weather.
Lercari returned without anyone's permission to Rome, but not to
the Cardinal's household. To the scandal of his office the Cardinal
went publicly to visit Lercari for hours at a time. He also wrote to him
endless letters. 'This is very innocent but puerile conduct which does
not contribute much credit to him who indulges in it,' Benedict
said. Nevertheless the Pope's denial of guilt implied that guilt had
been imputed by someone or other to the Cardinal's unorthodox
infatuation.

By July of 1752 father and son were on strictly non-speaking terms
although still living under the same roof. James ordered his son to
leave his palace. Then he threatened that if he left his palace he would
never speak to him again. Then he announced that if he did return he,
James, would leave the palace. He rushed off to consult the Cardinal
Secretary of State, who summoned Henry. The Secretary of State told
Henry that he must renounce either his father or his friend. He did
neither. Finally in September Benedict, sick to death of the whole
drama insisted upon the Chevalier not mentioning the subject to him
the whole of the forthcoming winter. By now he was disenchanted
with the Cardinal Duke who, he said, lacked knowledge of the world
and in allowing himself to be governed by young persons, was
infantile. He remarked that the English were emotionally unstable. In
his self-pity he compared himself with St Cassian who was martyred,
not by having his head cut off, but by a succession of knife thrusts
from his pupils.

By the autumn of 1753 the Cardinal's infatuation for Lercari had
petered out. By September he was frequenting once again the draw-

ing rooms of old ladies. The Chevalier was overjoyed and welcomed the errant son back to his bosom. Nevertheless relations between the King and Cardinal Duke were strained until the latter moved to the Piazza della Sagrestia of St Peter's where in his capacity as Arch-Priest of the basilica he had lodgings. So long as father and son were no longer living cheek by jowl under the same roof their basic mutual affection could be maintained. Before the world the Cardinal was always at great pains to preserve family unanimity and to insist upon unquestioning loyalty to the sovereignty of his father, his brother and ultimately himself. An acute sense of his own royalty demanded acknowledgement from all who came in contact with him. It was what exalted him in his eyes above his fellow Eminences. They were not all inclined to make obeisance to what could be deemed an archaic claim.

As the King grew older and feebler so the Cardinal Duke became more and more dutiful. He was constantly visiting his father's sickbed, proffering spiritual consolation and domestic advice, and keeping an eye upon the milling throngs of impoverished, discontented and bored Jacobite hangers-on. He was also a great comfort and support to his father's faithful and harassed private secretary, upon whose services of forty-six long years the Chevalier came utterly to depend. In James Edgar and then in Edgar's successor, Andrew Lumisden, the old King, who was unfortunate in many things, was most truly blessed.

The Treaty of Aix-la-Chapelle between Britain, France, Holland, Germany, Spain and Genoa signed in October 1748 embraced the condition that the Pretenders to the English throne might not reside within any of the countries which were parties to it. Accordingly Prince Charles was ordered to leave France. His father wrote strongly urging him to obey the French King's orders. The Prince paid no attention and pleaded that he possessed a letter from Louis stipulating that he might remain. He stormed. He raved. He saw everyone as his enemy. He looked everywhere for insults. He threatened to kill himself, which provoked the French Foreign Minister to remark, 'You must love the reigning King of England very much to give him that pleasure.' He was several times warned by special messengers that he must go. He stubbornly refused. Louis was persuaded to have him removed from Paris by force. One night in December the Prince was arrested on the steps of the opera house, pinioned hand and foot, and bundled into a carriage like a corpse. He was driven to the fortress at Vincennes where he was locked up. His humiliation was profound. The public was shocked by this treatment of their hero. The Dauphin burst into tears and even Louis was overheard to murmur, 'Poor Prince, how difficult it is for a king to be a true friend!' During the arrest and imprisonment the Prince behaved with splendid dignity.

After this experience he consented to leave French territory, and moved to Avignon where, incidentally, he had given his word to Louis that he would not go. In Avignon he stayed with his old governor Lord Dunbar and his sister, Lady Inverness. But he was not allowed to remain there more than a few weeks. Pope Benedict XIV, offended at not being sent the Prince's compliments and frightened by what the signatories of the Treaty might do, beseeched him to quit his territory. No one is absolutely certain where the wretched fugitive found shelter for the next twelve months. His occasional, curt letters to his father gave no address and were nearly all signed 'John Douglas'. Henceforth he must 'skulk to the perfect dishonour and glory of his worthy relations,' he wrote self-pityingly. 'What can a bird do that has not found a right nest? He must flit from bough to bough. Ainsi use les Irondel.' His spelling in French was as deplorable as it was in English. One rumour reached the French Foreign Office that he was living in disguise in a monastery in Bologna. During the summer he was probably in Venice, and the Chevalier told Pope Benedict XIV that he feared for his son's faith in that licentious city. In vain the Prince begged the Emperor and the Queen of Hungary for permission to stay as a private individual in their dominions. No wonder that whatever backwater he was washed into he took good care to keep secret lest he be driven away. It is probable that from September to December 1749 he was in Poland. If so he may have gone there through the offices of the Princesse de Talmond.

The only authenticated love affair of Prince Charles is the notorious one with Clementina Walkinshaw. That it was consummated we know. That it ended disastrously we are only too well aware. Considering his cavalier treatment of her from the beginning to the end of their liaison it is astonishing that it lasted as long as it did. It is difficult to say whether the beginning, the middle or the end brought the Prince the most discredit in the eyes of his contemporaries. All the Jacobites deplored that he, the last Stuart representative who ought to marry and beget heirs, was living openly with a woman not his wife; and they were shocked by the scandals to which the cohabitation repeatedly gave rise.

Clementina was the youngest of ten daughters of a small Scotch laird, John Walkinshaw of Camlachie and Barrowfield in Lanarkshire, who had worked and suffered considerably for the Stuart cause. He had joined the Chevalier in Lorraine after the Fifteen. Walkinshaw's only recompense was that the consort of King James III agreed to be godmother and give her name to his youngest child. Her dashing son first met Clementina either at Barrowfield or Bannockburn House, the seat of her uncle Sir Hugh Paterson where he spent most of January 1746 after the retreat from Derby. He was certainly nursed by her during illness, and the impressionable girl of nineteen fell in love with him. Legend has it that before separating, the two had come to the rather odd understanding that if the Prince's affairs should not prosper she would join him whenever and wherever he might dictate. If Clementina made a promise then she nobly fulfilled it, for in 1752 Charles, in dire misery, summoned her to him as though she were a last resource. It was not a very flattering invitation to a young woman. But Clementina leapt at the opportunity, for in the interval this impecunious daughter of a distressed Papist Jacobite had been eking out her youth in a chapter of noble canonesses at Douai. Miss Walkinshaw at once proposed to come to the Prince who happened to be living at the time a mere forty miles away, only to be told that she must go to Paris and wait for him.

For eight tumultuous years the Prince and Clementina lived together in Paris, Ghent, Liège, Basle and in Germany, as Count and Countess Johnson or Mr and Mrs Thompson. Between 1749 and 1766 the Prince called himself by more than twenty cant names. Together the couple drank and squabbled in public places. In a Paris tavern they actually came to blows before a startled audience. Reports of their scandalous behaviour, their flittings from one continental town to another – in 1755 Baron Stosch even believed the Prince to be dead, and then confined in a madhouse – reached the ears of loyal Jacobites and finally percolated the lugubrious recesses of the Palazzo Muti in Rome.

In 1755 an Irishman, by name Macnamara, was sent to France on behalf of the Jacobites in England to beg the Prince to get rid of Clementina. His reasons for the request were twofold. There was the moral harm being done to his reputation. There was danger to the cause in the fact that the mistress's sister was Bedchamberwoman to the Dowager Princess of Wales at Leicester House. Macnamara addressed the Prince with deference, which the Prince interpreted as insolence. Charles was enraged by the unjustifiable interference in his personal affairs and the suggestion that he ought, in Macnamara's words, 'to part with an harlot, whom, as he often declared, he neither loved nor esteemed.' It was then that Macnamara is reported as asking the Prince, 'What has your family done, Sir, to draw down the vengeance of heaven on every branch of it through so many ages?' Charles's grandfather and even his father would have had their ready answer, which was the sins of the flesh. It is unlikely that Prince Charles believed in the divine retribution for so innocuous a cause.

The estimable Cluny of MacPherson likewise remonstrated with the Prince. He met with the same non-cooperative reception, and was dismissed with a flea in his ear. So too was the sagacious Earl Marischal, the veteran Jacobite and intimate friend of Frederick the Great, who counselled the Prince to put Clementina in a convent, and if he really loved her, to take her out later without anyone knowing. The reply he received was that His Royal Highness would not send a dog to any convent. The Earl Marischal countered this observation with one of his own. It was that he would not give six sous to rescue the Prince from the bottom of a river.

The Chevalier felt constrained to write his son a letter of rebuke, tempered with the plea that, in abandoning a life of sin he should take a wife. To which in 1754 the son sent one of his rare replies, conveying his views on matrimony. 'Our family have had sufferings enough, that will always hinder me to marry as long as in misfortune, which would only conduce to increase misery, and subject any of the family who had the spirit of their father to be tied neck and heels.' These ambiguous words may be construed to mean that in the Prince's view matrimony was only tolerable with success, and was to be utterly eschewed in adversity, a philosophy implicit in the under-

standing reached with Clementina at Bannockburn. But alas! con-
cubinage also turned out to be unsatisfactory in adversity. By 1760
the break between the oddly assorted pair was complete.

The ultimate cause was incompatibility accentuated by the boredom of their lives, and drink – about which I shall have more to say
later, Clementina being by no means guiltless in this respect. She liked
to fancy that the reason was the Prince's unfounded jealousy of her.
She complained to Lord Elcho that he sometimes struck her fifty
blows in one day; and kept her a prisoner in the house. He surrounded her bed with tables on which he set chairs. To the chairs
were attached by a Heath Robinson device bells whose tinkling
would warn him of the approach of strangers. The story so closely
resembles similar complaints made years later by the Prince's wife
that one may read into it either a confusion of occasions, or if both
incidents be true, some curious Freudian significance, such as impotence.

That impotence, unless it was partial, was not the Prince's overrid-
ing affliction is borne out by the birth of a daughter Charlotte to the
pair in 1753. Within a few months of the event Charles wrote to
Colonel Goring announcing that he had discarded all his papist
servants, and since 'my mistress has behaved so unworthily that she
has put me out of all patience, and, as she is a Papist too, I discard her
also.' The threat was not in fact carried out. Nevertheless on 22 July
1760 Clementina fled with the child from Bouillon, where the Prince
was then living, to Paris. She left behind a letter. 'Your Royal
Highness cannot be surprised at my having taken my parrty when
you consider the repeated bad treatment I have matte with these eight
years past and the dealy risk of loossing life . . .' Mother and daughter
finally took refuge in a convent at Meaux. The Prince on learning
from the Principal of the Scots College in Paris that 'the old gentleman on the other side of the hills' had not only approved of
Clementina's walking out on him but even bribed her to do so, vowed
never to see his father again. After her separation Clementina liked to
be known by the title Countess of Albestroff, which at some time was
conferred upon her by the Emperor Francis I. She lived until 1805,
dying in comparative penury at Fribourg.

Clementina was undoubtedly shallow and weak. Her influence
upon Prince Charles was not positively harmful. Rather it was

negatively harmless. She came upon the scene at a time of great adversity when what he needed was a woman of strong character. Charles was the one who desperately lacked that moral fibre and common sense which she was constitutionally incapable of supplying. I do not think she should be wholly blamed for the undignified scenes in public which made their union a byword of squalor, brought him great discredit and lost him the allegiance of numerous followers. It is most improbable that Clementina, a well brought up Scottish lady of Catholic education, corrupted the Prince. It was he who corrupted her, and taught her to drink. Drink indeed had been his failing from an early age. This prevailing form of British intemperance was certainly aggravated by misfortune, extreme physical distress, disappointment, disillusion and the ultimate hopelessness of existence.

As early as 1742, when his beloved Carluccio at twenty-two was the spoiled darling of Roman society, the father recognized his tendency to drink more than was customary among Latins. He blamed his son's chosen companions, especially Francis Strickland for encouraging the tendency. After the Prince's escapade to Paris in 1744 news reached him of deplorable dissipations which the Chevalier again attributed to bad company, this time singling out the Revd. George Kelly as the chief offender. In August 1745 after the Prince had sailed to Scotland King James wrote about 'un peu trop de goût qu'il semblait alors avoir pour le vin.' If only it had been merely wine. Once the Prince was exposed to the rigours of a Scottish autumn and winter he found greater consolation in hard liquor. Lord Elcho, in so far as he can be believed, averred that during the march to Derby the Prince was often drunk. During the flight and the terrible hardships of the five months after Culloden, whisky and brandy whenever available became his staple solace. Neil MacEachain,* who was with him on the Long Island and Skye related that 'he took care to warm his stomach every morning with a hearty bumper of brandy, of which he always drank a vast deal; for he was seen to drink a whole bottle of a day without being in the least concerned.' And in June 1746 he drank for three solid days and nights with the Macdonalds in Glen Cora-

---

* Neil MacEachain of Uist (1719–1785). Attended Prince Charles from his landing in Scotland and accompanied him as far as Skye.

dale. But what man of twenty-five, surrounded by enemies out for his blood, sleeping in caves and fields under a canvas sail, in pouring rain, consumed by bugs and midges, and half starved to boot, would not have done the same, given the opportunity? Besides, as MacEachain attested, he was not 'the least concerned' by these prolonged boozes. When, however, the Prince ceased to live the hard way and commenced idling in Paris, the effects became only too apparent. As Andrew Lumisden, who loved him, wrote in 1749, 'I am afraid that there is not a single gentleman about him that has either sense or virtue, to manage that most ticklish point.' That was indeed the trouble.

The link-up with Clementina had coincided with the onset of Prince Charles's despair. Until he summoned her to live with him he still believed in his star. He still believed that the French government might advance the funds and the troops to bring about yet another invasion of Great Britain. He had not yet lost his over-weening self-confidence. He was not yet so undermined by drink that he could not make sense. He was never entirely to give up hope, even long after he made no sense at all, which explains why his late life was an utter burden and abomination to him. In 1750 he not only entertained hope but certainty that he was somehow going to regain that illusory throne. He felt pretty sure that when he was successful the old man on the other side of the hills would willingly surrender claim to it in favour of his victorious son. So he intrigued. And there ensued the clandestine visit – or were they visits? – to England.

Andrew Lang suggested that the Prince's motive for going to London was the old love of adventure coupled with the new love of the Princesse de Talmond, from whose nagging he wanted to escape. But there were additional motives. The way had been well paved in advance. The Prince went first to Antwerp where he ordered thousands of muskets to be assembled. They could only be needed for an invasion force at some unspecified date. On 12 September he left Antwerp and crossed the sea in 'an Abbé's dress with a black patch over his eye and his eyebrows black'd'. On the 16th he reached London, according to Joseph Forsyth 'in a hideous disguise, under the name of Smith', and in the company of a Colonel Brett. It was an extremely risky undertaking. The two men hired lodgings in Pall Mall. It seems that the Prince first made a totally unexpected appearance, presumably as Mr Smith, at the house in Essex Street off the Strand of Lady Primrose,* an ardent Jacobite who happened to be giving a party, notwithstanding the fact that she had on 21 August warned him by letter that some undesirable people were 'concerned in his family concerns'. Lady Primrose, taken absolutely unawares but recognizing her uninvited guest, kept her head and went on playing cards without paying undue attention to him until her other guests left. The incident was recorded by the great-grandson of Mrs Hetherington, an intimate friend of Lady Primrose to whom the latter related it, and who likewise claimed to have hidden him during this and a subsequent sojourn. The Prince and Colonel Brett also visited the Tower of London, where they actually inspected the defences.

Before leaving London on 22 September the Prince met some fifty secret sympathisers, the most influential of whom were the 4th Duke of Beaufort and the 7th Earl of Westmorland, and the most revealing Dr William King, Principal of St Mary's Hall, Oxford, with whom the Prince took tea in the doctor's London lodgings. King wrote that the Prince's schemes were wholly impractical and unprepared, and that by the time he left London he was undeceived by the strength of support he had been led to expect. As we have already seen the Doctor formed a low opinion of the Prince but admitted that, 'He is tall and well made, but stoops a little . . . He has a handsome face and good eyes.' The schemes which never hatched were for a rising, first in London, and then in the Highlands. They may have amounted to the so-called Elibank Plot, which on being discovered by the Government was rendered abortive by the execution of Dr Archibald Cameron in 1753. The Prince was at pains to impress upon his supporters that at all costs no violence was to be done to members of the Electoral family. It is said that George II, on being informed of the Young Pretender's presence in his capital and asked what he was going to do about it, replied with a shrug, 'I shall do nothing at all; when he is tired of England, he will go abroad again.' By now the Stuarts were regarded by the Hanoverians as a harmless, even amiable, anachronism.

The only positive step taken by the Prince while in London and one

* She was Anne Drelincourt, widow of the 3rd Viscount Primrose. She died in 1775.

which stood him in no useful stead whatsoever, was to renounce the Catholic faith and adopt that of the Church of England. Mrs Hetherington claimed to have had a hand in bringing about the ceremony which took place in a church in the Strand. Both St Mary-le-Strand and St Martin-in-the-Fields have been mentioned, but the former is the more likely candidate.* Horace Mann in a letter to Horace Walpole written in 1766 about the affair stated that 'the heir of Sir Nathaniel Thorold (a Romanist) who died at Naples, performed the abjuration in St Martin's church as a condition of the inheritance.' The Revd. Henry Thorold of Marston, a representative of this ancient Lincolnshire family, can throw no light upon this putative 'heir' of Sir Nathaniel, who died in 1764, leaving no legitimate issue.

That Prince Charles did apostatize there can be no doubt. A draft proclamation, never issued, made by him in 1759, confirms the action. It runs as follows:

'In order to make my renountiation of the errors of the Church of Rome the most authentick, and less liable afterwards to malitious interpretations, I went to London in the year 1750, and in that capital did then make a solemn abjuration of the Romish religion, and did embrace that of the Church of England as by Law established in the 39 Articles in which I hope to live and die.'

He had never had strong religious convictions and only his father's undeviating faith and efforts to inculcate the necessity of his son's adherence to Catholicism prevented him from renouncing it before the Forty-Five. The irony of the story lies in the Prince's wavering. Had he boldly apostatized before he set out for Scotland he would probably have succeeded in his expedition and rallied that large body of secret Jacobite sympathizers who could not stomach the prospect of being ruled by another papist Stuart. There is no record of his attending a single Mass all the time he was in Britain. In September 1745 he once attended an Episcopalian service in Perth. During the

---

* Horace Walpole and Horace Mann writing in 1765 and 1766 respectively, both mention St Martin-in-the-Fields. David Hume in a letter to Sir John Pringle mentions 'the new church in the Strand', by which throughout the eighteenth century St Mary-le-Strand was indicated. Mrs Hetherington also mentions St Mary-le-Strand.

flight after Culloden he was sometimes questioned about his beliefs. To Hugh Macdonald of Balshar he said, 'Do you know what religion are all the princes in Europe of? They have no religion at all.' This was hardly true and pre-supposes a desire in the Prince to accommodate himself to whatever was required of him. Father Allan Macdonald remarked in May 1746, 'Faith! I have reason to think that the Prince is not a great Papist.' He certainly was not. But he had not the courage to admit it when the telling might have benefited him. His desperate bid to acceptance by apostatizing in 1750 was too late. He liked to maintain the fiction that he was a true convert to the Anglican Church – the spark of hope never being completely extinguished – even after his return to Rome as *de jure* King of England, and would parade on Sundays with the English Prayer Book under his arm, although there was no service for him to attend. The prayer book, printed in 1766, is now in the National Library in Edinburgh. When he came to die however Prince Charles accepted, as other renegades have done before and since, the last rites of the Church into which he was born.

Whether the Prince paid subsequent clandestine visits to England is not certain, but is quite likely.* Mrs Hetherington affirmed that she helped to hide the Prince during his sojourns – she used the plural – in London. There are legends, unproven, that he stayed at Mereworth Castle in Kent with Lord Westmorland, at Cornbury Park in Oxfordshire, where the Charlbury barber sent to shave him recognized him, and at Arlingham Court in Gloucestershire with the Yate family – all between the years 1752 and 1755. The pastel portrait of the Prince at Stonyhurst College, signed 'Saunders pinx. Gloucester July 7th 1752' provides plausible evidence of the last visit. At Westbrook Place, Godalming his ghost is said to haunt a bedroom. There is the romantic legend, unconfirmed, that he attended the coronation of George III in 1760, and that when the hereditary King's Champion threw down the gauntlet in St George's Hall, Westminster, Prince Charles picked it up, and let fall one of a pair of white kid gloves he was wearing. Sir Charles Petrie does not reject this story as totally unfounded, and suggests that possibly some enthusiastic Jacobite

---

* On the 8th June 1752 Prince Charles wrote to Lady Primrose asking if she had any advice to give about another visit to London.

made the touching but ineffectual gesture on the Old Chevalier's behalf.

The flight of Clementina in 1760 seems to have taken the Prince greatly by surprise. He did not lament her loss, although his pride was deeply wounded. On the other hand he was genuinely saddened by the loss of his daughter, and even swore he would not shave until she was returned to him. He gravely resented Clementina's audacity in abducting her. Piteous letters flew back and forth between the Prince and his attendants and those people representing the Countess of Albestroff. After an interval Charles dispatched a letter to an intermediary, the Abbé John Gordon, Principal of the Scots College in Paris: 'I take this affaire so much at heart that I was not able to write what is here above [penned by a scribe]. Shall be in ye greatest affliction until I greete back yee Childe, which was my only comfort in my misfortunes . . .' And his devoted friend Thibault* followed up this cry by a letter on the Prince's behalf to Gordon. He thought his master would die if the daughter was not returned to him. Thibault wrote again describing the condition to which distress had reduced the Prince. He had developed 'un gros rhume avec un accès de fièvre à la suite duquel les hemoroides étaient sorties, elles l'ont obligée à garder le lit, ne pouvant pas s'asseoir.' However he soon forgot his little 'Pouponne' whom he was not to see for many a year – until in fact, it suited him to send for her. What is more, he resolutely declined either to answer the mother's frequent appeals for help or to send any money for their support. Charlotte was in the meantime obliged to remain within the convent of the Dames de la Visitation, making only occasional sorties in the great world of Paris.

The solitary wanderer went from bad to worse. There were reports in 1761 that he was drunk as soon as he rose until he was carried senseless to bed. He was fretful and quarrelsome, and he led his servants and few attendants a dog's life. Most of his friends were alienated by his perpetual recriminations.

The Cardinal Duke to his infinite credit never once sought to alienate his father's affections from Prince Charles for his own

---

* Monsieur Thibault, who was President of the Sovereign Court of Bouillon, had been called upon to make domestic arrangements for Prince Charles. He became devoted to him, and turned into his amanuensis, confidential adviser and willing slave.

material advantage. It was just not in his nature to do such a thing. On the contrary he did all in his power to bring about a reconciliation between the father and the first-born. For years the Chevalier had been beseeching Prince Charles to return to him before he died. He longed to forgive and embrace him once more. But no. Prince Charles would not budge. When the old king fell into a decline and was unable to write any more heart-rending letters, the Cardinal of York broke the eighteen-year old silence between the brothers. He took up his pen and in February 1765 wrote urging Charles to set aside his grievances and come to Rome. Thereafter he appealed again and again to him to visit their father before it was too late. He made Charles the offer of a pension from his own pocket, and again undertook to renounce in his brother's favour anything he might stand to inherit under James's will. He even sent him somewhat tactlessly, for he was a simple man, the Princesse de Talmond's love. The Prince did not acknowledge this indirect message from his former mistress. He steadfastly refused to come to Rome unless Pope Clement XIII would undertake to recognize him as King of England when his father should die. Pope Clement would undertake no such thing.

All of a sudden, because of some whim, Prince Charles consented to come. He set out from Bouillon where he was then living, by slow stages. He was at the time in a state of great lassitude. His legs were so swollen that he could barely walk, and every movement brought him pain. On the road he was met by a messenger with the tidings that on New Year's Day of 1766 his father had died. Not a word of sorrow or remorse escaped his lips. He was far too preoccupied with a determination to assert his sovereign rights on arrival in Rome. The knowledge that he was at last *de jure* King of Great Britain gave him strength to endure the appalling journey through snow and ice. Did he, one longs to know, reproach himself, as the heavy carriage lurched along the rutted roads, for his reprehensible neglect over the years of the father who had loved him, the father whom he had not once troubled to visit since as a young man he fell upon his neck and said farewell to him this very month twenty-two years ago?

The Cardinal Duke, who, in spite of his honest conviction that the Stuart cause was utterly hopeless, would not relinquish one jot of his family's hereditary rights, used his utmost endeavours to obtain the

Vatican's recognition of them in his brother's favour. The moment King James III was dead he set to work. Andrew Lumisden, the faithful secretary, confirmed that the Cardinal Duke left no stone unturned in paving the way for Charles's reception in Rome as *de jure* sovereign. He interviewed the most influential cardinals. He obtained audiences of the Pope. He even presented the Pope with a memorial on 'The indispensable necessity for the Holy See to recognize the house of Stuart as the only true and legitimate sovereigns of the Kingdom of England.' He stressed that in his father's lifetime his brother had been treated as heir apparent from birth, had been handed swaddling clothes by Pope Clement XI at his birth and as Prince of Wales had always been given an armchair at papal audiences. The tone of the memorial was plaintive and aggrieved. Clement XIII allowed the memorial to be circulated to the curia for their opinion. The French Ambassador, although without any authority in the deliberations, urged a favourable reply. But the majority of the cardinals headed by Alessandro Albani who was in close touch with Horace Mann – "ce diable Monsieur Mann', as the Most Catholic King's ambassador termed him – were definitely hostile to the idea. Clement XIII (1758–69) was also extremely reluctant to antagonize Britain, and refused to accede to the memorial. Had Prince Charles only come to Rome earlier when so piteously requested by his father and brother he might have received the recognition he now craved. So long as King James was still alive the Vatican would undoubtedly have continued to acknowledge him as Prince of Wales. It could hardly have done otherwise. And in the course of events, had he dutifully closed his father's eyes and followed his remains to the grave, he would perforce have been proclaimed by the Pope *de jure* King Charles III. It would have been difficult for the Pope, who revered and was fond of the father to have withheld the empty hereditary title from the son and heir, however much George III's representative in Florence protested. But certainly not now, in the present circumstances.

On 23 January news reached Rome that Charles Stuart would shortly enter the city. Hastily Andrew Lumisden prepared Queen Clementina's rooms in the Palazzo Muti for his reception. Having completed this task he went to meet his new sovereign on the road between Bologna and Florence. The actual arrival in Rome was pathetic in the extreme. No representative from the Vatican came to greet him. There were no trumpets to herald his approach, no triumphal arches for him to pass under, no fireworks to acclaim him. He was met by his brother the Cardinal at a small inn outside the walls on the Flaminian way. It was their first meeting for nineteen years. The worldly fortunes of the brethren were reversed. The poor, insignificant little Prince Henry was now an opulent prince of the Church. The handsome, dashing hero of the Forty-Five, of whom the other used to be in awe, was a raddled, middle-aged wreck. He had to be helped to descend from his shabby carriage by a valet. He could not walk without support. He was pushed and shoved into the Cardinal's resplendent coach and driven down the silent Corso to the Palazzo Muti, where he was received by a dwindled band of disillusioned Jacobites. He retired straight to bed where he remained for two days recovering from the fatigues of the journey.

Pope Clement was adamant. He received the Cardinal Duke's renewed pleading that his brother be recognized as King with the tart reminder that in 1750 the Prince had apostatized and joined the Church of England. He even withheld the right by which James had set great store, of nominating to Irish bishoprics. Evidently the Cardinal believed that his brother was fully reconciled to the Church of Rome, and a year later wrote in a letter that for this reason there was no call for Prince Charles to circulate an apologia to his bemused subjects. Unwisely the Cardinal Duke in driving his brother in his coach through the steets of Rome had made him sit on his right side. Since a cardinal might only defer this place to a reigning sovereign the gesture was interpreted as defiance of the Pope's refusal to recognize the Prince as such. The heads of the English and Scots Colleges openly prayed for King Charles III of England at High Mass. They were dismissed from their offices for their pains. While the Prince was away for a little shooting at Albano in April the Pope had the royal arms of England removed from their customary place above the entrance to the Palazzo Muti. This disobliging act was another deep mortification. Henceforth the Prince would not set foot outside his door even to go to the opera. He ostentatiously declined to receive Roman society at his court since he was not recognized as King by the head of the state in which he was dwelling. Lumisden wrote, 'He says he is like one on ship-board; he converses only with his own little crew.' Things could not go on in this way. In the end the Cardinal Duke had to persuade his brother that if he intended to remain in Rome and live upon the Pope's bounty he must toe the line. There was no alternative to his consenting to be received at the Quirinal Palace as the Count of Albany.

The papal audience duly took place. There was further irony in the fact that whereas the younger brother was by virtue of his office given a chair to sit on, the elder was obliged to kneel (a physically painful operation for him) like a penitent, only not in sackcloth and ashes, until given permission to stand before the Pope. His Holiness was nevertheless all sweetness, though unyielding; and the audience was brought to a close with compliments and expressions of good will by both parties.

The tribulations which the Cardinal Duke had to endure on account of his brother were endless. Although at the time of his succession the Prince was much enfeebled he was still very much alive. Drink was of course the cause of most of his troubles. It made him touchy, fractious, unpredictable and extremely quarrelsome. The Cardinal wrote to an unknown correspondent on 29 April 1767 that 'his difficultys and odd notions are such that it is indeed enough for to make one run madd,' and he referred to 'the home things [truths] I sometimes let drive at him,' to little avail. One notion that the Prince could not get out of his head was that he was destitute. The result was he withheld payment from his attendants. The Cardinal had to intervene. To the same friend the Cardinal wrote on 20 May, if only 'cou'd wee but gett the better of the nasty Bottle which every now and then comes on by spurts.' The bottle must, he averred, soon kill him unless it could be laid off. The Cardinal Duke went through agonies of embarrassment over the drunken scenes in public and the physical violence which sometimes accompanied them. It is remarkable that however deeply this man of God deplored his brother's conduct he was never overtly censorious these days. Yet the Prince showed him not the least gratitude for getting him out of countless scrapes. Instead he put obstacles in the way of anyone who tried to help him. The Cardinal admitted in 1767 that at times he was tired of the whole business, which necessitated the constant strain of assuaging the hurt feelings of his brother's victims and endeavouring to keep up appearances.

Then in 1768 an unfortunate incident occurred. One evening Prince Charles was all set for going to the oratorio. He was lolling in his carriage waiting for his attendants. They were Sir John Hay of Restalrig the major-domo, Andrew Lumisden the secretary, and Captain Urquhart the equerry, three true and trusted servants. The Prince was so distressingly drunk that they flatly refused to accompany him. He was obliged to be helped out of his carriage and hauled upstairs. He stormed, and sacked all three attendants on the spot. And when next day he recovered his senses, he would not withdraw the dismissal. Thus he lost their services. Hay returned to Scotland where he died in 1784, and Lumisden rejoined his sister Mrs Strange* in Paris, whence every year he wrote an affectionate letter of birthday greetings to his dear 'wild man', as he termed the Prince. The Cardinal on being informed of the affair told Lumisden that he and his colleagues had behaved correctly. Lumisden's last office was to prevent the episode bringing about a rift between the royal brothers. He was rewarded by the Cardinal with a small snuff box which had belonged to the Chevalier, but which the recipient did not consider an over-generous recompense for twenty-three years of dogged and faithful service to the house of Stuart. Since the Prince's return to Rome Lumisden had endured every kind of provocation with exemplary patience. Just before his dismissal he told Sir John Graeme (then Earl of Alford),

'Altho' indeed I have a right to demand at the Post Office any packets and letters addressed for me, yet I shall never dispute with my King on this or any other account. He is at full liberty to open and read every letter I receive or write. He will find that I carry on no correspondence to his detriment. On the contrary he will thereby see how many services I render him, often unknown to himself. However after he has read my letters he might be pleased at least to return them to me; but this I do not expect.'

Yet Prince Charles was fool enough to lose this pearl of a man, this living quintessence of rectitude and loyalty.

* Isabella Lumisden was as fervent a Jacobite as her brother. She only consented to marry Robert Strange, the celebrated engraver, on condition that he fought for Prince Charles in the Forty-Five.

Two further thorns in the Cardinal's flesh were his brother's ex-mistress, Clementina Albestroff, and their daughter Charlotte. Even since Prince Charles discarded these unfortunate women in Paris in 1760 they had been financed by the Chevalier. When he died their allowance ceased. The onus of their support fell upon the Cardinal who then gave them half of what they had been getting hitherto. They became solely dependent upon him for subsistence. But the mother, dissatisfied with the amount she now received, threatened to pretend that she had been married to the Prince. The Cardinal was appalled. He was obliged to bribe her to sign a written statement that no marriage had taken place.* Even so he was pestered again by the Countess and Charlotte, who on learning in 1772 of the Prince's true marriage hastened to Rome and pressed their claims to further financial aid. The Cardinal, at the instigation of the Cardinal Secretary of State, had the disagreeable task of persuading these unwelcome women to leave Rome immediately.

Descriptions of Prince Charles between his return to Rome and his marriage vary. Lumisden on seeing him in January 1766 after a long interval was, like all royal servants, discreet. He wrote to a friend that the Prince still 'charms everyone that approaches him,' which was very probably true, when he was sober. In 1767 an English lady who had been received by him said, 'He looks good-natured, and was over-joyed to see me; nothing could be more affectionately gracious. I cannot answer for his cleverness, for he appeared to be absorbed in melancholy thoughts, a good deal of abstraction in his conversation, and frequent brown studies.' His memory had become bad and he was finding concentration a difficulty, which should not have been the case with a healthy man of only forty-seven. 'As for his person,' she went on, 'it is rather handsome, his face ruddy and full of pimples.' No wonder! But in 1769 Bishop Robert Gordon – he was a Jacobite – recorded, 'Not a blot, nor so much as a pimple was in his face, though maliciously given out by some as if it were all over blotted; but he is jolly and plump, tho' not to excess, being still agile

* Sir John Coxe Hippisley, who knew both the Cardinal Duke and the Countess of Albany, left a note to the effect that Prince Charles 'was unquestionably married to Miss Walkinshaw by the law of Scotland.' Unfortunately he did not expatiate upon this categorical statement.

and fit for undergoing toil.' He clearly had his bad and his less bad periods.

In 1770 we catch a glimpse of him through the eyes of Lady Anne Miller who was passing through Rome. She noticed that he stooped exceedingly. He was corpulent, and his small mouth was lost in an inflated jowl. 'He appears bloated and red in the face, his countenance heavy and sleepy, which is attributed to his having given in to excess of drinking.' Nevertheless she was impressed by his 'noble presence' and 'graceful manner'. Lady Anne commented, 'Upon the whole he has a melancholy, mortified appearance.' There exist portraits which confirm this distressing description. That painted by H. D. Hamilton is very dreadful. Hardly a vestige of the Bonnie Prince can be detected in the elderly roué with pendulous cheeks, dewlap, and bags under the disillusioned eyes. These appear blue, although a little filmed, and the outline of the apple-like chin can be traced in the folds of fat behind it. The portrait drawn by Ozias Humphry in 1776 shows an even more marked declension.

This then was the man who had the temerity to woo. It is perhaps fairer to suggest that he did so less from personal inclination than a sense of duty. For the Jacobite followers – and there were still many left, particularly in Scotland – earnestly clamoured for a Stuart heir. If there was to be one at all the urgency was pressing. The Prince was fifty-two and his physical condition such as we have described it. The question of a suitable marriage for him had been discussed ever since his birth, the first serious proposition having been put forward by Lord Mar when the bridegroom-to-be was but three years old. In 1723 Mar wrote to the Chevalier suggesting an alliance with the Regent of Orleans's daughter. Years later the Prince had entertained the notion that a daughter of Louis XV would be desirable and is said to have drunk her health with his bandit friends in Glenmoriston Forest after Culloden. But the royal house of France was then far too firmly established to welcome alliance with a throneless family, however exalted. Instead Louis XV arranged, just as his great-grandfather had arranged the marriage of Prince Charles's grandfather James II, what he deemed a less illustrious yet in the circumstances suitable enough union with the daughter of a mid-European princeling. It was still in the interest of France to manipulate the Stuarts as political pawns on the European chessboard. And in spite of

Charles being totally disabused of Louis's intentions to grant him military aid and bitter about his repeated failures to do so he was still intermittently dependent upon that King's bounty.

The Prince's finances were always something of a mystery. His conditions fluctuated between extreme indigence and comfortable affluence. On his return to France in 1746 he was in desperate straits. In 1748 he was said to have collected much money from the various countries he had visited principally for that purpose. After his father's death in 1766 he was so hard up that he had to cease buying the English newspapers. In 1779 the revenue from his Polish estates brought him more than £5,000 a year. In 1782, again reduced to a low ebb, he nevertheless refused to sell the great ruby of Scotland which would have cleared off his debts. And in 1783, long after Louis XV's death, he was desperately trying to get renewed his pension from France, which had lapsed. So serious was the situation that he was not too proud to enlist the influence with Louis XVI of the King of Sweden, who even offered to give him money as well as sympathy. The truth is that Charles was both incurably extravagant and never in receipt of a steady income. The pensions promised him by various sources were frequently withheld or not paid at all. On the other hand his mother had brought him a large share of the Sobieski fortune upon which, after the Chevalier's death, he could rely, thanks largely to the Cardinal Duke's renunciation of his portion. It alone however was not enough to meet his requirements.

With the offer of the hand of Princess Louise of Stolberg-Gedern in 1772 went the welcome promise of a French pension of 40,000 crowns a year (which incidentally was never honoured). The pair were affianced by Louis XV and married by proxy in Paris.

III

QUEEN OF HEARTS

The nineteen-year-old girl whom the fifty-two year old Prince Charles Stuart married in 1772 did not belong to one of Europe's great reigning families. Yet she came of royal stock on her father's side; and her sixteen quarterings, that is to say the arms of all her great-great grandparents, by which continental patricians of the eighteenth century set the greatest store, were impeccable. In her marriage contract she was described as Most Serene Highness. Her father Prince Gustav Adolf, who had been killed in 1757 fighting for the Empress Maria Theresa against Frederick the Great at the battle of Leuthen, was the elder son of Prince Friedrich Karl, sovereign Prince of Stolberg-Gedern. The grandfather was to survive his son for another ten years. Prince Friedrich Karl inherited Gedern, one of several little provinces in the Harz mountains of central Germany, which had been ruled by different branches of the Stolberg family since 1210. He was created a Prince of the Holy Roman Empire in 1742. Since Prince Gustav Adolf had no son, the province of Gedern went to his younger brother in 1767. For this reason the widow, left with four young daughters,* found herself in serious financial straits. And because her husband had died fighting for Maria Theresa, she and her young family were taken under the Empress's protection.

Although the Stolbergs were a Lutheran family Prince Gustav

---

* They were (1) Louise, of whom we are treating; (2) Caroline Augusta (1755 –1829), married firstly Charles Bernard FitzJames, Duke of Berwick (d. 1787), and secondly in 1793 Domenico, Conte di Castelfranco (d. 1808); (3) Françoise Claude (1756–1836) married 1774 Nicolas, Comte d'Arberg et Valangrin (d. 1814), General in the Imperial Army; (4) Thérèse Gustavine (1757–1837), unmarried and a Canoness of Thorn.

Adolf's wife was Catholic. Princess Elizabeth was a daughter of Prince Maximilian Emanuel de Hornes by his wife, Lady Charlotte Bruce. The Hornes, although not royal, were one of the most ancient and illustrious families of the Netherlands. They were Spanish princes to boot. Lady Maria Charlotte Bruce was a daughter of Thomas 3rd Earl of Elgin who was also 2nd Earl of Ailesbury. In other words Louise had a Scotch grandmother through whom she was related to the families of Bruce, Grey, Shirley and Manners. Lord Elgin and Ailesbury, a Protestant, had refused to take the oath to William and Mary, was a loyal supporter of James II, whom he accompanied in the barge to Rochester during the King's first flight in 1688, and was even imprisoned in the Tower of London for plotting to restore him in 1695. On his release he was obliged to leave the kingdom. He resided in Brussels where he met and married his second wife, Charlotte d'Argenteau, Comtesse d'Esseneux and Baronne de Melsbroek from Brabant. In his *Memoirs* this great-grandfather of Prince Charles's wife wrote of her husband's grandfather, James II, 'I do affirm he was the most honest and sincere man I ever knew, a great and good Englishman,' and he added, 'a great patriot too.'

Prince Gustav Adolf and Princess Elizabeth of Stolberg-Gedern's eldest child was christened Louise Maximilienne Caroline Emanuele at Mons in Belgium where she had been born on 20 September 1752. Mons had since the Treaty of Aix-la-Chapelle been an Austrian possession which explains how Prince Gustav Adolf was representing his overlord the Empress in this important outpost at the time.

Soon after her father's death at the age of thirty-five, Princess Louise was sent to the Chapter of St Wandru in Mons, one of four establishments in the Low Countries for the education of the daughters of what today would be termed distressed gentlewomen, and were then the scions of noble families whose only asset, but that a considerable one, was an illustrious title. At the age of six the little Louise was appointed a canoness which set the seal upon her semi-royal eligibility in the marriage market. So long as she remained at St Wandru she received a free education and comfortable board until a suitable husband should be forthcoming to relieve the Chapter of the expense of keeping her. Her marriage to the *de jure* King of England, although socially the most brilliant, was not the first of the four sisters' marriages. Already the Princess of Stolberg's second daughter Caroline had been wedded to the Marquess of Jamaica,* a FitzJames descendant of the 1st Duke of Berwick, (James II's illegitimate son) and a cousin on the wrong side of the blanket, of Prince Charles Stuart. It was largely through the Marquess's mediation between Louis XV and Prince Charles that Louise's marriage was brought about.

We do not know what the Princess thought about her impending nuptials with an exiled, middle-aged prince with a romantic past, a fairly squalid present and a dubious future, as she was conducted from Mons to meet him in Italy. We do know what she thought of the circumstances of her marriage in retrospect. Years later she told her friend Teresa Mocenni, 'In order to get rid of me she [her mother] married me to the most insupportable man that ever existed, a man who combined the defects and failings of all classes, as well as the vice common to lackeys, that of drink.' Indeed a very ancient servant of the Cardinal of York who remembered Prince Charles at the time of his marriage told the authors of *The Stuarts in Exile* that 'no street-porter could equal him.' His usual after dinner allowance was six bottles of strong Cyprus wine, 'and he seldom missed being drunk twice a day.'

Once the terms of betrothal were settled no time was wasted in seeing the marriage through. The ceremony was completed with almost indecent haste. The meeting place was a remote little town in the Marche, called Macerata, twenty miles inland from Ancona. Prince Charles had driven in an open carriage from Rome in Holy Week of 1772 and set himself up in the palace of Count Campagnoni Marefoschi. Princess Louise arrived at the palace at 6 o'clock on the evening of Good Friday with one lady-in-waiting and Lord Caryll, a great-nephew of Mary Beatrice's secretary, who had been sent to fetch her from Loreto. Before she had proper time even to look at her bridegroom she was married by the Bishop of Macerata at 7 o'clock in the minute chapel. A plaque on the walls records the event.

After the ceremony the Bishop presented the bride with two bunches of asparagus, some fresh flowers and two carnations. The following day he sent her six bowls of sweetmeats for which the Prince rewarded the bearer with a gold piece. Let us hope these

---

* He eventually became 4th Duke of Berwick.

offerings were some compensation for the Princess's presumed disappointment with her bloated, dropsical husband. As soon as the couple had been declared man and wife one of Prince Charles's attendants left the chapel and announced to the assembled company, 'Long live the Queen!' The Governor of the district awaited the King and Queen at the head of the palace staircase, made a short speech of congratulation and was graciously dismissed. On Easter Saturday the local nobility were received and music and conversation ensued until three in the morning. On the afternoon of Easter day there was another reception with singing and refreshments. And at half past four the whole party left Macerata with eighteen post horses for Rome and the Palazzo Muti.*

The canoness bride was at the time of her wedding extremely fetching. Vernon Lee's phrase describing her as 'a bright, light handful of thistle-bloom', has a whimsical as well as misleading undertone. The young princess had far more substance to her than this. Although her fair hair and pale skin gave an impression of fragility, she was physically and mentally robust. There are two portraits of her as a very young woman by unknown artists. In the portrait at Badminton she wears a hat with feathers and holds a black domino. A small dog crouches at her feet. She is seated on an old-fashioned baroque chair against what looks like a northern landscape. This portrait – which judging from the unformed, almost child-like face was an early one – must have been painted before marriage, probably in Belgium. In the other, hanging in Stonyhurst College, she has the self-confident poise of a married woman. She wears a pile of curly hair with a pink rose pinned to one side of it. Her long thin neck is clasped by three rows of choker pearls. The low, square-cut dress is edged with lace. She is shown playing a guitar, an instrument at which she was proficient. The head is held high. The face is oval, the nose well-fashioned. The luminous hazel eyes under pencilled brows and the rosebud mouth are merry and mocking. Altogether she is very assured and very pretty. Her whole tenue is elegant. For at this time of her life Louise was well dressed and well groomed, whereas in middle age she was to take no interest either in her clothes or her appearance.

* A letter from the son of Count Campagnoni Marefoschi to his uncle the Bishop of Osimo, dated 11th April 1772, lent me by the late Mrs Louise Dentler.

The bride of the Stuart prince was naturally intelligent, quick-witted and tolerably educated. Although her views on literature and art were still superficial she had a keen desire to learn and to associate with people of intellect. When the couple took up residence in the Palazzo Muti these aspirations were not generally apparent. Louise was the distant object of sympathetic curiosity and speculation in Roman society. But for some time curiosity could not be satisfied or speculation verified owing to the pig-headedness of the husband. On the eve of his marriage the Prince had made fresh overtures through his secretary Lord Caryll to persuade Pope Clement XIV (1769–74) formally to recognize him and his wife as King and Queen of England. The Pope however turned a deaf ear to hints, requests and expressions of hurt feelings. On the couple's establishment in Rome Caryll bluntly demanded a papal audience for his sovereign and his consort. He was handed by the Cardinal Secretary of State this communication: 'I have acquainted His Holiness with the arrival of the Baron de Renfrew and his wife, and he has commanded me to assure them that he will be very glad to receive them, but as he is now very busy he wishes to defer it till he is less engaged than at present.' The Prince was so incensed by the content of the Cardinal Secretary's communication with its reference to him as the Baron de Renfrew, which was one of the titles he had assumed for himself and Clementina Walkinshaw when they were living together in sin, that he made Caryll decline to receive it officially. In consequence he would not suffer his wife to accept visits from or return visits to members of Roman society so long as the Pope withheld his and her proper titles. From the outset Cardinal Henry of York entreated his brother not to press these claims for fear of forfeiting the Pope's financial support. In fact the behaviour of both brothers was a repetition of the stand each adopted in 1766 when the elder returned to Rome after their father's death. On this occasion the Cardinal Duke's entreaties were more stoutly resisted. The Prince wrote to Cardinal Marefoschi, his new friend, 'I pay no regard to my brother or to anyone else when the maintenance of the dignity due to me is concerned . . .' All that he got was another politely veiled snub from Clement XIV. His fury against the Pope and his brother knew no bounds.

Although at first it must have been a disappointment to the young bride that she might not publicly enjoy the empty title of Queen, she soon supported her brother-in-law's entreaties. Eventually the Prince with a very bad grace desisted, although he never consented to forego his right.

The Prince's obduracy at the start of their married life was the cause of much unhappiness to his wife. Louise was young, naturally lively and gay. The closed society of English and Scotch Jacobite courtiers, who for the most part were old, disgruntled and out of touch with the world, contributed little to her enjoyment or edification. The fact that the Romans, whom she was not allowed to meet, were prepared to like her, made her lot worse. The secluded existence of the 'Regina Apostolorum' (Queen of the Apostles, for the Palazzo Muti stood at the northern end of the Piazza Santi Apostoli), or Queen of Hearts, as the Romans called her, fascinated them. Furthermore, Rome was at this time brimful of writers, historians, savants, artists and collectors from every country in Europe. It was after Paris the greatest intellectual centre of the continent. Louise, residing in the midst of all these brilliant cosmopolitan people was denied the benefit of consorting with them. What they saw of her was a distant, beautiful young woman accompanying night after night a middle-aged husband to a box at the theatre or opera, speaking to and being addressed by no one. Out of sheer loneliness Louise took to reading by the hour. What began as a solace turned into an intellectual appetite and the enduring necessity of her life. It was not long before the exigencies of protocol and grandeur, rendered doubly false by the poverty of the Jacobite court, struck her as fatuous and insupportable. Boring though her husband soon became to her, he had at least given up drinking during the first twelve months of the marriage. That pastime was soon to be resumed, for in December 1773 Horace Mann wrote that he was seldom quite sober and that Lord Caryll was threatening to leave him on this account. Alas, matrimony had induced another 'spurt of the nasty bottle'. The Cardinal Duke was highly embarrassed by his brother's inebriation, which somehow seemed more scandalous now that he had an attractive young wife. Only when the couple left Rome to live in Florence was the Cardinal Duke relieved of compromising scenes on, as it were, his own doorstep.

It goes without saying that no woman in the first flush of youth and beauty will be satisfied for long solely with books and an elderly husband who does not even share her interests. It is hardly surprising too that gallant young men were intrigued by the romantic and neglected princess. Louise's first admirer was an old Etonian of twenty on the grand tour.* He was extremely good-looking. Thomas Coke came of a Whig family; but even dashing sprigs of the Whig nobility let their curiosity outstrip discretion when they were away from home. And the Pretender's court had a dangerous fascination for them. It also gave them, however Hanoverian their background, a sound welcome. There was always a chance that the king over the water might, by receiving the son of a powerful minister or an influential landowner in Britain, bring about another conversion to the Stuart cause. It is said that the Princess and Thomas Coke met in 1774 at a masked ball where she presented this particularly Whiggish youth with the white Jacobite cockade. Either Prince Charles had by this year relaxed the injunction that the Queen must not accept invitations, or she flouted it by attending a ball behind a domino without detection. At all events Thomas Coke carried on a brief but brisk flirtation with her. The Princess commissioned Pompeo Batoni to paint him. The portrait of the handsome youth, proud as Theseus, wearing a pearl grey satin suit and rose silk cloak trimmed with ermine, is one of Batoni's most sumptuous creations. Coke is made to stand in a nonchalant pose, plumed hat in hand, his spaniel gazing adoringly at the lovesick, beardless face. The background is appropriately sculptural and Coke's left arm is supported by a stalwart plinth on which reclines the famous swooning figure of Ariadne abandoned on the isle of Naxos. Louise is said to have identified herself with Ariadne whose face she imagined hers resembled. Coke took the portrait back to Holkham Hall where it hangs today.†

Temperamentally and politically Louise and Thomas Coke were poles apart. Even if the young man had not gone home to England the affair would doubtless have petered out fairly soon; the future

* Thomas Coke's attentions may have been preceded by those of a less exalted person. Among the Stuart papers at Windsor (470/32) is written evidence, dated 30.11.1773, by one Giorgio Ghalt, an informer against Louise's relations with Bernardo Rotolo, Prince Charles's first lackey. According to Ghalt, Rotolo attested that the Princess assured him that she loved him. There exists no evidence that Prince Charles heeded the informer.
† Thomas Coke, later known as Coke of Norfolk, was made 1st Earl of Leicester of the second creation in 1837.

agriculturist would have few charms for the future blue-stocking. As it was, 'The young Mr Coke is returned from his travels in love with the Pretender's Queen,' Horace Walpole wrote to Seymour Conway on 18 August 1774. Evidently London was buzzing with the news.

Louise's intellect as well as her affections were stirred by her next encounter. Karl Victor von Bonstetten was a sort of Swiss passionate pilgrim. By 1773 he was twenty-eight, rather handsome with a round smooth face, and a cheerful, endlessly enquiring manner. An irrepressible love of life invariably got the better of those romantic posturings which every young man of sensibility was expected to adopt. Once only he had contemplated suicide because of unrequited love. He lay in his shirt on the floor of his chambers between a pair of loaded pistols. Suddenly from behind a cloud the full moon stepped forth in all her glory. That was enough for Bonstetten. He changed his mind, and leapt to his feet. By the time he reached Rome he had already travelled to Holland and England in pursuit of eminent men of letters, who flattered by his youth and attentions put up with his society which was engaging if not edifying. He calculated that before 1773 he had lionized more than eighty celebrated persons, including Voltaire and Rousseau. In Cambridge he sought out Thomas Gray in his claustral retreat of Pembroke College. He totally bewitched the elderly don-poet, causing much havoc with Gray's desiccated heart which had never, to his friends' knowledge, been touched before, only to rush off to France upon another lion hunt. 'My life is now but a perpetual conversation with your shadow,' Gray wrote dolefully to the fickle creature after his departure. 'The known sound of your voice still rings in my ears. There on the corner of the fender you are standing, or tinkling on the pianoforte, or stretch'd at length on the sofa.' Bonstetten had no intention of returning. Gray was heartbroken. He was never to be the same man again. It is hardly an exaggeration to affirm that he died of love less than a year and a half later.

Literary, intelligent, earnest but slightly ridiculous, Bonstetten next assailed the Palazzo Muti in a gush of bonhomie and bombast. He was enchanted with the miniature court he found in the old palace, a King and Queen of nothing, surrounded by two or three chamberlains and *dames d'honneur*, mostly of a very old-fashioned sort. Over them presided Louise, who was high-spirited and sparkling. 'The Queen of Hearts when I knew her in Rome,' he was to write, 'was of medium height; she had dark blue eyes [in her portraits they are hazel], a slightly turned up nose, and the complexion of an English girl. Her expression was bright, mischievous and sensitive, that she turned all heads.' He recollected that her 'natural gaiety was somewhat laced with malice, her malice was sometimes friendship, or better than that' – an ambiguous understatement.

The first time that Bonstetten dined at the Palazzo Muti he begged in his impulsive, boyish manner to be allowed to carve the turkey which was deposited by a footman in front of the Queen. Louise, guessing that he had never done such a thing before, gave her consent. Whereupon he made a terrible mess of the bird and splashed his neighbours with gravy. He was overcome with confusion and the Queen convulsed with merriment. He soon became a popular and regular visitor. His host liked him because he spoke English and appeared to enjoy listening to the Prince's interminable stories, every sentence of which, Bonstetten observed, was punctuated by the interrogation, 'Ha capi?' His hostess relished his disregard for ceremony, his uncurbed spontaneity and his incessant prattle about the intellectual giants he had conversed with in different countries. He introduced to her the writings of Voltaire and Rousseau in which she steeped herself to such an extent that, as she wrote to Bonstetten afterwards, she wished to forget 'all grandeur and become absolutely republican'. The extreme sentiments of extreme youth are soon exhausted by their very fervour.

Bonstetten was to confide in his memoirs many years later: 'I was in love with the Queen without admitting it to myself.' It is probably nearer the truth that he was more in love with her image than reality. Immature, naive lion hunter, he was about as captivated by his quarry of the moment as the stalker is enamoured of the game he is about to shoot. The moment the kill is over and done with he embarks upon the pursuit of another victim. Voltaire, Rousseau, Gray, or the titular Queen of Great Britain were all the same to Bonstetten. He was in love too with notoriety. Yet it is only fair to state that he was not fickle in his friendships. He remained a faithful friend to Louise for the rest of his life, and after one long interval a regular correspondent. He went on to write in his memoirs: 'She loved me without saying so.' But she did say so as near as makes no odds. There are preserved in the Fabre Museum at Montpellier five letters of hers addressed to Bonstetten during the winter of 1775, several months after he had left Rome, pathetic little letters, indiscreet, compromising, girlish letters. It is to Bonstetten's credit that he kept them to himself. 'Vous êtes le plus aimable des hommes et le seul crée pour captiver non coeur mon esprit et mon âme . . . Madame de Maltzam me dit souvent Monsier le B était le seul homme qui aurait été dangereux pour vous . . . voilà que je demande un amant.'

Lucille de Maltzam, Louise's principal lady-in-waiting and confidante had all the time, in the way of Mozartian comedies, been carrying on a more serious affair with Bonstetten's humble travelling companion, Schérer. Again Louise wrote that she preferred a really charming man to the greatest lord who would bore her. For her to be madly in love would be something unique. Ah, how delightful that would be! 'But I have not yet found a man to my taste, one deserving a constant love. Only you would be able to touch this heart of rock.' It was of very malleable substance. 'Let us go and live in some little corner of the globe where we may live according to our whim . . .' And, 'these sentiments which I feel for you it [sic] is sweet it is calm we will love each other madly we will never talk of disagreeable things.' The random, ill-written, unpunctuated outpourings of the poor little princess evoked, as far as we know, no responses.* And in 1776 Bonstetten, back in his native Switzerland once more, having concluded his youthful lion-hunts and verging on thirty, married a prosaic wife who brought him little happiness.

Thirty-three years elapsed before Bonstetten found himself again wandering through the streets of Rome and reviving memories of the days when he was entertained and petted by the inhabitants of the most exclusive palaces in Europe. In 1807 he wrote to Louise from the capital of the ancient world, 'I never pass through the square of the Apostles without gazing at the balcony and the house where I first saw you. It seems that I have a whole life time to recount to you.'

* Louise's letters to Bonstetten, as to all of her friends, were written in French as the first of these quoted extracts indicates.

In 1775 Prince Charles decided to leave Rome. He believed that he would suffer fewer slights to his regal dignity in Florence than in the Papal states, and might even receive from the Grand Duke of Tuscany the honours due to him. In this regard he was to be disappointed. The Grand Duke would not allow him to have a *baldacchino*, which was an emblem of sovereignty, suspended over his boxes in the several theatres he frequented. He would only permit him to line his boxes with silk hangings. In spite of these setbacks Charles at least had the sense to adopt the style of Count of Albany, the dukedom of which was one of the ancient subsidiary titles of the royal Stuarts. It was as Countess of Albany that Louise was henceforth to be known until the day of her death.

Full of hope the Stuart court rented the Palazzo Corsini in the Prato, a quarter between the present railway station and the Cascine. It is a large, long building of the late sixteenth century, with a fine garden at the rear glimpsed through an open entrance. Here the Albanys established themselves with a household of forty-three persons, compared with fifty-four in Rome. While in the Palazzo Corsini the Prince's behaviour towards his wife was fairly decent. He kept off the bottle. He showed no overt objections to Louise holding a literary *salon*, although not much of a reader himself and awkward in the company of intellectuals.

In 1777 the Prince bought and moved into the Palazzo Guadagni (now San Clemente) in the via San Sebastiano (now Gino Capponi), a street running in a straight line northwards from the Duomo into what was open country. The Palazzo Guadagni is a splendid late Renaissance building. The main front facing south has two wings with wide projecting eaves. The square tower of the recessed centre was crowned until very recently with a weather-vane perforated with the initials C.R. and the date 1777. From an enclosed portico for carriages a large door at either end gives access to an arcade. A bronze lantern, fashioned with a crown, swings in the breeze. The ceiling of the spacious entrance hall is painted with arabesques surrounding the figure of Religion brandishing a cross. From a wide archway under the royal arms of Great Britain, as fresh today as when they were painted, a steep and narrow staircase leads from the hall to moderate sized rooms on the *piano nobile* with decorated ceilings and decorated doors. On the west side of the palace a large area used to be the garden packed with cypress and ilex trees and a superabundance of statuary and urns. It is now a tarmacked car-park.*

By the time the Prince went to live in Florence he had given up actively intriguing for an invasion of Britain. Now he merely cherished dreams. These he was never to abandon. He even kept under his bed a strongbox full of sequins in case he might at a moment's notice be called home. He dismissed out of hand a project that he should accept the crown of America because that dignity was not compatible with the hereditary duties of a King of England. Until he took to drinking heavily again he enjoyed fencing and playing the violin, and even reading sentimental poetry to his guests. In 1775 that old maid Horace Mann – 'Mini' to his friends – his ear constantly to the ground, his eye to every keyhole, reported to the Secretary of State in London that the Prince's legs were grotesquely swollen and discharging pus; and that when they ceased discharging there would be fear for his life. The Prince's doctor had told Mann so, and that he suffered from colic and diarrhoea; and that he was also intensely bored with life. Occasionally he would touch 'two or three very low people' for the king's evil, a diversion which reminded him pleasantly of his royal prerogative. His chief daily recreation was an interminable crawl, it cannot be termed a walk, attended by four servants in livery and his wife, in the public gardens where he would with singular affability doff his hat to those visitors he recognized to be English. His favourite evening pastime was the opera, where he went to sleep on a sofa in his box, only leaving it to be sick in the public corridor. He was subject to epileptic fits between bouts of drinking. He would often lose his temper. In a fury with the son of Senator Guadagni for declining to lunch with him and daring casually to drop in for coffee after the meal, the Prince, having hidden behind a door, leapt upon the youth and delivered a mighty kick upon his posterior. In 1774 he was involved in a brawl in the opera with a French officer who meekly said he supposed the Prince was unaware whom he was insulting. The reply he received was, 'Je sais que vous êtes français, et cela suffit!'

In March 1775 a Scotch boy having begged for an audience was

* On my last visit to Florence, entry to the lovely Palazzo Clemente was impossible. It was occupied, barricaded and defended against the police by Maoist students. The condition of the interior, glimpsed through the doorway, may easily be imagined.

called into the Prince's dressing-room where he fervently kissed hands. Charles asked him who he was. The young man told him, and waited for some golden words to treasure for a lifetime. The Prince with an effort stammered, 'My lad, I wish you well,' and withdrew. The young man observed, 'He looks old in complexion and is pretty stout in person.' Sir William Wraxall gave a happier picture of him in 1779. Determined to get a close view of the Prince he posted himself at the head of the opera house staircase at the end of a performance. On quitting his box the Prince noticed the young officer in British uniform. He gently shook off the servants who were guiding his steps, removed his cocked hat of which the brims were drawn up to the crown with gold twist, and saluted Wraxall with an old-fashioned formality. Having done this he beckoned to his servants to escort him to the carriage awaiting him below. The little incident took place the year before his marriage broke up.

Relations between the Albanys steadily worsened. Louise became horribly bored by the daily walks in the public gardens, followed by the four servants in livery. Owing to his infirmities the Prince could now only shuffle with the support of a human arm. Still he persisted in the dreary routine during the heat of July afternoons until Louise could endure it no longer. Dr Moore, who was bear-leading the young Duke of Hamilton on his grand tour, met her on one of the paths of the public gardens. He pitied her. 'She is a beautiful woman,' he wrote, 'much beloved by those who know her, who universally describe her as lively, intelligent and agreeable.' When she refused to act any longer as nurse companion on these tedious perambulations the Prince took to driving. But he insisted upon his wife accompanying him slowly round and round the streets in his open carriage. She feared she might get sunstroke. She wrote him a note of remonstrance, beginning, 'Since your Majesty does not want to listen to reason when I address you . . .' and continuing with a list of her grievances. Further notes grew acrimonious, as his demands became less and less reasonable. He suggested that she should rise earlier in the mornings to attend to his daily ploys. She who in her middle age was indeed to become a very early riser and early retirer, protested in mockery that he 'who had always passed for a gay dog [un gaillard] should have become so degenerate as not to want to spend more than a few hours in bed with a young woman who was pretty and who loved him.' This is an example of Louise's disingenuousness, for by now quite the last thing she wanted was to remain in bed with him an instant longer than was absolutely necessary. And she no longer, if she ever had, loved him at all.

Evening after evening the Prince, having again taken in no uncertain measure to the nasty bottle, would eventually reel to the bed which he forced his wife to share. In bed he coughed all night when he was not actually puking. Horace Mann's informers in the Stuart household, who included the royal physician, told him in 1779 that the Prince had 'a declared fistula, great sores in his legs, and is insupportable in stench and temper; neither of which he takes the least pains to disguise to his wife – whose beauty is vastly faded of late.' There were few bedroom disclosures with which 'Mini's' sordid spies among the Albany servants, richly rewarded for their disloyalty, were not eager to regale him, down to the condition of the marital sheets. Oddly enough the Prince, when relations with his wife were on the verge of breaking point, adopted the same bedroom tactics as he did with Clementina Walkinshaw just before the end of that liaison. He had all entrances to Louise's bedroom barricaded by tables and chairs piled one on top of another. To the chairs were attached little bells whose tinkling would warn him of the approach of strangers. By now husband and wife were not on speaking terms. Yet so sanctified was the marriage-bond and so universally accepted were conjugal rights that the wretched young woman continued to submit without protest to the indignities of a whore. The devoted Madame de Maltzam was the only person aware of the misery her mistress was undergoing. The fuddled prince, furious with his wife and himself, half in love with her and wholly out of love with himself, and impotent besides,* desperately attempted to wreak nightly vengeance. The feast of St Andrew in 1780 was the occasion of the ultimate humiliation. On this anniversary Prince Charles, tormented by memories of days of Scottish glory, his near victories and final defeat, drank to excess while singing Jacobite songs till the tears poured down his cheeks. Then, vilely intoxicated, he turned upon his wife. 'He ill-treated her,' Mann wrote gleefully, and this time there is

---

* Mann actually boasted that Prince Charles informed his friends that he (Mann) gave Louise money with which to buy a potion to make her husband impotent.

reason to suppose, truthfully, 'in the most outrageous manner, by the most abusive language and beating her, and at night by committing the greatest indecencies upon her, in bed, and attempting to choke her. Her screams roused the whole family, and their assistance prevented any further violence.'

This was the last straw. Louise was no mouse, no 'wee, sleekit, cow'rin', tim'rous beastie'. For her the accepted code of what a wife owes a husband had its limits. They were reached. She came to a rapid decision. No matter what the cost to her reputation as a woman and a queen, or to the Jacobite cause to which she had contracted herself, she had to escape.

Let it not be supposed that Louise's sole cause of unease or her sole incentive to escape was a besotted husband. Far from it. Nevertheless I think we can dismiss the extraordinary anxiety of Dr Moore on behalf of his ward the Duke of Hamilton, as wholly groundless. But since it illustrates the sort of charges that were being levelled against Louise's conduct during these unhappy Florentine years, the following extract of a letter, dated 1 June 1776 from the tutor to the Duke's mother, the Duchess of Argyll, is worth quoting.

'Though the Duke's mind is preoccupied this does not make him blind to the Countess of Albany's charms, and if there was a possibility of his forming an acquaintance with her without making an acquaintance with her husband, I imagine he would be glad of such an opportunity. I have not omitted to hint the Impropriety of such an Intimacy, and if it could be supposed possible that it might be carried a certain length I have represented with equal zeal and loyalty how very ungrateful it would be to His Majesty [George III] to run the risk of begeting Pretenders to his Crown, at the very time when he was fixing honours upon your Grace and the Duke's family. I hope your Grace will put my zeal on this occasion in a proper point of view to their Majesties, that in case the Stewart line should be continued by the Duke's means, I may not incur their disapprobation . . . for the reanimation of the cruel, tyranical, bloody, papistical race of Stewart when it seemed to be expiring.'*

---

* *Intimate Society Letters of the Eighteenth Century*, ed. by the 8th Duke of Argyll. I am indebted to Mr Brinsley Ford for drawing my attention to Dr Moore's letter.

The Duchess of Argyll can hardly have been so tactless as to mention the matter to the chaste King George and Queen Charlotte. As for Louise, she was probably quite unaware of the nineteen-year-old Duke of Hamilton's aspirations.

By 1780 there was another and paramount incentive to attain freedom. It had in fact been agitating the Countess for a year or more. If Thomas Coke's puppy affection and Bonstetten's honey-tongued adulation had ruffled Louise's heart, the tornado of passion she was now experiencing was enough to sweep her off her feet, even had Prince Charles been the pattern and mirror of conjugal perfection – enough to sweep her away to the ends of the world.

We are vouchsafed much information about the course of the Countess of Albany's affair with Count Vittorio Alfieri from the lover's own words. Great tragic poet though Alfieri is recognized by his compatriots to be, of all his works the autobiography, which he began at the age of forty-one in 1790 and finished in 1802, is far and away the most readable. *La Vita di Vittorio Alfieri, scritta da Esso*, puts him in the rank of classical autobiographers such as Cellini and Rousseau for candour, bombast and picaresque adventure. In other words we cannot form a picture of this extraordinary man without looking at him through his own eyes.

The author recounts how he was born in 1749 at Asti of a noble family. His father died when he was a baby and his mother remarried. At the age of ten the young Count, for this he was, went to the Turin Academy where he spent eight lonely years, learning a little if we may believe him, 'of counter-education, an ass among asses and under the tutelage of an ass'. Certainly during his formative boyhood he learned to have no respect for authority, sacred or profane. He seems to have spent very little of his vacations with his mother and stepfather. His only friend and guardian throughout these years was a cousin of his father, whom he called uncle, Count Benedetto Alfieri, the King of Sardinia's chief architect, and indeed a Baroque architect recently raised from obscurity to a high plane in the estimation of modern art historians. Perhaps the best known work of this disciple of Juvara is the delicious parish church of Carignano in rose pink brick, with a nave shaped like a fan. Benedetto, of whom Vittorio became very fond, lived in a house close to the Theatre Royal in Turin (which he had built), a house where the university student was made welcome at any time of the day. The old Count was a worthy, kind-hearted, simple man. He held the great artists of the past in profound reverence, and never mentioned the name of Michelangelo without doffing his hat or bowing his head.

When his studies in Turin were deemed to be completed Vittorio was at the age of eighteen free to do whatever he wanted. He was rich. He had no responsibilities to anyone or anything. His estates were managed by resident agents. He admitted in the autobiography with compelling candour that he was spoilt, self-centred, self-pitying, petulant, neurasthenic and apathetic. So for lack of anything better to do, he travelled. He went practically everywhere, pursued by a restless demon, without purpose, in pursuit of he knew not what, unless adventure, constantly shifting ideals, and love were objectives. But he became dissatisfied with all three, and disliked everything he saw and everyone he met. He was presented to Louis XV and Frederick the Great. He took against all monarchs and despised the sycophancy of courtiers. While professing to loathe tyrants he refused, when he had the chance, to meet the apostle of freedom, Rousseau, considering his demagogic principles beneath attention, and his writings too silly to be taken seriously. Yet he liked to consider himself an advanced radical. In reality the aristocrat in him despised the proletariat much more than the radical in him despised the rich and privileged. For the French nation he developed during the Revolution a bitter contempt and loathing. His youthful disapproval of the autocracy of Versailles was superceded by a middle-aged fear and horror of mob rule, which impelled him to champion Louis XVI in all his writings and conversations.

It may well be asked wherein lies the importance of this mercurial contradictory, disagreeable young man? Many rich adolescent males do not know what they want, lead frivolous lives and are of no interest to anyone. But Alfieri was different from these long before he turned into a poet. His restlessness, his self-depreciation, his dissatisfaction were symptomatic of the age in which he lived, the age in which the intelligentsia were beginning to question, then rebel against the accepted canons of the feudal past. He was a precursor of the democratic movement of the following century. In his unspecified discontents he anticipated Childe Harold, the romantic wanderer. In his licence he also anticipated Don Juan, the picaresque roué. Unbridled passion was the quality which distinguished the young Alfieri from his contemporaries. I mean passion in feeling, thinking and expression, as well as in loving. Ultimately passion in writing.

In *La Vita* he records his amatory adventures with engaging frankness, beginning with an interest at the age of twelve in the choristers whom he lusted after while they served the priest at Mass in Asti cathedral. No doubt Alfieri dramatized his love affairs preposterously. He dramatized every event that pertained to himself. One evening in Florence he asked that virginal lady, Miss Cornelia Knight, to take to England the manuscript of *Miso-Gallo*, the satirical treatise he had written on the French Revolution. She readily consented. The next morning he rushed breathlessly to see her. He assured her he had not slept one wink all night for having narrowly submitted her to so dangerous an undertaking. If her luggage were searched and the offending manuscript discovered, and read by the guards at the frontier, she, virtuous Miss Knight, would without question, instantly be guillotined; and he, Alfieri, would be solely responsible. Her blood would for ever rest upon his head. Mildly surprised, Miss Knight retorted that the guards were almost certainly illiterate and she was perfectly prepared to take the risk.

In Turin he fell so desperately in love with a lady living in a house opposite his own in the Piazza San Carlo that to prevent himself forcing his unwelcome presence upon her he first cut off his red hair (wigs were not worn at the time), and when this self-inflicted affront to his vanity was no deterrent to his desire, made his servants tie him with ropes to a chair. It is typical of his analytical mind that he believed resort to these extreme measures was induced by his mistress's unworthiness of him. At the age of nineteen he tried unsuccessfully to bleed himself to death. His love for a lady in Holland was requited, but almost immediately she was obliged to accompany her husband to Switzerland. In England he had an affair with Penelope Lady Ligonier, which caused great scandal and his total undoing in society. It led to a duel with the husband in the Green Park between the acts of an opera which both combatants happened to be attending at the Haymarket Theatre. They fought with swords and Lord Ligonier, seeing how unskilled his opponent was, behaved very handsomely in sparing Alfieri's life, an act of mercy which the poet had the grace to acknowledge: 'I did not kill him because I could not;

and he did not kill me because he would not.' Nonetheless Lord Ligonier divorced his wife who throughout the affair with Alfieri had been sleeping with his Lordship's groom. In fact the man out of jealousy betrayed Alfieri to his master.

In Cadiz Alfieri at the age of twenty-three caught venereal disease which was probably the cause of eventual softening of the brain and his premature death. The only solace from amatory distractions which he claimed to derive was prolonged autumnal wanderings among the gloomy forests and wastes of northern Sweden. In the desolate twilit north he found the sublimity and melancholy which his soul craved. Here too the ardours of his passionate blood were temporarily cooled.

Back again in Turin in 1772 he fell in love with another lady of deficient qualities, the Marchesa Turinetti de Prié, who suffered from an unspecified ailment. He spent hours sitting at her bedside, tormented by agonies of desire and bored to tears. At least this unrequited affair turned the languishing swain to literature. Alfieri was inspired to write one act of a drama which he presented to her, or rather, for such was her indifference to things of the mind, which he stuffed under the cushion of her chair. After several weeks of incubation the manuscript was retrieved by him, and immediately four further acts were hatched. His first drama, *Cleopatra*, was performed in Turin in 1775. From now on Alfieri acknowledged literary fame to be his supreme goal; and love to be his only incitement to writing.

This was the individual who in 1776 happened to be in Florence, an angry young man of twenty-seven. Ostensibly he was learning to perfect his Italian in the capital city where the Tuscan tongue was most purely spoken. For although Italian by birth and breeding this cosmopolitan poet was primarily French speaking. He found that the first writings in his native language were stilted, over-refined and incorrect. His Italian grammar always remained shaky. As for his character he was at this date, in the words of Margaret Crosland, 'autocratic, violent, arrogant, lazy, vain; he was tyrannical and hated tyranny.' In build he was tall and thin, very handsome with commanding eagle features and a mane of bright red hair which sprang from his forehead like the jagged rays of a sun through thunder clouds. While in Florence Alfieri frequently noticed 'a beautiful, amiable and very distinguished foreigner'. She was unlike the usual run of visitors in that she observed works of art as though she liked and understood them. One day in the Uffizi Gallery he overheard her admire a portrait of Charles XII of Sweden. He was struck by her intelligent comments. But he decided to avoid meeting her so as not to be distracted from the composition of a drama, *Filippo e Polinice*, which he had in hand. Within the restricted social circle of Florence this proved impossible. Alfieri was soon taking stock of the lady's appearance. 'A subdued fire in her exceedingly dark eyes, united, as rarely happens, with a very white skin and fair hair, gave her an outstanding beauty and it was difficult not to be impressed and captivated. She was twenty-five;* she had a great inclination for the fine arts and letters; a nature of gold.' It was no good. He fell. Within a short while he was a frequent attendant at the Palazzo Guadagni.

For the first time in his life Alfieri's new passion was not overwhelmingly physical. There was in his early relations with Louise a blending of intellect with emotion. As he put it in retrospect: 'In the present [situation] the mind had a sentiment of esteem, mingling with love, which rendered this passion, if less impetuous, at least more profound and durable.' Durable it certainly was to prove. Nevertheless both Alfieri and Louise dramatized their love. He could from his very nature do no less. Margaret Crosland sums up the relationship well.

'Louise and Alfieri had created a drama of their own, distinct from the little comedy in which they were joined by the Prince. Theirs was a drama of will power. Alfieri had made himself into a poet, and Louise had made herself into a reader of poetry; she had chosen the 'outstanding man' she believed she needed. Now they were forced to live up to themselves and each other. It was not always easy. If they had not both been brought up on the remnants of morality and literature of *le grand siècle*, adapted to the living conditions of the eighteenth century, they could never have acted out their little play together. To them the play was a very serious thing indeed; to us it is less serious, but with a piquancy of its own, for this love affair, always worldly, sometimes cynical and perhaps artificial, transformed an infuriated poet into a great writer.'

* Actually twenty-four.

The only phrase in this passage which I dispute is the four words, 'always worldly, sometimes cynical', as governing their relationship. Artificial the manner of it may occasionally have appeared to be, for the fashion of the age was to overcharge love with sentiment. Worldly and cynical it never was. On the contrary when their passion was spent their mutual devotion endured until the very end.

Louise's part in the ensuing duet was a rare achievement. It is not often given to a queen, however inclined to the fine arts and literature, to shape the career of a living creator of genius. And this is in effect what she did. If she was no profound intellectual, she was a highbrow. She was earnest. She became the incentive behind her partner's work by purveying that implicit love which he had stated was the prerequisite to the fulfilment of his genius. She dedicated all her care and all her being to fostering that genius which she treated as though it were his and her child. When away from Louise Alfieri was unable to write at all. He declared that in her absence 'all my faculties were reduced or dormant.' Instead scalding tears washed away the seeds of inspiration before they could take root. It can be argued that a love so dependent upon literary ambition is an unorthodox love. Anything can be argued. In their case their love, whatever its nature, worked. Like Dante, Alfieri referred to her with reverence, almost humility, as 'my lady', 'my inestimable friend', 'my beloved mistress' and rarely as 'my love'. To her he was always succinctly 'the poet'.

For four years the couple, left-overs of *le grande siècle*, as Margaret Crosland sees them, were if not content, then reconciled to having a clandestine love affair. It is very probable that throughout these years of waiting for the death of the old Stuart prince, their love was not consummated. They were seldom alone together. In the midst of a miniature court there were obstacles to intimacy. By ingratiating himself with the sozzled husband Alfieri contrived to gain free entry into the Palazzo Guadagni. While Prince Charles fell asleep after dinner Louise would strum on her guitar, if Vittorio did not read aloud extracts from his latest drama, or whisper surreptitious words of love into her willing ear. They conversed in French for Louise could barely speak Italian. At her request he wrote *Maria Stuarda*, though somewhat against his inclination, because he felt obliged to whitewash too thickly the Scottish queen's part in the murder of

Darnley. The compromising preface, in which the relations of author and dedicatee were made abundantly clear, was added later.

In waiting for Louise, Alfieri took an unprecedented step in the annals of lovers. For her sake he disfranchised himself by casting off his Piedmontese nationality, so ceasing to be a subject of the King of Sardinia. He had long been irked by the Piedmontese law that a landowner must seek the King's authority whenever he wished to go abroad. To the cosmopolitan Alfieri it was intolerable to beg on bended knee for a privilege which anyway ought to be an individual's right. The restriction was indicative of a narrow and philistine provincial society, of which he disapproved. Each time he went through the process permission was granted with reluctance; and the longer he made each sojourn abroad the greater was his sovereign's suspicion. Worse still, he could not as a Piedmontese subject publish in another country any writing of which his sovereign might disapprove. The truth is that his sovereign did not disapprove, because he was on the whole a tolerant and enlightened man. When Charles Emmanuel IV was chased from his throne by Napoleon in 1798 and fled to Florence, Alfieri, inconsistent in all things, hastened to pay his respects. 'He was my King; he is now unhappy. My duty is to condole with him,' he protested. The poet obtained an audience, and the poor king in opening his arms wide so as to embrace the delinquent ex-subject, exclaimed, 'Behold your tyrant!'

The voluntary act of self-disfranchisement meant that Alfieri had to surrender his estates to his next of kin, who was his sister. To her he gladly relinquished his immense properties, retaining by arrangement only a small allowance of money. Seldom can a lover have divested himself of his worldly goods in order to maintain the heart of a queen. But Alfieri was not the man to put worldly demands before those of the emotions. Nevertheless it is characteristic of his contradictory character and also of his vanity that for a time he continued wearing Sardinian uniform, to which he no longer had a right, because it suited his appearance. With his usual candour he wrote: 'What will philosophers say when I frankly acknowledge the reason for this? It seemed to me that I looked better and handsomer in this than in any other dress.' He eventually abandoned the uniform in favour of a simple blue suit for the daytime, and a black suit for the evenings.

The proceedings of the night following the feast of St Andrew in 1780, distasteful though they were at the time, were a blessing in disguise. They provided a splendidly righteous excuse for the Countess of Albany to leave the husband with whom she was totally disgusted and devote her life to the lover with whom she was infatuated. Without delay she concocted with Alfieri a plan of escape. The support of the Grand Duchess of Tuscany, who was only too ready to lend a hand in punishing an errant husband – her own was not a model of propriety never looking for diversion beyond the conjugal bed – and who besides abhorred Prince Charles's drunkenness, was essential. It was quickly obtained. One morning in early December when the royal carriage drove up to the door of the Palazzo Guadagni for the Prince's matutinal drive, Louise condescended with unusual compliance to accompany him. She brought into the carriage with her a friend, Signora Orlandini,* and her Irish lover, one Gehegan, who had been breakfasting in the palace. On the pretext that the Countess wished to inspect some needlework done by the little white nuns, they drove to the via Mandorlo (now via Giusti) a stone's throw away. On reaching the Convento delle Bianchette, the two ladies rapidly ran up the steps and pulled the bell while the suspicious prince, who would never let his wife out of his sight unless he fell asleep, slowly and painfully followed on the arm of Gehegan. By prearrangement Louise and her companion were at once admitted and the doors slammed in the prince's face. His rage knew no bounds. He banged on the doors with his stick and shouted to no avail. Through the grill the mother superior blandly announced that any woman seeking to escape physical violence from a husband's hands was offered sanctuary within her portals. The Prince had no alternative to withdrawal. Back at home he threatened to shoot Gehegan for his collusion in the escape, thought better of the matter and apologized. Gehegan in his turn saucily challenged the Prince to a duel for calling his friend Alfieri a 'seducer', thought better of the matter and let it drop. Frustrated, the Prince vented his fury by smashing some furniture in the palace and refusing to send Louise her clothes.

After a few days in the Florentine convent, where Louise was at

* She was the wife of a Florentine General, and was born Thérèse Butler.

least able to collect her thoughts and lay plans for the future, she set off for Rome. The rumour that Alfieri accompanied his *inamorata* seated, disguised as the coachman, on the box of the carriage, and armed with a musket to ward off possible attempts on the part of the outraged husband to abduct her, was false. Actually the poet, in a state of pitiable anxiety over the fate of 'my lady', followed her at a discreet distance.

Once again the Cardinal Duke of York found himself drawn into family trouble that was no immediate concern of his. Once again he was to have dealings with and be hoodwinked by a woman. In the person of Louise of Stolberg he was to suffer yet another thorn of the flesh, and the sharpest of the lot. Against his will he was obliged to take sides in the unseemly brawls that ensued between his brother and his brother's wife.

Henry had been the first to welcome the marriage in 1772. He was as eager as the Prince that an heir should be begotten to the family so long as no begetting was expected of him. Since becoming a cardinal in 1747 he had always laboured under an anxiety as well as a sense of guilt. For he knew only too well that in cases of extremity cardinals had before now been obliged by dynastic pressures to surrender their sacred office in order that they might propagate. Pope Benedict XIV had actually written to Cardinal de Tencin in 1748 that if Prince Charles were to die he would grant the Cardinal of York a dispensation to marry. Undoubtedly Henry was aware of this hideous possibility. So he fervently hoped that a pretty and loving wife with character, which his sister-in-law possessed, would not only be an influence for good on the Prince's habits, but might provide him with children. In both respects he was to be disappointed. However in 1772 the prospects looked bright. He accepted Princess Louise of Stolberg-Gedern with open arms. He sent the young bride some splendid presents, including a gold lace court dress and a diamond snuff box containing 40,000 Roman crows, the equivalent of £10,000 in English money. Louise plunged eagerly into what Henry considered frivolities, and no heir was forthcoming. Rumours reached his ears that she had admirers, but only admirers; and then that the husband's drinking bouts had begun all over again. The bright prospects were somewhat dimmed. Suddenly in 1780 he learned that the marriage was completely on the rocks. A piteous letter came from Louise about her deplorable situation. Another, dated 9 December, followed, announcing that she had taken refuge in a Florentine convent. It was his mother's story all over again, only worse. To Louise's letters the Cardinal Duke replied on the 15th offering help, and suggesting that she might move to the sanctuary of the Ursuline nuns in the via Vittoria, Rome where his sainted mother had passed so many months in fasting and prayer, there to remain until relations with her husband could be patched up. The Cardinal Duke did not yet know his sister-in-law. She had not the slightest intention of ever returning to her husband; or of making a long stay in the Rome nunnery. Holy practices were not at all her way, and isolation from the temptations of society was by no means attractive to her.

Brian Fothergill in his admirable biography of the Cardinal of York questions whether his subject's natural obstinacy prevented him from opening his eyes to the true fact, which was that Louise had a lover in the poet Alfieri, now in hot pursuit of her. I am inclined to think that the Cardinal was incapable of deliberate self-deception. He did not shut his eyes to scandal. His eyes were closed to it. They were only opened when his nose was rudely rubbed into it. Meanwhile the talented, exuberant, beguiling poet, who was also a count and very much a patrician, went out of his way to charm the purblind Cardinal. Alfieri was constantly calling at the Palazzo Cancelleria. The Cardinal was impressed, and touched by the solicitude. So kind of the poet to interest himself in Louise's horrid predicament! So laudable his gallantry – if a trifle unorthodox in the circumstances perhaps – to champion a lady in distress!

In Rome the lady moved obediently into the convent of the Ursuline nuns on the advice of her brother-in-law. She had to find some temporary resting place in a hurry; and this one was as good as any other. Meanwhile she lost no time in appealing as a gravely injured spouse in dire need of protection and funds, not only to the Cardinal but to the Pope and Queen Marie Antoinette as well. When we consider what a scandalous offence it was for a wife to leave her husband in the eighteenth century we must pay tribute to Louise's courage and pertinacity. Her situation was made worse by an absolute dependence for existence upon people who must strongly disapprove of her action. From the Pope, whom she completely bamboozled at a meeting in the sacristy of a Roman church, she extorted agreement that half the pension he was paying to Prince Charles should at once be handed over to her as well as whatever possessions in the Palazzo Guadagni she might require. Through the French Queen's help and sympathy she obtained the pension which the Versailles court had already offered to the Prince and he had spurned for being too little.

The Cardinal of York was flattered by the appeals of his pretty and seductive sister-in-law for protection. He had no illusions whatever about his brother and readily believed the horrifying tales of his conduct with which she regaled him. Besides he liked and admired Louise. It must be admitted that Louise returned this guileless man's affection with ingratitude, unkindness and duplicity. To her he appeared a religious bigot and a simpleton. She made use of him shamelessly when it suited her, and when she had nothing further to get out of him, mocked and abused him. The Cardinal's understanding of women was deficient. He mistook Louise's character in supposing that it must resemble his mother's. He too readily assumed that she would be content to remain incarcerated in the Ursuline convent until through tears and piety she might persuade her errant husband to mend his ways and live with her again in a state of God-fearing uxoriousness and sobriety. When he discovered that this was not by any means her intention he made arrangements for her to quit the convent he had found for her. With the Pope's consent, which he solicited on her behalf, he let her move into the second floor of his official residence, the Palazzo Cancelleria. It was a spontaneous and generous action.

For several months all went well. Louise behaved with tact; Alfieri, who only reached Rome in May of 1781, installed himself in the Villa Strozzi on the Esquiline with discretion. The pair met clandestinely, and often. When they were together it was a blessed relief not to be incommoded by the hovering shadow of Prince Charles. On the whole it was a fairly happy time for both lovers. Although still living in different establishments, they had plenty of leisure to pursue and discuss their mutual concerns.

The poet could not for long disguise his irritation over the whole farcical subterfuge. It sickened him to be obliged to kow-tow to the Vatican, merely for the sake of a roof over his beloved's head, and to pretend to the Pope and that egregious ass the Cardinal of York that their relations were strictly above board. He felt shame in deigning to present himself, at Louise's request, to her brother-in-law in the guise of her disinterested protector, with the gift of a superbly bound Virgil, an edition which she had ascertained the Cardinal did not already possess. To hell with respectability and cant! Then in the autumn of 1782 the couple overreached themselves. All was no longer well. Louise, in order to promote her poet's fame, arranged for a performance of his tragedy *Antigone* by a cast of dukes and duchesses and Count Alfieri himself, at a private party given by the Spanish Ambassador. The cream of Roman society, including several cardinals, was present. The occasion was reckoned a brilliant gathering, and the performance a resounding dramatic success. As a result the true relationship of the Queen of England and Count Alfieri likewise resounded across the city and reached the ears of the establishment in the Quirinal and Vatican palaces. Even so the Cardinal of York in his innocence was still without suspicion.

The Spanish Ambassador's party at which Louise and Alfieri appeared together for the first time in, as it were, flagrant intimacy, was followed in April 1783 by the news that Prince Charles was at death's door in Florence. The Cardinal, who lately had again been in the Prince's bad books for championing his runaway wife, nevertheless dashed to the sickbed where he found his brother well on the road to recovery. The patient was very voluble. In unequivocal terms he unburdened himself of his injuries, hints of which in writing had hitherto been ignored by the Cardinal. He undeceived His Eminence. He told him that his wife had cuckolded him, the King of England, and had by a deceitful ruse run off with her lover with whom she was, whenever she had the opportunity, so he chose to suppose, living in sin. The Cardinal Duke was absolutely horrified. He could scarcely believe his ears. He rushed – the Cardinal Duke drove everywhere at top speed – back to Rome and instantly poured out the full story into the hearing trumpet of Pope Pius VI. He railed against the infamous pair of lovers and demanded their instant punishment. The Holy Father's agreement to banish Count Alfieri from Rome within fifteen days, because he could not well countenance such goings-on once they had been pointed out to him, was anticipated by the poet's leaving of his own free will on the 4th of May. The Pope being more accustomed than the Cardinal Duke to the habits of normal men and women did not express the same unfeigned horror of their conduct. And he had the sense to dissuade the Cardinal from insisting upon Louise's return to the Florentine nunnery. An unwilling recruit, he asseverated, would not benefit herself thereby, and might merely corrupt the other inmates. 'The cat,' exclaimed Horace Mann exultantly, 'is at last out of the bag.'

If Alfieri was annoyed with the Cardinal Duke for what he had done, the Countess of Albany was beside herself with indignation. She maintained that her brother-in-law was responsible for creating a scandal out of nothing, or very little. It is true he had created more scandal than was absolutely required. 'It is said,' wrote Miss Cornelia Knight, 'that taken aback by the revelation made to him in Florence [the Cardinal] told every postillion on the road from Florence to Rome the bad opinion he had of his sister-in-law and Count Alfieri, and he held the same discourse with all the shabby people about Frascati.'

'See what unpleasantness you would have spared me,' Louise wrote to Henry, 'if (as we had originally agreed upon) you had confided your views of the matter to myself, and had not most unnecessarily informed the Pope.' Henry, ever one to offer the other cheek, accepted the rebuke, but without admitting that he had acted wrongly. By way of amends he made her an offer of the Stuart diamonds, which she self-righteously declined. 'Being your brother's wife, I naturally have a right to the diamonds . . .' was her ungracious reply. 'I only ask for your affection,' she continued disingenuously, returning with a barbed thrust, 'In any case everybody will hear you wanted to give them to me, for I shall mention this to all my friends.' Her friends in Roman society took her part as was to be expected of them. Their unanimous verdict was that the Countess's case was a grievous one and that the Cardinal had acted like a spoilsport. Next year her husband, having fully recovered, was to complain to the King of Sweden that Henry was keeping from him the diamonds that were rightly his.

IV

FAMILY FOREGROUND

The rather sordid row between his brother and sister-in-law co-incided with an unusually busy time for the Cardinal in his capacity of Vice-Chancellor to the Holy See. Owing to the Emperor Joseph II's declared policy of Erastianism, more particularly styled Josephinism, which entailed the state taking upon itself in Austria and the Low Countries reform of the monasteries, and the curtailing of papal authority in Church affairs, Pope Pius VI (1775–99) was much perturbed. Being a reasonable man he decided to go to Vienna in 1782 in an attempt to sort things out with the Emperor face to face. In consequence many responsible duties fell upon the Vice-Chancellor during the Holy Father's absence. A further vexation was the malicious rumour which Alfieri put about that the Cardinal intended to assassinate him. Needless to say it had absolutely no foundation whatever. On the contrary an attempt was made that year by a disgruntled lunatic to assassinate the Cardinal in Frascati. It was happily foiled.

After his initial disclosures of Louise's affair with Alfieri to all and sundry the Cardinal behaved with commendable reticence. He also accepted the inevitability of the royal couple's separation. When a legal settlement – concerning which I shall have more to say in a later chapter – was brought about between the estranged husband and wife in 1784 Henry was only indignant that Louise had failed to consult him about the terms. He wrote reproving her for having surrendered to Prince Charles an allowance which he, Henry, had been paying to her. It certainly was an act of presumption on her part. But then she always held the Cardinal in profound contempt. She treated him cavalierly, yet took from him whatever she could get. In a letter of 1798 to her intimate friend Teresa Mocenni she complained that he exceeded all other cardinals in his extravagant prejudices, those of his birth and condition and, too, in his absurdly extravagant living. She said he was whimsical and yet very dull. 'He is one of those amphibious beings who have been raised to be seen from a distance, but whom circumstances have made seen from close to: they would all seem alike if one were obliged to live with them, as with this comical figure, my brother-in-law.' She derided his simplicity which she interpreted as outright stupidity. She wrote: 'When he was in the middle of the ocean he gave orders for the ship to be stopped. Can you believe such a thing possible?' Could anything be more droll, she asked. The answer is that the royal Cardinal's ancestor King Canute thought along somewhat similar lines. Other stories were told to illustrate his imbecility. In Louise's eyes he was at best a figure of fun, at worst an interfering busybody.

Two such diametrically different characters, the one sharp, the other soft, could hardly be expected to fraternise. And after Louise left the Cardinal's roof they did not meet again. Nor did they often correspond. When he learned – incorrectly as it happened – that she had accepted a pension from George III he was outraged. He spoke of the insult she had brought to his family, adding that he would sooner have died than accept one. Did he remember these words when in 1800 he was driven to do this very thing? Yet the Cardinal who finally came to dislike her – after all, she brought his brother no happiness, and no children – never spoke ill of her. He continued, even throughout the period in exile when he was practically reduced to penury, to pay her allowance, as he did that of the Countess of Albestroff. Louise did not volunteer to forego hers. And when she believed him to be dying in 1806 she hastened to Rome in order to make sure that by some means or other her annuity would not cease with his death. He bequeathed her a picture and, amongst a few other objects, a watch on which he had had her cypher engraved. Perhaps it is to her credit that she said, on receiving these tokens, 'she would have been satisfied had she been left only a pin as a remembrance.'

Meanwhile Prince Charles was left in Florence in parlous circumstances. He was old, ill, demoralised, and miserable. He was intensely lonely. Long before his lamentable behaviour had lost him his wife it had driven away the best of his servants. Colonel Henry Goring's position as confidential aide-de-camp had become so untenable that after years of faithful allegiance he enlisted in the King of Prussia's service in Berlin. Hay, Lumisden and Urquhart, as we have already seen, had left in 1768. Caryll (described by a cousin as 'one of the genteelest, best-bred men I ever knew. He has not even dogs-wages for his trouble, but does all for stark love and kindness.') was driven to resign from the Secretaryship of State in 1777. What was the royal dipsomaniac to do now? He would not whistle back the Countess of Albestroff. That was certain. But there was his daughter Charlotte, his little 'Pouponne', whom he had not seen for twenty years. We do not know much about the way mother and daughter had managed to eke out an existence in Paris after being abandoned by Prince Charles in 1760, and only a little after the Cardinal chased them from Rome in 1772. We know that on their return to France they retired to a convent, called La Miséricorde at Meaux-en-Brie, cheaper than the one they had previously occupied in Paris.

Prince Charles's behaviour towards his ex-mistress and only child had all along been deplorable. He neither contributed a penny towards their well-being nor answered the agonized appeals for help with which they bombarded him. Those from Pouponne to her adored Papa were admittedly couched in a style ingratiating or accusatory, and certainly not calculated to mollify the heart of the tenderest father. The heart of the Prince, until it suited him to feel paternal, was stony. In 1784 it did suit him. He was desperate. He simply had to have someone to tend, humour and, if possible, love him. In July he sent Colonel John Stewart, his major-domo, and almost the only friend who had remained in his service, to fetch Charlotte from Meaux where she was living with her mother. And not only with her mother.

In spite of her protestations of anxiety to rejoin her father Charlotte took a long time to come. Prince Charles could not understand the reasons for delay. It is very doubtful if he ever was to, or if he ever even suspected that for several years past his daughter was the mistress of no less exalted an individual than Prince Ferdinand de Rohan-Guémenée, Archbishop of Bordeaux, the brother of that Cardinal Édouard de Rohan-Guémenée, who was compromised in the scandal of Marie Antoinette's diamond necklace. The reason for Charlotte's delay in going to Rome was quite simple. She was recovering from the birth of a son. The child, baptised Charles Edward was in fact the third of Charlotte's illegitimate children by the Prince Archbishop, and the only one whose history has been traced. The secret had been so carefully kept that not even Horace Mann was aware of the full lengths to which the affair had gone. There can be no doubt that if he had had the slightest inkling, he would have been agog with the news. In 1784 he merely recorded that Charlotte was 'not obliged to conform to any of the rules of the convent [at Meaux], she is frequently absent from it,' preferring the society of the Archbishop, ostensibly for her spiritual benefit. Charlotte did not reach Florence and the Palazzo Guadagni until October.

Charlotte at this date was a buxom young woman of thirty-one. She was described by a contemporary as 'a tall robust woman of a very dark complexion and coarse grained skin with more masculine boldness than feminine modesty or elegance, but easy and unassuming in her manners.' Certainly her portrait by H. D. Hamilton in the Edinburgh National Portrait Gallery is of a rather unprepossessing tomboy. It depicts her with chestnut hair and her father's hazel-blue eyes. But her plump and freckled face denotes silliness allied with slyness.

At this stage of her existence she was very loth to be parted from her three children and her lover, as well as her mother. To the last she was sincerely devoted, and kept up a regular correspondence with her from Italy, often writing two or three times a week. She was very guarded in what she wrote, for letters were frequently opened and read by spies. Nevertheless hers contained cryptic references to 'mon amis', 'l'amis' and 'les amies' (her written French was astonishingly erratic), indicating the Archbishop, who was 'jealous as a tiger', and to 'le jardin', meaning the children. But she realised that it was politic to be accepted and recognized by her moribund father, for all their sakes, and that this necessitated living under his roof until his death. In a sense she behaved dutifully towards him and having put her hand to the plough, she did not turn back. It is questionable how fond of him she was, judging by the tone of her letters to her mother. Why indeed should she be? She wrote to Clementina about the probable length of her stay in Italy. 'Cela sera long – j'ai peur! Oh mon Dieu, que de patience!' which does not suggest deep filial affection. And again, 'although he is dying, he drags himself about everywhere. He likes parties just as if he were fifteen.' Was she at all sincere? For when Prince Charles died she told Clementina that she was 'crushed by sorrow' at losing 'the best and tenderest of fathers'. Or had she grown genuinely attached to him by the end? When she added, 'I know how much you loved him,' one begins to question it, since her mother had overtly loathed him for years.

When the Cardinal first heard in 1784 that his brother had created his illegitimate daughter a duchess and installed her in his palace in Florence he was shocked and indignant. It was one further degradation of the Stuart kingship which he regarded as sacrosanct. A tactless letter from Charlotte to 'her very dear uncle' announcing her new rank and reminding him of their close consanguinity did nothing to mollify him. It merely confirmed his opinion that the young woman was brazen, which she was. Pope Pius did not improve matters by recognizing in his usual kindly way her legitimation and her title of Duchess of Albany. The conferring of this particular title on his brother's bastard was very provoking to the Cardinal in that the dukedom of Albany, having since the fourteenth century traditionally been bestowed upon younger sons of the Stuart sovereigns, should by rights be his. The Cardinal Duke of York sent one of his long protests to the Prince in Florence and another to the Pope, deprecating 'this person', as he termed Charlotte, and her 'pretended legitimation'. He found 'this business so disgusting; which he protests for his part to regard as null and void.' Above all he objected to her assumption of the prefix H.R.H. before her new title. Such presumption was not becoming in one whom he had been supporting out of charity over the past eighteen years. The Cardinal was so put out that he even joined with Louise in mutual protestations. This was a mistake because news of the alliance soon reached the Palazzo Guadagni. In consequence relations between the brothers were once again at rock bottom. Furthermore, of all the people whom Charlotte most detested, her step-mother headed the list. And when the Cardinal eventually relented, which because of his naturally benignant disposition he was bound to do sooner or later, Charlotte did not forget that he had once joined forces with the woman who pronounced her vulgar and made mock of her.

Charlotte, to all appearances undeterred by the Cardinal's opinion of her, continued to persecute him with reproachful and ingratiating

letters, purporting to give him news of her father's improved health
and spirits since she had gone to live with him. The Cardinal was
determined not to succumb to these blandishments. But he could not
prevent himself. Gradually his disapproval melted under the warmth
of his niece's manner. Her total disregard of his dislike was dis-
arming. Her submission to his opinions was gratifying. And the good
effect she was having upon her father was most edifying. It alone was
enough to win him over. Guardedly but gradually he responded to
her overtures. Anyone less simple than the Cardinal would have seen
through them as patently insincere and calculated to gain his favour
against the day when her father should die and he become king. For
Charlotte after laying flattery upon her uncle as with a trowel,
proceeded at first to make sly innuendoes about Louise, to whom she
always referred offensively as 'Madame', and Alfieri, and then to
level very bitchy animadversions against the two lovers. 'I am sure,
Monseigneur,' she wrote, 'you must be greatly distressed at the
conduct of M. Alfieri and his influence over Madame; your feelings of
delicacy, and your principles must be shocked at the neglect of what
is due to your house.' It is pertinent to wonder how much more
shocked the Cardinal's feelings of delicacy might be were he made
aware of the existence of Charlotte's three illegitimate children by the
Archbishop of Bordeaux. Not even Prince Charles was privy to those
little peccadillos. The Cardinal evidently swallowed Charlotte's bait,
hook, line and sinker. He, the most correct of men, did not even
wince at her reference to Count Alfieri as 'Alfi'. He consented to meet
the Duchess at Monte Freddo near Perugia, where he fell for her head
over heels. On his return to Rome he informed the Pope that he had
been mistaken in his earlier estimates of his niece's character. She
possessed all the goodness and charm that any woman could desire.
By cunningly winning her uncle's favour Charlotte also succeeded in
reconciling Charles and Henry, and in finally ostracizing Louise from
the sympathies of the latter.

On 29th October 1785 Prince Charles sent the Cardinal from
Florence an affecting letter in which he thanked him for preparing the
Palazzo Muti for his and his daughter Charlotte's homecoming.
'Dearest Brother, With infinite pleasure and deepest satisfaction I
have heard of your safe arrival in Rome.' The Cardinal cannot have
come from further than Frascati, a journey which he frequently made

there and back in one day. But no one knew better than Charles how and when to turn on the taps of charm and pathos. 'I desire with all my heart, the moment I shall arrive, to express to you in person my affection and attachment in Rome itself.' He assured him that he now wished to be known merely as the Count of Albany. He related how for days on end he was kept to his bed by torments of suffering. He proffered his humble reverence to His Holiness.

The Cardinal must have been delighted with this show of submission to good sense, and saddened by the account of his brother's debility. He galloped off to Viterbo to meet the prodigal and his daughter, and accompany them back to Rome. On 8 December the three reached the Palazzo Muti. The Prince was not to leave it again alive.

The Cardinal at once became his niece's sugar daddy. He plied her with gifts. He prepared the way for her reception by the most illustrious and respectable families in Rome. After she had re-established her father in the Palazzo Muti the Cardinal paid frequent visits there, as much for the enjoyment of her gay society as for the relief of the Prince's tedium. He was captivated by her care of her father and apparent affection for himself. Further proof of her generosity of heart was manifested to him by her agreement – wholly unnecessary as it happened because she had no stake in their possession – to her father's transfer to him of the family jewels in January 1786. The Cardinal loved jewels and had a high sense, often keenly developed in childless persons, of family continuity. Charlotte's true feelings for the Cardinal are summed up in the following lines of a letter written about this time to her mother. 'My sainted uncle comes to see me three times a week and leaves me no time to breathe. He came for the fête of St Charles but brought no present.' The omission on this particular occasion was unusual.

At the same time the good Cardinal was worried lest the Prince might not have made adequate provision for his daughter in his will. He urged him to do justice by her, since he had been made aware during his brother's last illness that he had left most of what he possessed to John Stewart, who completely dominated the household of the Palazzo Muti. Even the Duchess of Albany was obliged to defer to Stewart's authority. He was one of the very few servants who, having accompanied the Prince to Italy after the Chevalier's death, stuck to him. The Cardinal never liked him, and when his brother dismissed Lumisden and the two other high ranking courtiers in December 1768, regretted that John Stewart was not among them. The Prince created him a baronet in 1784, and in his final will directed that Sir John, whom he described as his 'maestro di casa' should receive a pension of £750 a year and a free apartment in the Florentine palace. The Cardinal however refused, when the time came, to concede this sum and compromised with a smaller pension.*

One gets the impression that there was an *arrière pensée* in everything Charlotte did. She could not stop playing to the gallery. She was bored to tears by the best that Florence and Rome had to offer. The monuments of Rome, which she called 'old stones to break your neck,' left her totally unmoved. What she loved was buying fashionable clothes and wearing the Stuart jewelry at the lavish receptions held in the Palazzo Muti. She tried hard to live up to a position for which the early years of her life had not equipped her. She delighted in the title Duchess of Albany which her father conferred upon her, and the rather equivocal legitimation which he had first obtained for her from Louis XVI. With it went the coveted privilege of a *tabouret* had Charlotte ever been received at the court of Versailles. 'Tout cela est une belle Arlequinade qui n'a pas le sens commun,' her step-mother the Countess of Albany observed tartly. At any rate these high sounding honours flattered the daughter inordinately and encouraged her whose situation was in many respects unenviable. She revelled in the semi-royal state conferred upon her; and her positive recognition by George III's brother and sister-in-law, the Duke and Duchess of Gloucester, when on a visit to Rome, was balm to her innate sense of insecurity. Perhaps she found some affinity with the duchess whose marriage had only lately been acknowledged by King George after a long interval, she too having been born out of wedlock.†

By the time Charlotte rejoined her father in 1784 his state of mind

---

* John Stewart married a Roman girl, Rosa Fiorani. Their son Charles became an officer in the papal army, which he commanded during the siege of Gaeta by the French in 1848. He died in 1864 and was buried in S. Lorenzo in Lucina, Rome.
† She had been Maria Dowager Countess of Waldegrave, and was the illegitimate daughter of Sir Edward Walpole.

was, according to Mann, verging on imbecility. But for another four years his decrepit body held out. One is almost glad after reading Mann's catalogue of denigration of Prince Charles and unseemly gloating over his declining health to learn of the old gossip's sudden demise in November 1786, more than a year before that of the wretched victim of his acidulated pen. The last two years of Charles's topsy-turvy life were spent harmlessly enough. He drank comparatively little now that he was approaching dotage. He received few visitors at his court. English people came but rarely, and Italian people did not amuse him. Mrs Piozzi watched him one evening at the opera making an old fool of himself. He got on to his high horse over some slight or other. 'He called Mr Greatheed up to him, and said in good English, and a loud though cracked voice, "I will speak to my own subjects my own way, Sare. Ay, and I will soon speak to you, Sare, in Westminster Hall!"' The Duchess of Albany who was with him looked embarrassed and merely shrugged her shoulders. The old make-believe that he must be called to England was still buoying him up. There was little else to make life worth the living. Music was certainly a solace. Domenico Corri who then held a post at the Prince's court recorded: 'I usually remained alone with him every evening, the Prince played the violincello, and I the harpsichord, also composing little pieces of music; yet these tête-à-têtes were of a sombre cast. The apartment was hung with old red damask, lighted only by two candles, and on the table lay a pair of loaded pistols.

Bertie Greatheed was an indifferent dramatist who may then have been a provocative young cub. He was evidently a tactless one. Ewald relates how Greatheed 'happening to be alone with the Prince one evening studiously turned the conversation on the events of the Forty-Five. At first Charles appeared unwilling to talk on the subject and shrank from the topic as if its reminiscences were painful to him. But his visitor with more curiosity than good taste' persisted with his enquiries, and prompted the Prince.

'Gradually the panorama of the past ran vividly before the dull brain . . . so vividly that for a brief moment the Prince was no longer the ruin of himself, but again the hero of the '45. His eyes brightened, he half rose from his chair, his face became lit up with unwonted animation, and he began the narrative of the campaign. He spoke with fiery energy of his marches, his victories, the loyalty of his Highland followers, his retreat from Derby, the defeat at Culloden, his escape, and then passionately dwelt upon the awful penalties so many had been called upon to pay for their devotion to his cause. But the recollection of so much bitter suffering – the butchery around Inverness, the executions at Carlisle and London, the scenes on Kensington Common and Tower Hill – was stronger than his strength could bear. His voice died in his throat, his eyes became fixed, and he sank upon the floor in convulsions. Alarmed at the noise, his daughter rushed into the room. "Oh Sir!" she cried to Mr Greatheed, "What is this? You must have been speaking to my father about Scotland and the Highlanders! No one dares to mention those subjects in his presence."'

This story of the broken old man being overcome at the close of his life by revived memories of his distant past is poignant. It confirms that even in extreme old age Prince Charles could never reconcile himself to his miserable lot as an outcast, and the misfortunes which fate heaped upon shoulders not broad enough to bear them. His absolute belief in the divine right of the Stuarts to the throne of the United Kingdoms was as deeply and firmly entrenched in his mind as it was in those of James II and James III. The fiction must at all costs – and how high these were – be maintained to the very last. The most creditable part of the story is I think, Prince Charles's grief over the barbarities inflicted upon the Highlanders by Cumberland. All his life long he was haunted by them. One of his most outstanding qualities was clemency towards his enemies. This virtue was mistaken by his more ruthless companions for weakness. When the prisoners he took at Prestonpans broke their parole by escaping and were recaptured, instead of having them shot, he shut them up in Glamis Castle and again put them on parole. When after the victory of Falkirk the question arose what to do with the large number of prisoners the Prince indignantly refused to allow their right thumbs to be cut off in order to prevent a future use of the musket. On 10 September 1745 he wrote to his father, 'There is one thing, and but one in which I had any difference with my faithful Highlanders. It was about the price upon my kinsman's head.' He was shocked by other people's inclination to retaliate with vengeance. 'Your Majesty knows,' he went on, 'that in my nature I am neither cruel nor revengeful.' In the same letter he referred to 'the errors and excesses of my grandfather's unhappy reign ... Can anything be more unreasonable than to suppose that Your Majesty, who is sensible of, and has so often considered the fatal errors of your father, would with your eyes open, go and repeat them again?' This youthful compassion and consideration of the feelings of others was very commendable. And his soldiers and the companions of his flight, especially the humble, loved him because he shared their privations and provisions like one of themselves. Indeed servants, who are often more tolerant than educated persons of venial weaknesses like drink, mental instability and even bad temper, put up with him when he was vilely intoxicated, pain-wracked and horribly exacting. To the lower classes he was nearly always affable, whereas to his courtiers he could too often be insufferable.

On 11 January 1788 news was brought from Rome to Cardinal Henry at Frascati that his brother was gravely ill. Early next morning the Cardinal drove across the Campagna at breakneck speed to the Palazzo Muti. Here he found Charles at death's door in one room and the Duchess of Albany suffering acute pain in another. In truth she was too ill to attend to her father and was genuinely distressed by his condition as it was reported to her. The Cardinal administered to his brother the last rites of the Catholic Church into which he had been born and which he had vainly renounced. On the 30th, Prince Charles died. Immediately six altars were erected in the antechamber and 200 Masses said for the repose of his soul. In the death chamber the office of the dead was chanted by Irish Franciscan monks throughout the thirty hours which elapsed before his body was transferred to Frascati. A plaster mask* was taken of his face. It showed the long, slightly hooked nose drawn a little to the left as though by a final stroke; the chin prominent and pointed; and the mouth, although tightly closed by death, retaining even after the last agony that seductive charm which all who loved him found irresistible. A wooden crown and sceptre were secretly placed under the coffin lid for fear of causing offence to the papal court if displayed upon the outside.

* One cast is in the Inverness Museum; another in the Fort William Museum.

On 3 February the Cardinal, having failed to obtain the Pope's permission to accord his brother royal obsequies in St Peter's, conducted the funeral service in the cathedral at Frascati. He took his seat upon the episcopal throne in the presbytery, and was observed chanting the office of the dead while the tears trickled down his cheeks. His voice faltered but he controlled his sobs. As a temporary measure Prince Charles's body was interred in the cathedral by the central west door. Under the musicians' gallery a large stone slab, surmounted by the royal arms of Britain in painted metal, recalls the name, titles and dates of birth and death of the second uncrowned Stuart King of England. On the pavement in front of the epitaph is carved that seemingly unnecessary single word, 'Praecordia'.

It is a pity that the pages of Henry's diary for 1788 which must have recorded his brother's last illness and death, and presumably his own feelings and grief, were torn out. Did the Cardinal on re-reading them find the record too poignant? Or did the pages contain extracts which on reflection he considered unfavourable to his brother's memory? Who else but he would have thought fit to destroy them?* In spite of the excisions the diary of this year gives us the most detailed information we have about the Cardinal's day to day life at Frascati.

The Duchess of Albany did not long survive her father. For years she had suffered from a cancer which, attacking the liver, was eventually to kill her. As long ago as 1768 her mother, in endeavouring to enlist Prince Charles's sympathy had written that their daughter's ill-health was caused by grief and disappointment at not being recognized by her father. In fact the early stages of her fatal illness were already apparent. When Charlotte joined Prince Charles in Florence in 1782 the growth had got a firm hold of her.

During the few months after Prince Charles's death and before Charlotte's departure from Rome in desperate search of a cure, niece and uncle saw a good deal of each other. She frequently drove from the Palazzo Muti or from the villa at Albano to Frascati. Sometimes she was accompanied by the Abbé Waters, the Procurer-General of

---

* *Diario per l'anno 1788 di Enrico Cardinale di Yorck* (1876). In fact the diary was begun long before 1788 and may have continued beyond that year. The first marginal numeral in 1788 is 406; and there is in the text a reference to a diary entry made in 1775.

the English Benedictines in Rome. In the summer months dinner would be at 7 o'clock. Some fourteen covers were habitually laid for the Cardinal King's household staff in addition to those for guests. Charlotte who, although she had an eye firmly fixed on the main chance, was certainly lavish, would bring over expensive presents. She had inherited from her father more than fifty chests of precious treasures in the Palazzo Guadagni, Florence. The Cardinal's diary records that on 13 July she gave her uncle a circular table centrepiece in four compartments for salt and various condiments. It was made of gold and enamel encrusted with superb emeralds; Cleopatra was represented sitting on the lid in the nude, her stomach fashioned from a huge pearl, and her breasts from two smaller pearls: a curious gift, one may think, for this prudish man of God. Charlotte would sing to her uncle after dinner, or discuss with him the wretched state of her health. At midnight she would drive home across the Campagna beneath the stars.

Although Charlotte's inheritance was by no means inconsiderable she evidently thought she was entitled to more. There is a draft appeal* by her to the British nation for arrears of Queen Mary Beatrice's jointure which she claimed as her due. If the appeal was ever dispatched it met with no response, which is hardly surprising. Charlotte sold the Palazzo Guadagni and had the contents removed to Rome. Even so, the unfortunate woman was too ill to reap much benefit from her enhanced financial position. Nor was she in a fit state to enjoy that independent status in society to which she had so greatly looked forward. She wandered aimlessly around the papal dominions, and tried the baths of Nocera for relief of her sufferings. She never returned to Paris. Nor again did she see her mother, her children or her lover. Did she fear to confront them in her pitiably wasted condition? She died in Bologna on 17 November 1789 at the age of thirty-six. Cardinal Consalvi who mourned her as an intimate friend, attributed the immediate cause of her death to inadequate nursing during a mild attack of smallpox.

The claim to her friendship by a man of Consalvi's distinction and intellect suggests that Charlotte may not have been quite so shallow

* In the Fabre Museum Library, Montpellier. For the story of Queen Mary Beatrice's jointure, see pages 166–7.

as her letters indicate. She was certainly silly and pert, and in spite of her distress at the time of Prince Charles's death, her attitude towards him during his life was callous to say the least. But she had suffered all her youth from his neglect both of her and the mother who came first in her affections, even transcending her lover the Prince Archbishop. Her equivocal situation, first as a royal bastard, and then as a semi-legitimate daughter of a crownless, exiled monarch, as well as her chronic disease, rendered her short life a sad one. The *mémoire* which she addressed in 1774 to Louis XV pleading for financial help, contains a sentence about her own character which is probably not far from the truth: 'les dépits de vengeances et les considérations de l'état ne pouvoient pas anéantir la nature douce quand on le [*sic*] suit mais impérieuse et dominante quand on la brave.'

V

CARDINAL KING

The Cardinal Duke of York was sixty-three when Prince Charles died in 1788. He did not waste a moment in asserting his hereditary right, which was indisputable, to the throne of Great Britain. At the same time he was the first of the Stuarts in exile to make no attempt whatever to regain the throne. He did not even insist upon being granted that appendage of royal power, which had meant so much to his father and was denied to his brother, namely of nominating bishops to Irish sees. Of all the 'pretenders' he was the one best qualified for it. In his simple wisdom he realized that a Stuart restoration was at last out of the question. To expect Britain, now entrenched in Protestantism, to adopt a childless cardinal as sovereign was too ludicrous for him to contemplate seriously. Some people have seen nothing but arrogant folly in the old man issuing a manifesto and circulating a memorial to foreign courts demanding for himself recognition as *de jure* King of Great Britain. But it was one thing to expect restitution of rights, and quite another to renounce them. Besides Henry had always been a stickler for hereditary titles, and before his succession had insisted upon being addressed as 'Altezza' rather than 'Eminenza'. While he was Duke of York the scribe who penned his diary in the third person referred to him unfailingly as S.A.R. He was not now going to relinquish claims which were indubitably his, even though they would never be honoured. He knew too that after his death his lawful successors would not trouble to remind the House of Hanover that they were usurpers. So it was his duty as the last of the Stuart dynasty to underline this fact. He had a silver medal struck to celebrate his succession. Did he recall the dual medal struck when he and Charles were children? Then around his brother's boyish effigy the Horatian tag, *Micat inter Omnes* (He shines above all others) was quoted, and around his the mere mark of difference, *Alter ab illo* (the other one). Now things were different. The dignities were his. He had inscribed around his effigy on the obverse the arresting abbreviations, 'Hen IX.Mag.Brit.Fr.et Hib.Rex.Fid.Def.Card. Ep.Tusc.' and on the reverse of the medal the figure of Britannia holding like St Helena, a large cross, with at her feet the British lion, and in the background St Peter's basilica. The inscription on this side is poignant. 'Non desideriis hominum sed voluntate Dei' (not accepted by men but chosen by the will of God). It was his interpretation of that divine exhortation – those whom God hath joined together let no man put asunder. Henry IX was by right divine wedded to the kingdom of Great Britain. The inhabitants of those distant islands might not want him. Never mind. They could not annul the union which God had ordained. The Cardinal had always implicitly believed in the sanctity of kingship. For the last time he would set the seal upon this tenet.

Henceforth the Cardinal's old title of Henricus Dux Eboracensis Nuncupatus (Henry styled Duke of York) was dropped. He had the crescent, which is the mark of cadency, removed from his arms, and the royal crown blazoned under the cardinal's hat. Friendly ambassadors frequently addressed him as Majesty in the third person; his household and servants always. Most of his guests avoided doing so unless they particularly wished to give him pleasure, like his young friend Lord Cloncurry, and only when no Hanoverian spies were likely to overhear them. Till his dying day the Cardinal referred, with a cold smile, to George III as the Elector of Hanover. And when Pius VI in 1792 formally recognized George III by receiving Sir John Coxe Hippisley (who soon was to prove the Cardinal's initial benefactor in his straitened circumstances) he protested in writing at prodigious length. 'Oh God, what a blow!' the memorial ended, 'What anguish of soul for me to note in a pontifical brief, which must of necessity fall before my own eyes, that, by a stroke of the pen, as it were, I myself have been betrayed and deprived of the benefit of that maxim, which had been upheld by the Holy See with unswerving fidelity for upwards of a century!' Pope Pius being a kindly man may have blenched under the long-winded reproach.

There was however one prerogative which the Cardinal King exercised without feeling bound to consult anyone for authority, not even the Pope. It was that of touching for the King's Evil. He was the last British sovereign to do what had been practised in Saxon times. He had struck and he used a silver-gilt touch-piece engraved with a ship in full sail on one side, and an angel on the other. It is said that among the patients assembled in Rome for healing on one occasion was George III's delinquent brother the Duke of Gloucester, whom the Cardinal pretended not to notice and touched all the same. The Cardinal King was to come into still more direct contact with another member of the Hanoverian family. On 18 August 1794 his carriage met the Duke of Sussex's in a narrow street in Frascati. Both coachmen drew up, and the Cardinal from his carriage complimented the Duke with much affability. Sussex, a younger man (he was George III's son) had the courtesy to descend. In the short conversation that ensued he addressed the Cardinal several times as 'Your Royal Highness'. The Cardinal expressed unfeigned pleasure at the opportunity presented of showing no prejudice, as he put it. Both princes parted delighted with one another. They were to meet again in more intimate surroundings.

Frascati was where the Cardinal's heart lay. The Roman Palazzo Muti in which he had been born, had never been a happy home for him. It was associated with early memories of his father and mother's marital troubles, her death, the departure in 1744 of the brother he idolized and the loneliness that followed; his youthful differences with his father; the mournful condition of his father's last years and death; and finally the return of his brother, with hopes dashed and physique now totally wrecked, to be followed by his death. The Cardinal's residence in the Piazza della Sagrestia and the Palazzo Cancelleria were merely tenancies attached to specific ecclesiastical duties. They were never homes. The first was too close to the Vatican Palace for freedom of movement, the second too urban for his content. For him home was the palace of La Rocca which he had chosen and purchased. Of all his residences – and there were others – this grim little fortress was the dearest. So dear was it that the Cardinal persuaded Pope Benedict XIV to accept it for the official seat of the Bishops of Frascati.

La Rocca, as it is called, is not an attractive building outside, although its situation on the edge of Frascati, on the slopes of the Alban foothills, facing the open Campagna to the north-west and the Subiaco hills to the north-east is very fine; or rather was very fine until recent years, before the Campagna was inundated by the concrete rash of Rome's dismal suburbs, now spread in uninterrupted waves from the ancient city walls to Frascati itself. La Rocca dates from the twelfth century, but the exterior appears to belong to the fifteenth. From a little *piazza* it is entered between two squat square corner towers. Being constructed on the steep hill it is higher on the rear side, whence one cylindrical tower acts as a buttress, with walls strongly battered at the base. Yet another large square tower, with battle-mented and machicolated crown, rises from the centre. Within the rather depressing shell the first floor rooms are surprisingly gay. They are approached by an open staircase from a courtyard, and owe their decoration entirely to the Cardinal of York. He had them frescoed in tempera in 1777–8 by a Polish artist, Thaddeus Kuntz, after a disaster in 1775 which nearly had fatal consequences for the owner.*

The Cardinal was entertaining a large company of guests when the dining-room floor gave way beneath the unwonted weight. The guests were ignominiously precipitated into the coach-house and stables below, and the Cardinal owed his life to the roof of his travelling carriage, upon which he was gently deposited. The walls of the *salotto* of La Rocca are covered with conjectural medallion portraits of all the bishops of Frascati in rows, ending with that of the Cardinal of York. The overdoors are adorned with delightful land-scapes and grotesques in a Raphaelesque style. Eleven white calf-bound volumes of the Cardinal's parochial visitations, a suite of leather-backed chairs made for him and bearing his arms, and a third-century sarcophagus which he bought (it is now in the courtyard) are further legacies of his long occupation of the building.

The Cardinal also enjoyed the use of the Villa Muti, half a mile

---

* The doors, now in the Sacristy offices of St Peter's, after removal from the Arch Priest's residence at the time of the Lateran Treaty, were painted for the Cardinal of York after 1788. They are clearly by Kuntz. They comprise floral emblems, cherubs and the royal arms of England, France and Ireland. Kuntz also decorated the Seminary which the Cardinal founded a little to the south of Frascati Cathedral. Both Seminary and Cathedral were practically wiped out by the bombing of 1943–4.

outside Frascati on the Grottaferrata road. The house is a large rectangular block, now yellow-washed, to which he resorted in the summer months. He loved to amble along the extensive terraces in the cool of the evenings, and contemplate the most beautiful geometrical box parterre in all Italy; to look down the long vistas through groves of ilex towards Rome and St Peter's dome in the far distance; and sometimes to sit on rustic benches in the wilderness of umbrella pines and planes. This villa was eventually bought in 1801 by his trusted secretary, intimate friend, and, ultimately, executor, Monsignor Angelo Cesarini.

The Cardinal dwelt in Frascati in royal state in that he was attended by innumerable courtiers and servants in livery. Ceremonial was strictly observed. For unlike Prince Charles, who had the habits and preferred the style of life of an English squire, the Cardinal behaved like a Roman patrician. Indeed he was a Roman from birth to death, having only spent twenty months of his eighty-five years outside Italy. Yet simplicity and propriety distinguished his personal tastes. His entertainment, when he received company, was hospitable without being lavish. He kept an open table at La Rocca. Lalande observed that any person once having been presented to the Cardinal of York might dine with him, a privilege rarely conferred on strangers by other cardinals, and then by invitation a long time ahead. He indulged in few comforts. The Comtesse de Boigne described how she was taken as a child of eleven into the Cardinal King's presence at La Rocca on a cold winter's day of 1792. She found him sitting in a large, bare, under-furnished room – doubtless the *salotto*. He wore a cowl over his head and two topcoats. His hands were in a muff and his feet on a charcoal pan. One tiny fireplace gave out a flicker of flame and no appreciable warmth. But then he was notoriously stingy over fuel and would pretend that his breathing suffered from wood and coal smoke.

A seemingly contradictory taste relished by this sedate and placid cleric was speed. He kept sixty of the fleetest horses in his stables. His coach-and-six was a familiar sight travelling at breath-taking rate across the Campagna. He employed a retinue of running footmen who in their scarlet liveries were required to keep pace with the carriage. An empty coach and four would gallop in the rear in case of an accident or breakdown. Nothing gave the Cardinal more delight than being summoned urgently by the Pope, or a member of his family to Rome, at a moment's notice. The greater the urgency the greater his satisfaction. He would have the grooms, outriders and postillions instantly alerted, the carriage drawn out of the coach house and the horses harnessed. While the horses were champing at the bit the Cardinal would step briskly into his seat. The whips would crack and the cavalcade would dash, jingling and clattering down the hillside. Or at a whim the Cardinal would decide to drive after the siesta hour to what was described in the diaries as the 'casino' behind St Peter's, and back again before midnight. The casino, now known as the Villa del Duca di York, was used for the informal 'villegiatura', or occasional country retreat. Comparatively small and compact, it has a high central stage, flanked by two lower wings, and is distinguished by a pair of domed turrets for spiral stairs. It stands on a hillock overlooking a delicious formal garden of terrace, steps and pool open to the fields. A perron from the terrace mounts to a hall on the *piano nobile*. Alas, today this enchanting retreat is in the last stages of desolation and decay! The octagonal marble floor tiles are smashed. The painted ceiling canvas is in tatters. The ox-blood walls retain but faint traces of a wide frieze of painted scenes, now indecipherable. A small room on the right of the hall has, or had (for maybe since writing these words the building has been demolished) a window with festooned *trompe l'oeil* curtains fashioned in stone, not dissimilar to the mezzanine recess of the Palazzo Muti also treated in this Baroque manner.

Whenever opportunity offered itself the Cardinal liked to wear full canonicals. No ecclesiastic knew better than he which ceremonial robes were appropriate for which saint's feast day. The number of his pectoral crosses seemed infinite. In his portrait as the young Cardinal in the Commune at Frascati he wears over a scarlet jacket a cross of emeralds on his breast. As for his magnificent cross of enormous Sobieski diamonds, it was the cynosure of all eyes profane as well as sacred, and became famous throughout Europe.

The Cardinal was not tall like his brother, yet he was spare. He kept his slim and elegant figure in old age. As a boy he looked pretty, as a young man personable, as a middle-aged man distinguished, and as an old man saintly. He was not so much handsome as striking.

1 Prince James Edward Stuart, by Alexis Simeon Belle.

2 (*below left*) A medal of Prince James Edward Stuart, struck in 1721.

3 (*below right*) A medal of Princess Clementina Sobieska, wife of Prince James Edward Stuart, struck in 1719.

4 (*left*) Prince Charles Edward Stuart at the time of the Forty-five (artist unknown).

5 (*right*) Prince Charles Edward Stuart in later life, by Pompeo Batoni.

6 Princess Louise of Stolberg, wife of Prince Charles Edward Stuart, probably at the time of their marriage (artist unknown).

7 Prince Henry Stuart, Cardinal Duke of York, by L. G. Blanchet.

8 (*opposite above*) View from the loggia in front of the Prince's room in the Ducal Palace at Urbino, temporary home of Prince James Edward Stuart.

9 (*opposite below*) The Palazzo Guadagni in Florence, the temporary home of Prince Charles Edward Stuart.

10 The Italian poet Vittorio Alfieri, by François-Xavier Fabre, 1794.

11 Princess Louise, Countess of Albany, by François-Xavier Fabre, 1794.

12 The tomb of the three Stuart princes by Canova in St Peter's Rome, 1819.

Battoni's portrait of him in the National Portrait Gallery was accounted one of his best likenesses. In this as in several of his portraits the Cardinal is made to hold a document which draws attention to his clumsy hands. His head, always held high is like most Stuart heads long and oval. His chin is pointed; his nose long and well shaped; his forehead high and sloping. His large eyes under raised brows are dark and sideward glancing. In this Battoni portrait the lips are depicted slightly pursed, which is to his advantage. For he had an unfortunate habit of keeping his lips, of which the lower was thick, parted when he was in repose, a habit that his father allowed to get the better of himself in old age. Whereas it gave James III a look of intense melancholy, it lent the Cardinal an air of fatuity like a sheep that is about to bleat. His bust, attributed to Canova, in the Vatican Treasury, was sculptured towards the end of his life. The hair, curled over the ears and under the calotte, makes the distinguished head almost jaunty: again the projecting underlip, and the mouth slightly open. By now the Cardinal probably had few teeth. Nevertheless the face is more than pleasing. It is good. The over-impressionable James Boswell who watched him officiating in St Peter's as long ago as 1765, remarked that he had 'the face of an angel'.

Henry Stuart was undoubtedly a good man, although he was no angel. In youth he was subject to fits of passion which were followed by sullen silences. These failings were inherited from his Polish mother. But whereas she, having given rein to uncontrolled scenes, would indulge her sulks for months on end, her younger son learned to discipline his temper. Like all Stuarts, however, he did not relish advice and was inclined to pig-headedness. When he was no more than a lad his brother wrote: 'I know him to be a little lively, not much loving to be contradicted.' And Cardinal Consalvi who knew him intimately recorded that he was deeply resentful of contradiction. Few people were in a position to thwart him in view of his exalted station. Successive popes however were, and did. When they told him flatly that he must stop trying to get his brother treated as a reigning sovereign the Cardinal Duke had reluctantly to obey. Even so he retaliated with long, aggrieved and querulous memorials of expostulation, which were usually disregarded. For the sad truth is that he was sometimes a bore. Benedict XIV, his father's friend, who made him a cardinal found this out. 'Cazzo!' this mundane and astute pontiff exploded after an unusually tedious audience with the Cardinal of York, 'if all the Stuarts were as boring as he, no wonder the English drove them out.' To be a bore is a distinct disadvantage. But it is not a sin.

His worst fault was pride. Because he was extremely sensitive about his royalty and the equivocal status of his family after three generations of exile, he was too ready to receive slights. To protect himself against them he assumed a defensive haughtiness and coldness which were in effect a negation of his natural humility. They merely served to repel acquaintances and strangers. Thus he was not popular with his fellow cardinals, none of whom came from quite such an exalted background as his, and nearly all of whom resented his insistence upon being addressed as a prince of royal blood and not a high ranking prelate. They resented too his insistence upon sitting in the pope's presence on a chair with a cushion embroidered with gold whereas they were obliged to perch upon wooden stools without cushions of any sort. People who met him for the first time mistook his reserve for churlishness. They did not realize how much he disliked being assessed merely as a curious relic of the past.

As he grew older he relied less upon royal prerogative. He became less exclusive, more human and more approachable. He was touchingly responsive to gestures of goodwill from strangers. It is true he always remained on guard against the idly curious and insolent British who flocked to Frascati hoping to get a foothold in his doorway and to gape at the last king over the water. But he received with ineffable courtesy anyone, prince or pauper, old or young, Tory or Whig, who sought to pay him respects. There was Lord Somers' son, Colonel Cocks; and Sir Charles Oakeley's eldest boy. John Forsyth, a schoolmaster from Elgin, was received because his grandfather had fought for Prince Charles at Culloden. He found the Cardinal 'an hospitable, warm-hearted, testy old man', and not melancholy like his father. On the contrary he was interested in events, eager to hear and exchange news. Mr Thomas Coutts the banker, was received at Frascati in 1790 with his wife and daughter. The Cardinal showed them his treaures and actually put upon the finger of Miss Coutts the ring which King Charles I wore at his coronation. The royal condescension was much appreciated by Mr Coutts, although the medal which his host gave him with his likeness stamped upon it, was to be lost to him. For when years later he showed with pride the medal to George III that monarch begged to be allowed to keep it, and could not very well be gainsaid. Mr Coutts wrote to tell the Cardinal this story, adding a trifle tactlessly that His Britannic Majesty expressed interest in and sympathy for his cousin. But this is to anticipate events in which Mr Coutts was to play a future part.

In an estimate of the Cardinal of York's character the imputations that he was a homosexual need not be overlooked, even though they were exaggerated by contemporaries given to gossip and eager to discredit by one means or another the exiled Stuart family. It has been, and still is the case, that whenever ill-disposed persons seek to denigrate an enemy, they instantly expose that enemy's presumed sexual aberrations, even though such aberrations may not indicate any reprehensible conduct. Mrs Piozzi after a visit to Rome wrote in her notebook. *Thraliana*, under 29 March 1794 what she doubtless confided to her friends and acquaintances:

'Can the stories told by Suetonius be all true? I scarce believe it possible . . . I might have heard similar stories in Italy all day, had I not hated lewd conversation as I do, Old Cardinal de York kept a catamite publicly at Rome while I was there, tho' a man of the *best character* possible, for piety and charity – with which as a person said to me – *that vice has nothing to do*. They consider'd it as mere matter of taste.'

Which only goes to show that 'they' in Roman society of the late eighteenth century had more sense about this subject than most people had elsewhere, and have had since. Mrs Piozzi then implied that Horace Mann shared the same taste by the way he gesticulated with his fingers, which she took to be an infallible sign. How indignant the prim and prissy Sir Horace would have been to be coupled with one of the Pretenders on such a charge!

Mrs Piozzi was either mischievous or misinformed in implying that the Cardinal of York publicly kept a catamite. This was most improbable, for the Cardinal was not only very correct but also very virtuous. An article* of the *casi riservati* of the diocesan synod of Frascati drawn up in 1763 reserved to the Cardinal Bishop sole authority to confess and shrive sinners guilty of certain forms of unnatural vice, forms so ludicrous that the mind boggles at them, first with amazement and then with amusement. Cynical persons may reasonably assume that someone as humourless as the Cardinal of York could not possibly have been addicted to such practices himself. I prefer to believe that his simplicity was untainted by any subconscious motives of the sort. By 'catamite' Mrs Piozzi probably had in mind some personable but totally innocent neophyte who happened to be in close attendance upon the Cardinal during the 1790s. For Henry certainly liked to be surrounded by handsome young clerics. If Mrs Piozzi was mischievous, Count Goranni was malevolent, as one has only to find out by reading his memoirs. Goranni boasted that in 1766 the Cardinal entertained him at Frascati very graciously, but put questions to him which were those of an ill-educated person. Moreover his company was far from lively. Yet after staying several weeks under the Cardinal's roof Goranni wrote that his host was highly unpopular with the people in his diocese (it happens to be untrue) because of his intolerance and aversion to their innocent pleasures. He wanted everybody to spend his life in church. He would arrest girls on the merest suspicion of misconduct, have them cruelly whipped and shut up on bread and water. The slightest departure from good conduct was enough to have a monk in the diocese arrested. This behaviour, Goranni said, was hypocritical in view of his own tastes. And, he went on

'his palace seemed to me to be filled with young adolescents of beautiful aspect, but in clerical dress. That made me suspect that this royal Eminence might well have the tastes of which several of his colleagues were accused. However not having the opportunity of questioning these young men [I should think not indeed] I was unable to gather any evidence which might confirm this suspicion.'

---

* Jam vero quicumque cum aliquo animali sive terrestri, sive aquatili, sive volatile, coierit, sive masculini, sive faeminei generis illud fuerit, etiamsi totum actum non consummaverit, ita ut non intra, sed extra animalis vas semen effuderit, ab hoc suo crimine non nisi a nobis absolvi potest. Sub hac quoque riseratione complectimur hominis concubitum cum daemonio, sive succubo, sive incubo, quodcumque tandem id sive viri, sive faeminiae, sive bestiae corpus assumat, ac praeseferat.

Andrew Lang, in a preface to Alice Shield's biography of the Cardinal of York, revealed that, 'In a letter to Charles, James touches on some unpleasant set of circumstances known to the Prince and says, in effect, that Henry, for whom marriage had been planned will never marry.' He does not mention which letter, and since there are 70,000 Stuart letters I have not been able to check Lang's reference. It may have been one of those written by the Chevalier to his elder son explaining away Henry's acceptance of the cardinal's hat. It is not out of the question that Henry was involved in some youthful liaison which would have seemed highly unpleasant to his father and which convinced him that since his younger boy was not of the marrying sort, he had better enter the Church and lead a life of cloistral celibacy. Again Princess Louise's letter to her friend Teresa Mocenni suggests that she may have known the truth of her brother-in-law's homosexuality. Did her reference to him as 'one of those amphibious beings' have a double meaning? The word 'amphibious' was in the eighteenth century the word polite society used for men who had this proclivity;* and women especially would never admit that real men existed who could be totally indifferent to their physical charms. Princess Louise was a highly sophisticated woman, and she could be tart right enough. Her contempt of the Cardinal was the contempt of a worldly woman for a male homosexual. Much evidence therefore points to the likelihood that the Cardinal of York was homosexual. In his adolescence the neurotic phase of religiosity which so worried his tutor suggests guilt over the discovery of his erotic inclinations, if not actions. In his youth the passionate friendship for and elopement with Padre Lercari, which so troubled his father, provide further data. We have seen that Pope Benedict XIV was drawn closely into this affair and made the recipient of the Chevalier's hysterical pleas for help. How this easy-going pontiff really interpreted the relationship we do not know for certain. He clearly thought the young Cardinal Duke was behaving indiscreetly. He believed him to be a good priest but puerile, and in need of a guiding hand. An ambiguous

---

* See Pope's devastating couplets, describing John Lord Hervey (Sporus):
> Amphibious thing! that acting either part
> The trifling head, or the corrupted heart,
> Fop at the toilet, flatter at the board,
> Now trips a lady, and now struts a lord.

phrase in a letter of January 1756 that he felt sure Henry would not spend the revenue from a French abbey recently acquired, 'en choses criminelles', suggests, but does not prove, that he was aware of the young man's temptations.

The Chevalier was troubled more than once by his younger son's friendships. After Lercari came Cardinal Gianfrancesco Albani in 1754 to occupy the heart of the lonely young prince. Gianfrancesco was the nephew of the Chevalier's great ally, Cardinal Annibale Albani who by virtue of his resourcefulness in European politics had been of help to the Stuart cause. He was also the nephew of that other brother Cardinal Alessandro Albani, the protector of English Protestants in Rome and colleague of the infamous Baron von Stosch, who did great disservice to the exiled royal family. It was on this score that James ostensibly deprecated Henry's intimacy with Gianfranceso. He need not have worried because Gianfrancesco was to remain his son's consistent friend until death parted them in 1802. Cardinal Gianfrancesco, who was five years older than Henry was extremely fascinating. He was also extremely handsome and witty. He was the brightest ornament of every function and party he attended. Before becoming a cardinal he had spent his youth in all the pleasures which Roman society so lavishly afforded. The young Cardinal of York was bowled over by his new friend, who was blessed with the very gifts of charm which he coveted but lacked. While staying with his father in Albano in the autumn of 1754 he dashed across the Campagna at least once a week to dine with Gianfrancesco, who in Pope Benedict's words, 'selon le caprice actuel occupe la place du jeune Lercari.' In fact Lercari was completely forgotten. The Chevalier pursed his lips in disapproval and refused either to receive the new Apollo in the Palazzo Muti or to meet him at his son's table in the Arch Priest's lodgings. Yet Cardinal Albani did not reciprocate the Cardinal of York's transports of affection which, he said, transcended the limits of sense and rather bored him. In spite of his social activities Gianfrancesco was a serious character, and like his friend a conscientious priest and respected member of the Sacred College. It fell to his lot to be present at the Chevalier's death. When the old King faded away he drove to the Palazzo Cancelleria and broke the news to the son, who was snatching a brief respite from watching by the sickbed. Gianfrancesco Albani eventually rose to be Dean of the Sacred

College, in which office he was succeeded by the Cardinal King. It is said that he only missed election to the tiara on account of an infatuation about his chamberlain, Mariano, who governed him like a despot. When Pius VI gently rebuked Cardinal Albani for exhibiting too signal favours towards his chamberlain he received the smiling retort, 'Ah! Holy Father, we all have our Marianos more or less.' This reference to the Pope's dependence upon his *camariere segreto*, Consalvi, met with a pontifical frown.

Ercole Consalvi, who was to become one of the leading international figures during Napoleon's domination of Europe, owed his first steps on the ecclesiastical ladder to the Cardinal of York. An orphan child of impoverished noble parents, he was educated at the Cardinal's seminary at Frascati. There he attracted his patron's attention by his good looks, his outstanding abilities and, above all his passion for music. He was a proficient performer on the violin. Consalvi was very soon taken into the Cardinal Duke's household at Frascati and treated like a son. The Cardinal could not be without him for a minute. It was, 'Ercole, come here!' Ercole, do this and do that! The young seminarist, although grateful to his benefactor and indeed attached to him, grew irritated by this familiar treatment. And in 1776 he persuaded the Cardinal to send him to the Accademia Ecclesiastica in Rome. Nevertheless he regarded La Rocca as his home whither he repaired during vacations. The Cardinal heaped favours and conferred upon the brilliant youth, before he was properly grown up, a vicariate of St Peter's which Pius VI, deeming it premature, countermanded. This did not however prevent the Pope from also taking a keen personal interest in him and enlisting him in the papal household at an early age.

By the date, 1807, of the Cardinal of York's death Consalvi, himself now a Cardinal, was the all-powerful Secretary of State to Pope Pius VII. To the last he remained one of the Cardinal King's closest friends – indeed he was a close friend of Charlotte and Louise also – in whose company the royal Stuart reserve dissolved. Perhaps because of his upbringing at Frascati Consalvi, in spite of being the great reformer of papal government, became a convinced believer in the divine right of kings. The doctrine led him to be a legitimist and supporter of Louis XVIII's claims to the throne of France. He was, as far as brain and wit were concerned, the most formidable opponent of the Napoleonic regime. Although he was made to endure the harshest sufferings, imprisonment by the tyrant's orders in the Castle of St Angelo, deportation from Rome among galley slaves, and for a time absolute penury, he was eventually to be responsible for the terms of the concordat between Napoleon and Pius VII which saved the papacy from extinction. He was the Emperor's consistent bitter opponent, and one of the European statesman whom Napoleon most feared. With implacable firmness and dignity he stood up to him and earned his hatred and respect. He was also the only man to demand and receive a public apology in Paris for the treatment which he, as the Pope's Secretary of State, had received from the imperial hands.

The Cardinal King left Consalvi in his will a diamond ring and a sum of money. Consalvi having twice in Henry's lifetime refused offers of money, likewise refused the legacy. He only consented to accept the ring because, he declared, the Cardinal King had cherished him so paternally. In his turn he devised it to the Countess of Albany.

In 1769 the Cardinal of York appointed as his personal secretary Canon Angelo Cesarini, a well born and cultivated young man of independent means who was as virtuous as he was lacking in ambition. The association was the least disturbing and the most satisfactory of the Cardinal's life. Cesarini was devoted and faithful. He made no intellectual demands upon his master's limited capacities and no inroads upon his susceptible emotions. When the Cardinal King became old and ailing Cesarini looked after him like a male nurse. Reliable and capable, he was the trusted servant, the beloved yet subordinate companion, and the absolute confidant of his every thought and wish for nearly forty years.

The imputation by Goranni that the Cardinal of York was un-popular in the diocese of Frascati is not borne out by evidence. The contrary is the case. He was revered for his piety and his wealth – primitive peasants admire, if they do not always love others for being rich, and no people esteem money for its own sake more than the Italians. His flock loved him for his fatherly concern for their well being. A cardinal bishop in the eighteenth century was regarded as a prince, and the diocese as his principality. Furthermore this particular cardinal was a prince of royal blood, which meant more to his flock than a mere prince of the Church. After 1788 he was actually a king, although a king without a kingdom, unless his diocese could be regarded as such. His revenues from the multitudinous ecclesiastical preferments he enjoyed were enormous. His income from abbeys and other pluralities in Flanders, Spain, Naples and France amounted to some £40,000 in English money of the time. He also held sinecure benefices yielding revenues in Spanish America. He owned territory in Mexico, which contributed largely to his income.

After his succession he was called upon to spend more money than he used to spend when Cardinal Duke. He was obliged to keep a regal court of a modest kind. He had a new dignity to maintain. Besides there were still many impoverished Jacobites to be fed and clothed out of his civil list. And he never allowed anyone who had worked or suffered for the Stuart cause to go hungry. He was open-handed to all his exiled compatriots while he was rich, and when he fell on evil days he still paid the pensions of those whose demands upon him were closest. At his lowest financial ebb he managed to send the Countess of Albany her quarterly allowance because he had promised not to discontinue it. To the poor his charities were boundless, as Cardinal Wiseman learned from people who had known him. Not only the people of Frascati were recipients of his generosity. He made an arrangement with the proprietor of a chemist shop (the shop still exists) at the street corner of a block facing the Palazzo Cancelleria in Rome whereby the poor might order whatever medicines they required at his expense. Within his diocese the destitute and the unemployed were scrupulously cared for and, whenever possible, given work. Their spiritual needs were catered for by priests sent among them for the purpose. The Bishop of Frascati set out to be provider and director of his people's material and moral welfare. They came to look to him for guidance in times of stress and crisis. When there was an earthquake in the hills of Tusculum the peasants panicked. They lost their heads. Marauders took advantage of the situation by pillaging and looting the stricken homes of the victims. Only the presence of their Bishop could bring about calm. He immediately went among them, heading a procession to the worst scene of devastation. In his hands he carried a little book called *Miracolosa Immagine di Maria Santissima*, opened at a page displaying an illumination of the Mother of God. After fervent prayers, and with presence of mind he quelled the disorders and allayed the fears, modestly attributing his success to the efficacy of the image. On every anniversary of the occasion flowers were scattered on the site and crackers let off by his credulous and grateful subjects. Over the long years Henry Stuart established himself in their eyes as a tower of practical strength and a bulwark of righteousness. If at times he was severe with delinquents he was ever ready to temper justice with mercy.

The institution in which the Cardinal of York took the greatest interest was the Seminary of Frascati for the training of young men in the priesthood. When the Jesuits were expelled from the Papal States in 1773 by Pope Clement XIV the Society was deprived of their college and church at Frascati. Clement handed over the property to the Cardinal Bishop, who decided to run the college himself on new lines. He rebuilt the seminary and chapel (a thunderbolt falling upon the new structure in August 1788 did some damage), added a concert hall, a theatre for masques and oratorios, and a library. He endowed the seminary handsomely. He set up a printing press which issued books highly prized today. Within a few years the number of pupils at Frascati had jumped from six in 1773 to one hundred. The seminary flourished as a first-class place of learning renowned throughout Italy. For this all the credit was due to its benefactor. His impressive marble bust by Agostino Penna dominated the long gallery, until it and the entire building were wiped out by the air raids of 1943–4. Although the Cardinal of York was not a notable scholar – his only known literary effort, apart from the otiose memorials, was an appropriate treatise, entitled *The Sins of the Drunkard* – he had a great respect for learning, and saw that the most eminent professors were engaged for the seminary.

His love of books and his collection of choice volumes rank him among historic bibliophiles of wide discernment. His bindings became famous. The surest way for a visitor to win the Cardinal's favour was to present him with a rare volume, taking care to find out first of all that he did not possess a copy already. Several of his most treasured books were inherited. He himself commissioned an innumerable quantity of manuscripts, including musical scores, which this music lover had bound in morocco stamped with his monogram, arms and cardinal's hat. One score is entitled *Magnificat a Otto Voci composta* *per espresso e venerato Comando di S.A.R.E^{ma}* Il Sig. Cardinal Duca di Iorch da Niccolo Porpora 1760.*

In 1769 the Cardinal transported his library from Rome to Frascati. A few years later he installed it in his beloved seminary where it could be enjoyed by the pupils. There it remained until 1944. In that disastrous year Frascati, having been occupied by German troops was under such constant bombardment by the allies that 83 per cent of the town's buildings were either totally destroyed or grievously damaged. When news reached Rome that the seminary had been bombed twelve noble Camaldoli monks decided to go and salvage what they could from the wreckage. During the severe fighting they drove a large lorry to the scene of devastation. They found that although the seminary was a total ruin the adjacent room which housed the Cardinal's collection of books had by some miraculous chance survived, buried under rubble. By dint of tireless digging and at the risk of their lives the monks succeeded in extracting 8,000 volumes and by relays piled them into the lorry. After four perilous journeys all the books from the Cardinal's library were stacked in the fourth floor of the New Deposits Gallery of the Vatican Library. There they presumably repose at the present time, as yet inaccessible to students of bibliography.

The Cardinal of York's first loves among the arts were then music and books (of which the bindings and illuminations appealed to him more than their content). Architecture was not specially venerated by him. He assessed the merits of old buildings by their suitability as domiciles or shrines for worship and religious instruction. As I have already said, he employed a competent Polish painter, Kuntz, to decorate the episcopal palace of Frascati, and an excellent architect to design the enchanting casino on the outskirts of Rome. He was also profuse in restoration and embellishment of churches in his diocese and under his jurisdiction, not for the sake of the stones and mortar, but for the glory of the Almighty. A tablet records that he restored the little Romanesque church close to La Rocca at Frascati in 1766. He built the neo-classical Cappella del Coro d'Inverno in Sta. Maria in Campitelli, his titular church in Rome. The wooden choir

---

* Niccolo Porpora was a versatile Neapolitan composer and one of the greatest singing masters Italy has produced.

stalls and the arch over the entrance to the chapel still carry the royal arms of England. He had little respect for classical remains and ruthlessly demolished the Temple of Jupiter on Monte Cavo in order to raise a Passionist convent on the site. This can only be described as wanton vandalism. He was, notwithstanding, a lover of intricate trinkets encrusted with gems. And when he returned to Frascati after his exile, having lost the greater part of his cherished possessions he started collecting all over again at the advanced age of seventy-seven.

It cannot be pretended that the Cardinal of York played a positive, or even much of a negative role in European politics. Unlike his brother he was no schemer. And unlike him too he was not treated as a pawn upon the dynastic chessboard of the continent, for his own claims to the English throne did not arise until nearly the end of the eighteenth century, by which time they had not the slightest value. He never pressed them beyond demanding recognition that they were his by constitutional right. He was not the least interested in politics for their own sake. He declined to play a part in matters of international concern. He did on the other hand advance any cause which he believed to be in the interests of Britain. Thus he thought fit to plead for, and was successful in obtaining from Benedict XIV, establishment of the feast days of the English saints George, Edward, Ursula and her virgins, Edmund and Thomas of Canterbury. He was an active supporter of the national colleges in Rome for the initiation of young men from the United Kingdom into the priesthood. With the influential help of Sir John Coxe Hippisley, then engaged by the British Government in negotiations with the Vatican, he persuaded Pius VI in 1794 to allow these missions to be run by British in place of Italian superiors. The government in London stipulated that the young acolytes should take the oath of allegiance to George III; and there arose the extraordinary situation of the Cardinal King personally ensuring that they did so. In the same spirit he once vigorously insisted upon the *commune* of an insignificant little town in the Papal States called Vetralla reinstating a marble tablet which it had lately covered up. The tablet recorded the protection of the town by one of his royal predecessors – of all kings, Henry VIII. Henry IX may have been born and bred on Italian soil but he never forgot or allowed others to forget that he was of British stock. His atavistic and royal instincts were ineradicable.

He performed his regular episcopal duties conscientiously, and his curial duties as these presented themselves in the course of a long career, with dignity. When his patron Benedict XIV died in 1758 he as the new *camerlengo* entered the death chamber, removed the veil from the pontiff's face, smote the bald forehead with a silver hammer, and called the dead man aloud three times by his personal name, 'Prospero Lambertini!' After a pause, there being no response, he announced to the assembled cardinals, 'The Pope is dead indeed.' According to age old custom he then formally broke the Fisherman's ring with a golden hammer.

It may be argued that these duties would have been carried out just as adequately by almost anyone else. So too perhaps would those of organizing the conclave for the election of the new pope which followed. But the Cardinal of York resolutely declined to advance the cause of the French candidate who was recommended by powerful influences. No, it would be against his conscience, he declared, to interfere with the proper course of a papal election, which must be secret and free. He was unmoved by arguments that individual cardinals had for centuries past been solicited, threatened and bullied to cast their votes according to the dictates of the great powers. He would not be a party to this traditional form of corruption, in spite of reminders that the defunct pope had exhorted him to show gratitude to the French king for favours to his family. In 1774–5 he again presided with exemplary patience and skill over the conclave following Clement XIV's death. It lasted 265 days and ultimately elected Cardinal Braschi as Pius VI. It was a most taxing period of responsibility for one man. Doubtless other cardinals *camerlenghi* have weathered similar periods in just as unruffled a manner. But would every cardinal have shown the same courage as he when summoned as Dean of the Sacred College by the dreaded Napoleon in 1804 to accompany Pius VII to Paris for his coronation? The Cardinal King, as he then was, stoutly refused to go. It was a bold stand for an old man of eighty to take, and it brought about a physical collapse. But he would not budge. Not for nothing was he a believer in the divine right of kings. On no account would he be a party to the crowning of an upstart usurper of the legitimist Bourbon throne.

The Cardinal had his loyalties, which no earthly considerations would tempt him to betray. What is more, when these loyalties were put to the test he sacrificed all he had to uphold them. He would gladly have offered his life for them if his life was worth the purchase. When the great moment of reckoning came he was already an old man. And an old man's life is counted for little.

To superannuated gentlemen of the Cardinal of York's way of thinking the French Revolution was anathema, and the execution of the French king, the Lord's anointed, was the ultimate act of wickedness against the natural order of events ordained by God. The Cardinal had all his life misprized the feeble efforts of the French monarchs to reinstate his family on the English throne. He bore deep resentment against the Regent of Orleans and Louis XV for failing to ensure victory to his father and brother in 1715 and 1745. Like his brother he accepted French financial aid as a sort of family obligation to the Stuarts on the part of their Bourbon cousins. Still the Bourbons were his cousins. And like the Stuarts they reigned by divine right which transmitted from distant medieval centuries, could not be appropriated by a new dynasty. This sacred right had been challenged and overthrown by evil men. The fate of his own great-grandfather Charles I was brought back to him by the terrible catastrophes of 1793. The Cardinal King with that propensity to ceremonial which distinguished him, personally conducted a most solemn requiem for the soul of his cousin and fellow sovereign, Louis XVI, in Frascati Cathedral.

The Cardinal's own calvary was at hand. The sequel to Louis's terrible murder gathered momentum. Napoleon's conduct of French affairs was scarcely less disastrous than that of the Jacobins. Those creatures were common assassins whose nefarious actions were more or less confined to their own unfortunate country. The Corsican was overturning Europe and the world. In 1796 Napoleon occupied the Papal States. On 11 January 1798 General Berthier marched on Rome. At the Vatican all was in confusion. Pope Pius VI was ordered to leave his capital. On 15 February the Roman Republic was proclaimed in the city. Hastily the Cardinal King packed up his furniture and belongings, distributing the smaller pieces for hiding in the houses of his poor dependents in Frascati. He was obliged to leave the larger in La Rocca where in due course they were looted by the French troops, or sold at auction by officials of the Roman Republic. Accompanied by his faithful companion and secretary Angelo Cesarini, and his valet Eugenio Ridolfi, Henry fled from Frascati to Naples.

In Naples he was able to take refuge until conditions in that capital became untenable. Cornelia Knight relates an agreeable incident which greatly cheered the fugitive Cardinal. One September day Sir William Hamilton, the British envoy, on returning from the King of Naples's palace met the Cardinal King in his carriage, and called upon his coachman to halt. Getting out of his carriage and taking off his hat Sir William said, 'I beg pardon of your Eminence but I am sure you will be glad to hear the good news which I have to communicate.' 'Pray, sir,' said the Cardinal, 'to whom have I the honour of speaking?' 'To Sir William Hamilton,' came the reply. 'Oh, the British Minister! I am much obliged to you, sir; and what is the news?' On being informed that Nelson had won the victory of the Nile the Cardinal continued, 'But may we depend on the truth of this great affair? There are so many false reports.' Hamilton reassured him. 'In that case, sir,' said the Cardinal, 'when you arrive in England do me the favour to say that no man rejoices more sincerely than I do in the success and glory of the British navy.' Fitting words from the grandson of James II, who did as much for the welfare of the British Navy as any man.

Unfortunately the Neapolitans were so elated by Nelson's defeat of the detested enemy that they prematurely launched a half-hearted attack against the French thus laying themselves open to reprisals from the occupied Papal States. The Neapolitan court was obliged to flee to Palermo. The Cardinal King could not remain in a capital invaded by French republicans and he too escaped in a tiny coasting smack for Messina. The voyage was undertaken in one of the worst storms on record (true to form the elements harried the last of the Stuarts as they had consistently harried his predecessors), and took twenty-three days. On reaching Messina the Cardinal badly bruised his right shin and as a result was crippled for the rest of his life. In Messina he met with a few other cardinals in flight and shared lodgings with them.

In February 1799 the Cardinal of York with Cardinals Pignatelli and Braschi (a nephew of Pius VI) crossed from Sicily to Reggio. There they hired a Greek merchant vessel. But another ghastly storm forced them to land on Corfu where they were courteously received by the Ottoman viceroy. After a respite they managed to embark again and reached their destination, Venice, where they were under Austrian protection. By now the Cardinal of York was exhausted, ill and destitute.

Notwithstanding his stricken condition the Cardinal Camerlengo soon had to set about organizing a conclave for the election of a new pope. The saintly Pius VI, while being driven from pillar to post and treated by the French with the utmost barbarity, had succumbed at Valence in August. The Venetian conclave reflected the greatest credit upon the Cardinal of York. The French Directory in sacking Rome and expelling the last pontiff, had declared that there was never to be another papal election. And it is true that in 1799 the fate of the papacy was probably at its lowest ebb in all its history. The Cardinal of York however refused to accept defeat. If an election could not take place in Rome, then it would take place elsewhere. It was his absolute duty to see that this happened, no matter what the political consequences. So in the face of disapproval of the greatest tyrant on earth an election took place. The Camerlengo summoned all cardinals who could get to Venice to assemble at the Benedictine monastery on the island of S. Giorgio, where they remained incarcerated for three and a half months. It is not a little ironical that just before the last Stuart king made history by organizing a papal conclave away from Rome, Napoleon on the crest of his victories and in anticipation of a conquest of England, was seriously planning to restore him to the throne from which his family had been ousted 110 years previously.* At the time the *de jure* King of England had lost his incumbencies, palaces, possessions, fortune and health. He was in his mid-seventies. What future was left to him looked bleak indeed. It is a pity that a formal offer was not put to him in these circumstances. The dignity and scorn with which it must have been rejected would have made edifying reading.

From being immensely rich the Cardinal of York was literally penniless. Since Messina he had been living solely on the proceeds of some silver plate he had managed to carry away from Frascati. By now the plate was exhausted. The fall of the French monarchy had

---

* Again when the Cardinal's death was announced to Napoleon in 1807 he said, 'If the Stuarts had only left a child of eight years old I would put him on the throne of Great Britain.'

deprived him of revenue from the abbeys of Auchin and St Amand given him by Louis XV. The Revolution removed his remaining French income. His Spanish income evaporated likewise. So too did his South American benefices. His Italian revenues had gone with his bishopric and various other offices. In spite of this diminution of his fortune he had sold nearly all his treasured family jewels in order to put the proceeds at the disposal of Pius VI for the payment of the exorbitant fines imposed upon that Pope by Napoleon. The treasures included the gold embossed shield given to his great-grandfather John Sobieksi by the Holy Roman Emperor Leopold, and the great Sobieski ruby which had reverted to him on his niece Charlotte's death. It alone raised £60,000. He also was obliged to sell several of the English crown jewels. He knew his duty to the papacy came before all personal and sentimental considerations.

It speaks well for the old English Cardinal that his friends were deeply concerned about his plight. The first person to take steps to relieve it, upon the news reaching his ears, was Sir John Coxe Hippisley, who had returned to London from his long Italian sojourn since 1796. While unofficial British representative in the Papal States Hippisley had become acquainted with the Cardinal of York, whom he held in high respect. He wrote a very solicitous letter to his old friend, Cardinal Stefano Borgia, the Prefect of the Sacred Congregation of the Propagation of the Faith, who he knew must be better informed than anyone else of the Cardinal King's circumstances. He tactfully suggested that an appeal to the British government for financial help would come better from Cardinal Borgia direct than from himself, an Englishman suspected of being on good terms with the Stuart claimant. At once Cardinal Borgia addressed to Hippisley a carefully prepared and extremely warm letter, dated 14 September 1799, giving an outline of the Cardinal of York's financial straits and appealing through him to the government in London to alleviate them. The letter made it clear that after paying the annuities to the Countess of Albany, the Countess of Albestroff and others he had nothing whatever to live upon. Hippisley forwarded Borgia's letter to a friend of his, Mr Andrew Stewart, M.P. Stewart in turn drew up a memorial on the subject which he forwarded to Mr Secretary Dundas, who showed it to Prime Minister William Pitt, who showed it to King George III. Through this roundabout channel Borgia's moving appeal finally reached the fountain-head. The soft-hearted King George responded at once. Relief must be sent urgently, and £500 for immediate necessities were despatched from the Civil List through Hippisley to the Cardinal of York, then immured on the island of S. Giorgio during the conclave. A pension for life of £4,000 was to be paid in two annual instalments. On 4 January 1800 Borgia wrote again to Hippisley informing him how the whole conclave applauded King George's munificence.

The Cardinal King was indeed deeply touched. On 26 February he dictated a letter of cordial thanks to Hippisley beginning, 'Dear Sir John, I confess I am at a loss to express my feelings.' He said that without this unexpected relief he would have been 'reduced for the short remainder of my life to languish in misery and indigence . . .' He ended, 'With all my heart I embrace you, Your best of friends, Henry Cardinal.' To Lord Minto, the British plenipotentiary in Vienna, who had communicated the official notification of the pension in a letter to the Cardinal, addressing him as 'My Lord', Henry replied on the same day, referring to 'your gracious Sovereign's noble and spontaneous generosity.'

In this story everyone comes out well. Cardinal Borgia and Sir John Hippisley behaved as true friends should towards a person in distress. King George did not need the encouragement he got from his son the Duke of Sussex to act spontaneously with cousinly feeling. The recipient of the Hanoverian bounty was not now ashamed to express gratitude with dignity. Yet there is some pathos in the proud old Cardinal King accepting bounty from the rival whom to his dying day he called the Elector of Hanover. All the more so in that he was morally and legally entitled to accumulated arrears of the jointure granted by Act of Parliament in 1685 to his grandmother, Queen Mary Beatrice. Those arrears amounted by the time of that Queen's death in 1718 to £2½ million. After 1688 his grandmother never received one halfpenny of the jointure which even William III did not rescind, but promised to pay at the signing of the Treaty of Ryswick in 1697. Needless to say, William did not honour the undertaking. In the Treaty of Utrecht of 1713 Queen Anne reiterated in a special clause the promise, which again was not fulfilled. The Chevalier tried in vain to obtain the sum, and so too did Prince Charles in 1785. He even bequeathed the right to the money to his daughter the Duchess

of Albany, who bequeathed it in turn to her uncle. And whereas both
the Chevalier and the Prince had been attainted, the Cardinal had
not. The British Government in 1800 were well aware of the Cardinal's title to his grandmother's money, yet Pitt, although the case
was brought to his notice, declined to raise it with George III, who
doubtless was ignorant of its history.

Nevertheless the Cardinal of York's pressing needs were satisfied.
It was not in his nature to haggle, especially over ancient and lost
causes. It did not occur to him to appeal personally to the British
government for reimbursement of Mary Beatrice's jointure. Instead
he went quietly on with his work within the conclave, well contented.
After a difficult three and a half months Cardinal Chiaramonti was
elected Pope on 14 March, and chose the name Pius after his
predecessor. He was crowned in the Benedictines' island church of S.
Giorgio because the Emperor of Austria, in whose suzerainty Venice
lay, knowing Chiaramonti to be opposed to Austrian claims, withheld permission for the ceremony to take place in St Mark's Cathedral. The Cardinal of York was called upon as *Camerlengo* to
pronounce the new Pope's eulogy. He did so, and in his speech
begged permission to welcome His Holiness at the door of St Peter's
when he should return to Rome. The request was granted and the
reception took place sooner than was expected. For Napoleon came
to realize that his entrenchment in northern Italy and even his status
in France could only be maintained so long as he recognized the
authority of the Catholic Church. In Chiaramonti he found a pope
anxious to come to terms with the new French constitution on
condition that the Church's freedom was guaranteed. Accordingly
Pius VII and a retinue of cardinals left Venice in May to reach Rome
on 3 July. The Pope had been preceded by the Cardinal of York who
was duly present on the steps of St Peter's basilica to receive him.

The very day, 25 June, on which the Cardinal King arrived in
Rome he set forth after dinner for Frascati, having somehow acquired a carriage and enough horses to gallop across the Campagna
in his old spanking style. The jubilation of the people of Frascati,
particularly the poor, at having back their bishop and benefactor
knew no bounds. They advanced to meet him with a brass band, they
surrounded his carriage with outstretched hands, they knelt in the
road beseeching his blessing. The air was rent with the clanging of

church bells, and the crackle and sparkle of fireworks in the twilight. At La Rocca a deputation of the clergy and *commune* of Frascati was assembled to greet him with acclamations and tears of joy. This was the homecoming to which for months past he had been looking forward. It was followed by a busy period of repairing, redecorating and refurnishing La Rocca and Cesarini's villa which had suffered grievous hurt from the provisional government during his absence. Indeed on 6 July Henry wrote to Hippisley announcing the 'total devastation of all my residences both at Rome and Frascati,' from the hands of 'those enemies of humanity' who had brought about the ruination of Europe. He described himself as 'a downright vagabond'. What was far worse, the poor Pope had not enough money to 'pay his very frugal dinner from day to day'.

Owing to his infirmities and to the undoubted fact that he found difficulty in expressing himself in English the Cardinal's letters were merely begun and ended in his own hand. The intervening parts were written by an Irishman, Father John Connolly, then superior of the Irish Dominicans of San Clemente. Whenever the Cardinal was obliged to answer, or even to read a letter addressed to him in English, he sent for Father Connolly all the way from Rome. On 19 July 1800 Connolly wrote a personal letter to Hippisley explaining the awkward situation and begging him when he next wrote to pen his letter more clearly. 'I read your two last letters to HRH as he could not read them himself, not being much accustomed to the ready, loose and smart way of writing of most of our English nobility.' Connolly also let fall how sensitive the Cardinal was about the way letters were addressed to him by English correspondents. He was very displeased that Mr Andrew Stewart, M.P., addressed him as Eminence, and not Royal Highness. The slightest upset these days threw him into a fever from which he sometimes took days to recover. Finally the Father asked if Hippisley would say a word in his favour to the Cardinal who, unless prompted, would not think of advancing him in his career, but the Cardinal must not know that he, Connolly, had suggested it. Whether or not Hippisley took the hint, Connolly ultimately was promoted to the bishopric of New York.

After his return in the midsummer of 1800 the Cardinal was never to leave his beloved Frascati again for more than a few days at a time. I have already mentioned how on the death of his old friend Cardinal

Gianfrancesco Albani in 1803 he succeeded as doyen of the cardinals to the Deanery of the Sacred College. The office entailed titular advancement to the bishoprics of Ostia and Velletri and permanent residence in Rome. But in view of Henry's advanced age and attachment to the little town where he had reigned for so many years, and to La Rocca the home which he loved so dearly, Pope Pius VII allowed him, after a token visit to Velletri of ten days only, to continue living at Frascati. The Roman domicile was also waived. It was a huge satisfaction to the Cardinal King to be able to entertain the Pope in his home town on 17 October 1802. His Holiness was accompanied by King Emmanuel IV of Sardinia. The two reigning sovereigns were escorted round the Seminary and given a sumptuous banquet in La Rocca by the throneless sovereign. Within a matter of months the King of Sardinia, with whom the Cardinal felt close affinity, abdicated in order to become a Jesuit.

We have pen sketches of the Cardinal King at Frascati in his last years after the return from exile. Although he was not to recover the immense wealth which previous to the Revolution he had derived chiefly from fruitful Italian pluralities and foreign revenues, he enjoyed with the help of his British pension a comparative affluence.

The 2nd Lord Cloncurry, an eccentric Catholic peer, ardent advocate of a united Ireland and opponent of the Union, who had twice been arrested by the English government on suspicions of high treason, and once imprisoned in the Tower of London, travelled to the continent in 1802. He several times visited and quickly made friends with the Cardinal of York, of whom he left an account in his *Recollections*. The Cardinal was amused by the stories with which the wild young Irishman regaled him. They exchanged compliments and gifts. The Cardinal accepted with delight from Lord Cloncurry an English telescope. Cloncurry referred to the other's frailty and greed, which must have accentuated with old age. The Cardinal's doctors prescribed a strict and moderate diet which their patient repeatedly disregarded whenever he got the opportunity. It was not very often, for his servants, who were obliged by protocol to set before him every course which was offered to his guests, whisked away the rich dishes before the Cardinal could snatch a morsel on to his own plate. His love of animals had always been a characteristic. At the end of his life his adoration of a stray King Charles spaniel was very touching. The dog had attached itself to the Cardinal King outside St Peter's and would never leave him. This was proof, its new owner claimed, of the Cardinal's royalty which the little creature instantly recognized. Joseph Forsyth, the Scottish antiquary, recalled that the dog was encouraged to play tricks on the dinner table. Forsyth was struck by the difference between the porcelain laid before the Cardinal and his guests at meals. To his surprise the guests were given the best services, painted and adorned with a gold crown and a cardinal's hat, whereas the host ate off the simplest china.

The Cardinal's face, even in his late seventies was handsome and strangely youthful. He had few wrinkles except upon his forehead. But he stooped and walked painfully as a result of the injury to his leg received in Messina. Forsyth described his ordinary dress at home. He wore a plain black jacket lined with scarlet silk, a black silk mantle, and black velvet breeches. His waistcoat and stockings were of scarlet; his shoes black with scarlet heels. His top-coat was purple laced with gold. Forsyth recorded that in conversation 'he says little and in that there is nothing.' His jokes were somewhat forced. He remarked that he had heard of the Scotch having second sight, but not foresight. The middle-class schoolmaster fresh from Elgin did not think this funny. But the truth was that the Cardinal King had difficulty in speaking English with fluency, and it irked him not to be understood. Besides – and one may sympathize with him – although ready to receive his countrymen out of courtesy he did not necessarily find them all sympathetic. One whom he was glad to welcome again was the amiable Duke of Sussex to whose influence the Cardinal liked to attribute the Elector of Hanover's pension. They chatted away in great amity, each 'Your Royal Highnessing' the other with the utmost regularity.

The ripe old age which the Cardinal of York reached was not predicted in his youth. As a child he was strong and active. But in adolescence he ailed. His contemporaries mistook neurasthenia for incipient tuberculosis, proclaiming that he would die early like his mother. But that affected and fractious young woman deliberately destroyed herself by fasts and lack of fresh air and exercise, in order either to oblige her confessor or to disoblige her husband. Certainly the youthful Prince Henry showed signs of going the same way, even if his motives were not tendentious. Luckily the 1745 expedition intervened, to be followed by the cardinalate and an active ecclesiastical life. Thereafter his emotional disturbances were controlled by his religion and a hard core of common sense. Nevertheless the Cardinal of York was from time to time afflicted with some of the prevalent diseases and pains that eighteenth-century flesh was heir to. He caught and recovered from smallpox, which may have affected his eyesight. He read with steel-framed folding spectacles with rings to go over the ears. The lenses were slightly magnifying. The spectacles were kept in a neat shagreen case. In 1763 Mann referred gleefully to the Cardinal's scorbutic body and the belief of his dependents that he could not long survive. Scurvy was a common complaint of the age, characterized according to the Oxford Dictionary 'by general debility of the body, extreme tenderness of the gums, foul breath, subcutaneous eruptions, and pains in the limbs due to malnutrition arising from the lack of suitable food'. 'Suitable' is the operative adjective, because the Cardinal's table did not lack abundance. Although the quality of food served at rich men's meals was entirely natural it was not necessarily healthy, and prosperous peasants often fared better owing to sparser and less lickerish diet.

The Cardinal's diary of 1788 makes repeated references to his frailties. He had swollen hands and feet – gout presumably, although he drank little wine – and could barely walk. He supported himself with a stick of which the ivory handle was carved in the likeness of Charles I's head. 'In carozza a far la trottata,' was an invariable distraction from the suffering, although one might suppose the jolting and swaying of the carriage at the speed the Cardinal liked to drive would aggravate rather than relieve the pain. And during this year he was also troubled with an inflamed right eye and swollen lid. However by dint of coddling himself he survived another eight years. He was observed in 1804 entering St Peter's in procession 'with a far away look in his eyes.' By 1807 he was senile. He died at La Rocca at 2 o'clock in the morning of 13 July. It was the forty-sixth anniversary of his enthronement in the cathedral of Frascati. Thither his body was carried and there it lay before being moved to Rome.

The last journey across the Campagna must have been the slowest the Cardinal of York ever took. On this occasion there were no outriders, no runners in scarlet liveries to accompany the dashing carriage and six spanking bays. No clouds of dust. No upright figure in the back seat urging the postillions to whip the horses ever faster. The funeral cortège was led by black horses, their mourning plumes nodding with each rhythmic step. The Cardinal was drawn supine in a black and gold coffin, within a heavy, lumbering hearse. In the Palazzo Cancelleria he lay in state, not as a defunct sovereign but as a prince of the Church, and Dean of the Sacred College at that. For sixty years he had worn the scarlet tasselled hat which now reposed at his feet.

The funeral was held, not in his titular church of Santa Maria in Campitelli – presumably it was not large enough for the great concourse of Romans come to pay their last respects to this venerable person whom the oldest could remember since their childhood – but in S. Andrea della Valle. Pope Pius VII, accompanied by twenty-seven cardinals officiated at the Requiem Mass. No function was neglected which the deceased, so scrupulous over ceremonial detail, would not himself have rigidly observed. No hitch occurred which he would have cavilled at. The remains were transported to St Peter's, encased in an urn, and buried in the *grotte vaticane* beside his father's. His brother's were brought from Frascati shortly afterwards. In 1939, through the offices of Sir D'Arcy Osborne, British Minister to the Holy See, Queen Elizabeth the Queen Mother had a tomb erected over the bodies of the last three Stuarts in the crypt of the basilica.

The Cardinal King long had in mind that a fitting monument might be erected to the memories of his father, brother and himself in the great nave. After all there was already one to his mother in the south aisle. The faithful Cesarini (made Bishop of Milevi in 1801) acquainted Pope Pius VII (1800–23) with what had been his master's dearest wish. The Pope generously commissioned the best known Italian sculptor of the day to design a neo-Greek monument in the shape of a gigantic *stele*, flanked by a pair of nude angels, to commemorate the three throneless kings. It is one of the most compelling of Canova's works, and certainly one of the most beautiful monuments in St Peter's.

There exists in the Fabre Musuem, Montpellier a letter from Canova to the French painter F. X. Fabre dated 22nd June 1820 announcing that he has just completed the epitaph on the monument to the 'Casa Stuarda', with the information that the Prince Regent, recently become King George IV of Great Britain, had voluntarily and spontaneously offered to contribute towards the expense of its erection. Stendhal, on seeing it shortly after its completion observed, 'George IV, true to his reputation as the most accomplished gentleman of the three kingdoms wished to honour the remains of those unfortunate princes, whom if alive he would have sent to the scaffold, had they fallen into his power.' He was wrong. I have no doubt that, had the Cardinal of York by some misguided impulse ventured to cross the Channel, the Prince Regent would have invited him to Carlton House, lavishly entertained him and seduced that susceptible prince with all the sophisticated charm he well knew how to exercise. Ever since 1788 the Hanoverian royal family were perfectly aware that, in spite of Napoleon's idle threats, they were sitting tight and would never be dislodged from the English throne by the Stuarts. The Prince Regent could afford to feel romantic about them. When he went to Edinburgh he wore the royal Stuart tartan to which he claimed the right through his tortuous descent from the Queen of Bohemia. It was of course quite unjustified. His niece Queen Victoria likewise indulged herself in orgies of sentimentality over the family's tragic fate.

We should not underestimate the change of attitude of the Hanoverian family towards the old, legitimist dynasty. George III and his sons behaved handsomely to the last of the Stuarts while he was alive. George IV honoured his memory. Besides he was always ready to promote a work of art at any cost. And Canova's monument to the Stuarts qualifies as a great one. Stendhal rhapsodized over the angels on either side of the entry of the tomb. He would sit on a wooden bench facing them for hours at a stretch, and found at nightfall their beauty to be celestial. He advised visitors to Rome for the first time who wished to learn how to appreciate sculpture, to make straight for the Stuart monument. Whether or not they found themselves profoundly moved by it would determine whether they had, or had not a heart capable of appreciating this particular art. If they were moved then they might proceed afterwards to study the Apollo Belvedere and, when they got to London, the Elgin marbles.

Cardinal Henry's last will which he drew up in English in 1802 after his return from exile, was straightforward enough. 'So great is our confidence in Monsignor Angelo Cesarini, Bishop of Milevi, and

Rector of our Seminary,' the document ran, 'that in him alone and to no one else we confidently leave' – everything. The testator went on to delegate to him, 'with whom we have daily spent the greater part of our life, who knows our every wish, absolute authority to dispose of all our effects as he knows best.' In other words the Cardinal's property in money, furniture, books, pictures, family heirlooms and treasures, then belonged to Cesarini who, had he cared to disregard his old friend's wishes, would have been legally entitled to keep or sell the lot, and nobody could have disputed with him. Naturally Cesarini, who was scrupulously conscientious, carried out to the letter what he believed to be the Cardinal's intentions.

The Cardinal did not, however, die a rich man. As for ready cash he had little, so little that Cesarini in a letter of 1808 to Hippisley informing him how glad he was that George III had granted a pension to the Countess of Albany, stated that she was already receiving 4,000 scudi a year from the Cardinal's estate, that the sum absorbed nearly all the assets left and in consequence the Cardinal's fifty-six dependants would get practically nothing. There exists a copy (among Lord Braye's papers) of a letter dated 30 August 1807 to the Prince of Wales from the Bishop of Milevi. It mentioned his intimacy* for more than thirty-eight years with the Cardinal of York which enabled him to testify to the Cardinal's gratitude to the English royal family for his pension, and his desire to show some mark of it. Among the belongings left by the Cardinal the only objects which he found deserving the Prince of Wales's acceptance were the cross of St Andrew set with diamonds, worn by Charles I and later by Prince Charles Edward in Edinburgh, and Charles I's ring engraved with a cross, which the Cardinal used to tell him was formerly placed on the finger of the kings of Scotland at their coronation. These things he, Cesarini, now offered to the Prince of Wales. The Bishop also threw in the 'george' worn by Charles I on the scaffold. Some of these pathetic relics were among the treasures which James II had smuggled to France in 1688. Indeed James managed to conceal the coronation ring (and his wife's diamond bodkin) in his drawers when the fishermen manhandled and stripped him at Faversham, rudely

---

* Cesarini wrote of himself: 'Il est plongé dans le comble de la douleur de la perte d'un Seigneur qui lui a donné la marque de son amour.'

calling him, as they did so, 'Old hatchet face!' puffing tobacco smoke at him and exclaiming, 'Damn it! If you can't endure smoke now, how will you endure hell fire?'

The relics were gratefully accepted by the Prince of Wales, and are now the property of Her Majesty the Queen.* The remaining English crown jewels which the Cardinal had inherited from Prince Charles or received as gifts from the Duchess of Albany, included the sceptre, enamelled collar, badge and star of the Garter, the cross of the Order of the Thistle set in diamonds, and the ruby ring, all once belonging to James II, and carried or worn by him at his coronation. But these crown jewels formed part of the treasure sold to help Pius VI in his extremity, and have disappeared. All that remains of the Cardinal's generous benefactions to the papal treasury is a gold chalice designed by Giuseppe Valadier and studded with what Sobieski brilliants were left over. The date of this handsome object is presumably early nineteenth century, which explains why it did not go the same way as the rest of the Cardinal's gifts to Pius VI in 1797. The quantity of silver and plate which the Cardinal presented to the seminary in Frascati was destroyed in the air raids of 1943–4.

It is nice to know that neither Sir John Coxe Hippisley nor 'Mr Thomas Coutts's services to the Cardinal King were overlooked. To Sir John Cesarini sent an edition of Plutarch in two volumes printed in 1470, a manuscript with illuminations, a gold medal and the veil of Mary Queen of Scots, which relics have passed to Sir John's descendants. To Coutts, who transmitted the Cardinal's pension from London and would take no commission on the transaction, he sent a gold enamelled snuff box with the Cardinal's likeness on the lid surrounded by a border of pearls, an *étui de voyage*, two small porcelain vases set in gold, and a gold medal of James II. These were a generous recompense for services which were not spread over more than seven years.

Although most of the Cardinal of York's possessions had been pillaged by the revolutionary forces in 1798 his books and papers were not taken. At the time nearly all his famous library of books was in the Frascati seminary. The papers, in spite of their vast number, marvellously escaped detection and destruction. Their subsequent

* At least I suppose they still are, for I have not been able to find out.

fate was strange. The Bishop of Milevi became their absolute owner. It is possible that he intended, had he lived, to provide for their future and even to have undertaken the formidable task of cataloguing, or at least sorting them. But he never got down to it because he did not long survive the Cardinal King. On his death he bequeathed the papers to Monsignor Tassoni, the papal auditor. Tassoni handed them over to the Abbé Lupi (a former amanuensis of the Cardinal) who had no idea of their interest and importance. He put them in an attic of the Palazzo Monserrato in Rome, where in 1816 they were discovered by a certain Dr Watson. They were then in a deplorable state, having been exposed to the weather and nibbled by rats. Watson, with an eye to the main chance persuaded Lupi, who obtained Tassoni's consent, to sell them to him for 170 piastres. The delighted Watson unwisely boasted to friends of the bargain he had made. The news reached the sharp ears of the Cardinal Secretary of State, Consalvi, who acted promptly. He forbade the papers to leave Italy, and had Watson's apartments containing them sealed. In fact he confiscated them, and had them put into five chests and entrusted to the Governor of Rome. He then ordered a formal enquiry into the deal. It transpired that Tassoni denied he had ever authorised the papers' sale, and that Lupi persisted in stating that he had handed to Tassoni the money he received from Watson. Consalvi offered the equivalent sum (170 piastres) for the papers to Watson, who refused it. Consalvi, whose authority none dared dispute, thereupon offered all the papers as a gift to the Prince Regent of England. The Prince unaware of the tracasserie involved, accepted them with pleasure. He was soon surprised to receive a demand for £3,000 from the irrepressible Dr Watson, for what His Royal Highness had supposed was a free gift to him from the Pope's Cardinal Secretary of State. The Prince Regent with his usual generosity and affability nonetheless offered Dr Watson £500, which was turned down flat. Dr Watson consequently received nothing for his pains in the transaction. Sixteen years later at the age of eighty-eight he hanged himself in The Blue Anchor Tavern, St Mary-at-Hill, Thames Street.

This is not the full story of the Stuart papers now at Windsor Castle. Another very large batch which never passed through the Cardinal of York's hands, likewise found its way there. The Abbé P. Waters, Procurer-General of the English Benedictines in Rome, wrote on 12 June 1805 to Sir John Coxe Hippisley that he was in possession of a quantity of Stuart documents which had been given to him by the Duchess of Albany. She had come upon them in her father's library when clearing out the Palazzo Guadagni in Florence. Waters claimed that he had brought them on the Duchess's behalf to the Palazzo Cancelleria in Rome. Since this was the Cardinal's residence it is probable that she meant them to go with several other family treasures to her uncle, and instructed the Procurer-General to deliver them to their legal owner. Waters asserted that on the Duchess's death he as her sole executor took them from the Palazzo Cancelleria for safe custody to his own lodgings. At any rate he yielded them through Hippisley to the Prince Regent in return for a small pension. Since he died in Rome shortly afterwards he derived little financial interest out of them.

The fact that the Cardinal of York left no specific instructions regarding the future of his family documents might have been disastrous. As things turned out the papers eventually came to be housed in the place most suitable for them. Among the voluminous Stuart papers at Windsor Castle none of Queen Mary Beatrice's are included. It is supposed that after her death in 1718 they remained in the care of her faithful secretary, William Dicconson who lived on at Saint-Germain until his death in 1742. During the French Revolution they may have been stolen, because at the very end of the eighteenth century one or two turned up in booksellers' shops in Paris. In 1842 two further hauls of Stuart papers were purchased in Rome by Baroness Braye and Mr Towneley Balfour of Towneley Hall, Drogheda from the Marchese Malatesta whose wife was Cesarini's heir. Fifty volumes of the Braye documents were deposited in the British Museum in 1877. The Cardinal's diary of 1788 was bought by Horace Walpole, Earl of Orford. Many of the Stuart papers have been printed in various learned journals, but several letters have not yet been deciphered, and others still await publication.

In spite of his personal gratitude to the reigning Hanoverian sovereign George III, and the goodwill he felt towards the Prince Regent, the Cardinal of York made sure that after his death there should be no doubts as to who was the legitimate claimant to the throne of Great Britain. For the benefit of Jacobite loyalists he nominated his successor in his will of 1802. The heir was the widowed and childless King of Sardinia, Charles Emmanuel IV whom he had entertained with Pope Pius VII that very year. Since this king abdicated a few months afterwards the heir at the time when the will became operative was his brother Victor Emmanuel I. They were the great-grandsons of Victor Amadeus II King of Sicily and Sardinia, who had married Anne Marie, the second daughter of Henrietta of England, Duchess of Orleans. The elder daughter Marie Louise having married the imbecile Charles II of Spain died childless. Thus the house of Savoy inherited the Stuart claims, but not for long. Victor Emmanuel I, who was the Cardinal King's second cousin twice removed, likewise abdicated in 1821 leaving no sons. His successor and younger brother Charles Felix died childless in 1831. His eldest daughter Mary Beatrice however married by special dispensation her uncle Francis IV Duke of Modena. Their granddaughter Marie Teresa married Prince Ludwig of Bavaria. Through this alliance the present Duke of Bavaria is the *de jure* King of Great Britain.

VI

ROYAL MISTRESS

As a consequence of Prince Charles's revelation made in 1783 to his brother the Cardinal Duke that his wife was having a rip-roaring affair with Vittorio Alfieri, the poet-Count under threat of instant banishment by Pope Pius VI hastily departed from Rome and the Papal States in early May, leaving his mistress behind him.

Alfieri described the year 1783 as a bad one for 'Psipsio and Psipsia', the onomatopoeic nicknames by which the enamoured pair addressed each other at this stage of their liaison. While Louise was obliged to remain in the Palazzo Cancelleria, Vittorio went off to Siena to stay with Gori Gandellini, a silk merchant and prominent member of the intellectual circle in that city, who was his most intimate confidant and one of two men – the other was the Abbate Caluso – who had some restraining influence upon his impetuosities. Gori was devoted to Alfieri, extremely proud of their relationship and enough of a scholar to give useful advice on the poet's compositions. From Siena Alfieri roamed around the north of Italy until October when he decided to visit England once more in order to satisfy the third passion of his life, since indulgence in the first two, love and writing, were, owing to his separation from Louise, temporarily suspended. This third passion was for thoroughbred horses, on which he had always spent more money than he could afford. The English visit was to result in his buying and bringing back to Italy fourteen more. He travelled by way of Paris where he succumbed to the prevailing balloon mania. 'What a majestic and noble spectacle,' he wrote ecstatically to Louise, 'more fitted for poetry than history! A discovery that!' She, incarcerated in Rome or in Genzano, a summer retreat in the Alban Hills where her movements were closely supervised by the Church, was much dejected by the ever increasing distance which separated them. She also disliked the prospect of her beloved revisting the scenes associated with Lady Ligonier. All she could do was to await developments, in other words the event which would change her status of a grass widow into that of the real thing. She did not hesitate to express these wishes on paper, and wrote to Gori, to whom as her lover's greatest friend, although she had not yet met him, she was already devoted: 'What a brutal thing it is to expect one's happiness through another's death! Oh God, how it degrades the soul! Yet none the less I cannot refrain from this desire!' At least hypocrisy was not one of the Countess's failings. 'I would surrender the remainder of my life to spend one whole day with him and then die contented. My devotion to him is unalterable, and his is towards myself.' And again she poured out to Gori her helpess, overpowering desire for her poet. 'I want him. I cannot do without him.' The fact is, if Alfieri's own testimony and what we know of the Countess of Albany's upbringing and respect for her queenly dignity are anything to go by, that after seven years of intense mutual attraction their love was still not physically consummated.

Meanwhile the poor old, tattered, discredited, yet living legend of the Forty-Five, the former Prince Charming, handsome, debonair and heroic, the winner of all hearts responsive to youth, gallantry and romance – which is to say the majority of mankind of both sexes – this person of the past and embarrassment of the present, persistently declined to die. 'The man of iron', his heartless wife called him. The once effulgent spirit, now thoroughly dimmed to be sure, nevertheless continued to flicker within a body swollen and putrefying. The frustrating quandary in which Louise and Alfieri were floundering might have lasted another four years until the Prince's eventual extinction, had it not been for the chance visit to Italy of a personage with just the rank and attributes necessary to put a term to it. Gustavus III, King of Sweden, happened in 1784 to be in Tuscany *incognito* on a cultural tour. This extremely intelligent, educated and civilized monarch was the very man to win the confidence of the English prince, who was sensitive about his equivocal status, and also of the Countess who revered anyone with artistic and intellectual leanings. Moreover Gustavus, on paying his respects to the old prince in the Palazzo Guadagni, was deeply touched by his sad condition. So much so that the first time he saw him the King of Sweden was reduced to tears. No doubt with his own domestic and political troubles well in mind Gustavus was qualified to sympathize. His marriage was wretched and he too was separated from his queen whom he cordially disliked. Constitutional affairs in Sweden were also in such a state of flux that the harassed monarch could easily visualise himself reduced to a similar extremity, and even exile. As we know, a comparable solution to his own problems was never to be reached, because his life was abruptly put an end to by an assassin's bullet in 1792. Gustavus upon whom his fellow monarch, the *de jure* King of England unburdened his distress, advised a legal separation as the most satisfactory conclusion to a broken marriage which he at once saw could not be mended. He counselled Charles to banish all dreams of a return to his throne as vain. He urged him to live for the present. Prince Charles accepted the advice proffered, and on 27 March wrote to the King: 'I consent absolutely to a separation from my wife and that she no longer bears my name.' The very same day he addressed to the King's equerry, Destours, a begging letter: 'At the moment of writing to you I haven't got a *sou*,' continuing with complaints about the Cardinal of York's ill treatment of him – and referring to 'the tyranny of my brother'.

In Rome the Swedish king next tackled Louise, persuading her to agree to sacrifice certain financial claims as the price of her freedom to live where and how she pleased – namely the Stuart diamonds, which she had her eye on again, and part of the pension she was receiving from the Vatican. He even induced her to return to her husband 1,690 books which she had somehow managed to purloin from his library. At first she demurred, declaring that a formal separation would make her feel humiliated in French circles. Gustavus undertook to put this right with Louis XV through his ambassador in Paris, the Baron Staël-Holstein. Louise soon fell in with the proposals. King Gustavus's task was made easy through the intermediary of a member of his suite, the aide-de-camp Baron Carl Sparre. As the individual who drafted the legal document of separation Sparre came into frequent touch with Louise. She was greatly attracted by his handsome person and engaging manner, and soon got on to flirtatious terms with him. She wrote her 'dear Senator' – he was governor of a province in the north of Sweden – lengthy letters, which were coy and even over-affectionate. She confided in him her love for Alfieri. She mocked the Cardinal of York. She affirmed that he was furious with her because he believed she had renounced her full allowance from him in return for a pension from the Hanoverian king. Could anything be more ridiculous? Long after Sparre's return to Sweden with his master she continued to assail him with sprightly letters, levelling cheap jibes at her husband, 'the old man of Florence,' as she termed him, and his ailments. 'It would be a good thing to deliver the world of his weight, with which it has been overcharged too long,' she wrote in 1785, not in the best of taste.

At all events, the King of Sweden and Baron Sparre earned the gratitude and devotion of both Albanys. Released from all obligations to her husband by legal decree, the Countess decided to throw to the winds those inhibitions which up till now had prevented her giving herself wholly to her lover; the inhibitions, yes, but the circumspection which hedges a royal person and that one still in name a queen, not yet.

When the legal separation was completed Louise persuaded her 'gaoler', as she now styled her brother-in-law, to allow her to leave Rome and travel in Switzerland for the benefit of her health. She went in the height of summer by slow stages. In her carriage she read; in the inns she played the harp. Her first resting place was Baden in the Aargau. Having taken the spa waters for six hours daily she moved to the Château de Martinsbourg on the Rhine, near Colmar in Alsace, the home of the ever-faithful Madame de Maltzam. Here she waited two months in a state of excitable anticipation for Alfieri, whose professed motives for delay were a desire not to risk injuring her reputation. At last the lovers met in the Two Keys Inn at Colmar at 8'clock in the morning of 17 August, after an interval of sixteen months. The jubilation of both was overwhelming. Alfieri recorded: 'I found myself again completely reintegrated in spirit, heart and mind.' And three days after the reunion Louise wrote affectionately to Baron Sparre, making mock once again of her husband and the state he was endeavouring to maintain in Florence. The only news brought to Colmar which marred the couple's happiness was that of the death of Gori in Siena. Alfieri was inconsolable over the loss of his closest friend and mentor. He gave vent to expressions of hysterical grief. The catastrophe and the presence of his mistress however impelled him to a frenzy of writing.

In mid-October the lovers felt obliged to part again for a period. Although legally separated from 'the man of iron', Louise was still his wife and could not contemplate setting up house with Alfieri until she was decently widowed. Moreover should the Cardinal suspect that she were living with him, he might get the Pope to stop her dowry, and Louis XVI her French pension. So while Vittorio went off to Pisa she moved to Bologna, all the while posting letters to Sparre, assuring the 'dear Senator' of her devotion to him and complaining that he sent her too few letters in return. Could he believe it, her husband was now claiming honours from the Grand Duke of Tuscany for his bastard daughter, giving balls and complaining of poverty at the same time? 'I assure you it is Harlequin's court, and the good man has to be carried from one room to another for he can no longer walk and he thinks he is king. It is enough to make you die of laughing.'

During the winter of 1784–5 Alfieri seems to have had a lightning affair with a Venetian beauty. More important still, he wrote what is perhaps his best play, *Mirra*, the plot based on a tale in Ovid's *Metamorphoses*, in which Mirra falls in love with her father, giving birth by him to Adonis. Alfieri treated the incest with greater delicacy than Ovid by making the father unaware of his daughter's passion for him. It is the only one of Alfieri's plays with a human theme, the others being concerned with the inexorable retributions of fate upon mythological or Old Testament shadows, whose agonies and ecstasies fail to move us. Byron, who saw *Mirra* with Count and Countess Guiccioli in 1819, was profoundly affected. 'The last two acts,' he wrote John Murray his publisher, 'threw me into convulsions. I do not mean by that a lady's hysterics, but the agony of reluctant tears, and the choking shudder which I do not often undergo for fiction.' He gave way to loud sobs, and hurriedly left the box. Alfieri had likewise burst into tears on first reading Ovid's more harrowing version of the story.

In May 1785 Louise arrived in Paris by way of Colmar. Her main object in going there was to correct the complaints which her husband, prompted by his daughter Charlotte, had made to the virtuous Louis XVI; and to secure her French dowry from the clutches, as she feared, of Charlotte whom she knew to be spreading malicious rumours that her stepmother and the amoral Alfieri had been cohabiting. For the next five years Paris was to be her home, with occasional visits to the Château de Martinsbourg in order to be alone with Alfieri away from prying eyes. These years were among the happiest of Louise's life. Her epistolary affair with Baron Sparre waned to extinction. Without the reciprocation which she demanded, how could it continue? Her relations with Alfieri after so many years of frequent partings were losing their turbulence. Their love was less charged with emotion and on that account more stable. Twice a week regularly he wrote to her. Meanwhile she had learned to live contentedly without him, so long as she felt sure that she retained the first place in his heart.

In Paris Louise was having her cake and eating it. She was treated as a sort of semi-queen, accorded the honours and attentions of royalty which few women spurn, with absolutely none of the obligations of sovereignty. She was also achieving her ambition of being the hostess of a *salon* to which statesmen, men of letters and artists resorted. Meanwhile in Colmar Alfieri was stricken with a serious illness of dysentry from which he nearly died. With his love of harrowing himself and others he afterwards recorded how he endured as many as 'eighty pestilential evacuations' in one day. He never properly recovered and was prematurely aged by his sufferings. As soon as he could travel he was reluctantly persuaded to join Louise in Paris. The din of the Paris streets was an intense irritation to his nerves. He hated the city and the inhabitants, few of whom had the slightest knowledge of his fame in Italy. Even now the lovers did not live under the same roof. She was established in the Hôtel de Bourgogne in the Faubourg St Germain, in old-fashioned state. She was addressed by her servants as Majesté. She was served with china and plate on which the royal arms of Britain were prominently painted and engraved. Much of her furniture, consisting of heavy Baroque pieces which had belonged to Mary Beatrice, was by the standards of Louis XVI's ébénistes considered lamentably out of date. She set up in her drawing-room a chair of state with a canopy emblazoned with the royal arms. Enthroned more like a pope than a queen under this preposterous reredos, she received her lions – Beauharnais, Madame de Staël, Madame de Flahaut and David. As late as 1817 Henry Matthews remarked upon the 'form and ceremony of a Queen Dowager', which she was to maintain at her receptions in Florence.

By 1787 Louise was thirty-five. She was already plump, but moved with agility. Her skin was still fair, her hair chestnut; her eyes were bright and her teeth perfect. Although she was of middle height her presence was majestic. Yet this woman, who never forgot her semi-royal origin and her more exalted status as consort of the rightful King of England, had a gracious manner which put those she met at their ease. Her approach to rich and poor, proud and humble was kindly, in spite of the acid remarks about individuals which she occasionally let fall. She was spontaneously open-handed to all in need. She was fairly accomplished at drawing and painting, proficient at the guitar and harp, and her singing voice was more melodious than her speaking voice which was often shrill. A nephew of Madame de Maltzam who met her at Colmar, observed that 'it was necessary to know her in order to understand her well.'

Cultivated rather than intellectual, direct rather than urbane, comely rather than handsome, Louise might be thought the negation of what Alfieri looked for in a woman. For the other women whom he had loved had been of mean intelligence, sugary disposition and sexually appetising. Louise represented something very different. She had the inclination but not the glamour of a cocotte. Her mind, capable of understanding and analyzing his writings, provided an essential stimulus to the genius which she never once hesitated to believe was paramount. In Alfieri's lowest moments, when his creative powers were dormant, she was there to inspire, encourage and praise, without ever stooping to flatter. And the extraordinary thing is how highly Alfieri's poetry was esteemed by his contempories. To us his personality is more interesting than his drama. The man Alfieri is the archetypal product of the eighteenth-century romantic movement. He was a precursor of Byron, who closely resembled him in temperament and tastes, and who incidentally admired his works.

The dramatist Alfieri is to us an egregious bore. His plays are static and interminably repetitive, irredeemably untheatrical. They take place in a sort of no-scene in which the heroes and villains, mostly the latter, all in the likeness of Alfieri, stand stock still declaiming vehemently about nothing in particular. Madame de Staël, alone among Alfieri's contemporaries, deplored the tediousness of his tragedies. She remarked that they failed to evoke sympathy because the characters lacked individuality. They merely reflected the author's own muddled sentiments. Their message was, she said, rendered nugatory by their unrestrained vehemence, just as Metastasio's verse was rendered cloying by its unrelieved sweetness.

When the news reached Paris that her husband had drawn his last breath in the Palazzo Muti on 30 January 1788, Louise was shocked. The death which she had dearly longed for had come in a sense too late. The obstinacy of the old prince in not dying sooner had frustrated her great love during its meridian in that it prevented her living in open sin. Now that fierce passion was spent. It was turned into something different, possibly better, a devotion based upon mutual dependence. Louise was not necessarily insincere in lamenting Prince Charles's passing. She was certainly remorseful for having so blatantly looked forward to what, now it had come, was a slight anti-climax. Alfieri testified that her sorrow was unfeigned. And Cornelia Knight wrote that, 'She spoke of him with great calmness and compassion, and thought, drinking apart, that he was a less despicable character than Cardinal York.'

Nevertheless the event eased Louise's predicament. Henceforth she felt free to abandon the irksome vestiges of respectability. There was no longer any call upon her to save face in the interests of Jacobitism for with Prince Charles Jacobitism was totally extinct. She could lead a life which no great lady of the age, who did not enjoy the privileges of a Queen Dowager, would dare to lead without forfeiting social position, namely of mistress to a man under one roof. The equivocal ménage was accepted by a cynical society because of the fame of both parties, their years, the length of their liaison, and the mystery, carefully fostered by the pair, whether or not they were secretly married. As late as 1807 Bonstetten assumed that a marriage had taken place because Louise on being asked if she often went to the theatre, let slip the words, 'My husband doesn't like it.' He was, however, wrong.

In the spring of 1791 the Countess of Albany fulfilled a wish long cherished, to visit England, the country of which she had for a few inglorious years been the legitimate queen. Her first motive for going was to advance Alfieri's literary reputation in a land which she had been led to suppose was capable of appreciating it. Her second was financial. With the oncome of the French Revolution, Louise saw her rents and pension from the Bourbons in peril. She intended to appeal for help from the English royal family instead. As it turned out she was in this respect unsuccessful.

She went from Paris accompanied, of course, by Alfieri, whose fourth visit it was. They stayed in England for four months, of which three were passed in London. The presence of this exotic pair and their romantic circumstances caused a great flutter of excitement in the capital. Horace Walpole wrote to Miss Mary Berry on 19 May that the Countess, presumably on her own, was 'at this very moment, I believe, in the palace of St James, not restored by as rapid a revolution as the French . . .' Instead she was presented at court by Lady Ailesbury, whose husband was her cousin. King George III and Queen Charlotte received her very graciously. The same evening Horace added a postscript to his letter.

'Well! I have had an exact account of the interview of the two Queens, from one who stood close to them. The Dowager was announced as Princess of Stolberg. She was well dressed, and not at all embarrassed. The King talked to her a good deal; but about her passage, the sea, and general topics: the Queen in the same way, but less. Then she stood between the Dukes of Gloucester and Clarence, and had a good deal of conversation with the former, who, perhaps, may have met her in Italy. Not a word between her and the Princesses: nor did I hear of the Prince; but he was there, and probably spoke to her. The Queen looked at her earnestly. To add to the singularity of the day, it was the Queen's birthday.'

Louise had in fact encountered the Duke of Gloucester when her husband's coach met his head on in a narrow Roman street in 1772. The Duke gave way and the occupants of both coaches, with windows down, saluted each other courteously. After the presentation ceremony at St James's, the Countess of Albany appeared at the opera in the Pantheon, seated in the royal box. She also attended the prorogation of Parliament, seated on the steps of the throne. Both these privileges were accorded her by George III. The contingencies to which the Stuart wheel of fortune had revolved three quarters of a circle were strange indeed.

It would be interesting to know what the Countess thought of the Hanoverian family. When years later she wrote to the Prince Regent a letter of condolence on the death of his father she reminded him of the enjoyable dinner party he had given for her to meet Mrs Fitzherbert. It would be nice too to know what she thought of Horace Walpole, whom she met a few days later at a small party which Lady Ailesbury gave for her. Evidently Walpole was not very impressed. She 'has not a ray of royalty about her. She has good eyes and teeth; but I think can have had no more beauty than remains, except youth. She is civil and easy, but German and ordinary.' Virtually she was neither one nor the other. Her upbringing was French, her character complex. Later on Walpole came round to her because she expressed a wish to see Strawberry Hill and bring Alfieri with her. On Saturday 2 July they breakfasted at Strawberry, and she expressed herself delighted with the place. Whereupon the susceptible owner of this Thames-side bijou villa found that she had more sense than he had realized at their previous encounter.

The Countess of Albany, keyed up by Alfieri's enthusiasm for England and all things English, was prepared to be enraptured by our country and countrymen. At first she was pleased but as the four months progressed she changed her opinion. It is true that Alfieri was the first to become disillusioned with the English climate, the philistinism of the upper classes and the dreary round of London social engagements. And Louise, who was always influenced by his moods, became disillusioned too. She kept a memorandum on four folded quarto sheets which have been preserved.* They contain some revealing comments on English habits and manners. Written in French, of course, in her neat, not very adult hand, but clear and firm, the notes to which she gave no heading, have been entitled by a later hand, 'Souvenirs d'un voyage en Angleterre'. Indeed they are a journal of a month's excursion into the country, interspersed with observations on the native ways of life.†

* Among the Fabre Papers (Fonds A 30) in the Library of the Fabre Museum, Montpellier.
† Louise acknowledged that, although French speaking, her French style of writing was not good. It is a sophisticated, cosmopolitan sort of style, inaccurate and slapdash.

She and Vittorio set out from London on 20 July. They had intended travelling to Scotland, but the bad weather deterred them. They were disgusted by the cold and the incessant rain. Their first night was spent at Park Place near Henley-on-Thames, which belonged to General Conway, Walpole's cousin and intimate friend whom he hero-worshipped. The Countess and Alfieri had met Conway at Lady Ailesbury's party. Conway, who had been aide-de-camp to the Duke of Cumberland, had fought against Prince Charles at Culloden. When a very young man he bought Park Place, to which he was much attached and where he spent his retirement planting trees, erecting grottoes, 'Gothick' cottages and a rock bridge. In 1791 he was in his early seventies, still handsome, cultivated and fascinating. Louise did not record whether she was charmed by her husband's old enemy. She conceded that Park was beautiful, as was the English landscape generally. But she complained of the tedium of the country house régime in England, of which that at Park Place was no exception. One lunched at 10 o'clock, walked a couple of hours, dined at 4, and again walked, always with the other guests. One was never permitted to walk and ruminate by oneself. Such a thing was just not done by a lady. Then came tea and supper at 10.30. Finally bed at midnight. The routine was invariable.

From Park Place the pair proceeded to Oxford, visiting Christ Church and New College libraries. They saw the Arundel marbles and several indifferent churches, including New College chapel with its recently painted glass from designs by Reynolds, which she did not think much of. They were allowed access to Blenheim Palace. She considered Vanbrugh's architecture deplorable, but admired the park. They walked up to the great Duke of Marlborough's column which she described as 'baroque', probably in term of disparagement, since this particular memorial is decidedly Palladian. She found Stowe more congenial than Blenheim; in fact its architecture was good for England, whose modern architects were signally lacking in taste. All English country houses presented a melancholy, deserted air as though they were unlived in, in marked contrast with French châteaux.

They slept at Daventry, which was in horrid country. The discomfort of most of the inns they stayed in was appalling, and the food! – 'la nouriture y étant affreux,' and very expensive. On 26 July they reached Birmingham of all places, with a view to getting first hand knowledge of an industrial centre. Louise had a good deal to say about the various industries of Birmingham. Her liberal instincts were shocked by the treatment of the non-conformists whom she called the Presbyterians. They could not find employment and were not suffered to stand for Parliament. They were justifiably discontented. Like most persecuted minorities, however, they were sensitive to slights and intolerant of others. 'The Presbyterians are even more tyrannical than the Catholics who since the Revolution of '88 have been treated like them.'

They left Birmingham without regrets. 'The little city of Worcester is gay,' she recorded. Would she think the same today of this county town, its remarkable medieval and Georgian centre vandalized and practically gutted, one asks oneself? On the 29th they slept at Upton-on-Severn. Worcestershire was 'the most beautiful county imaginable and the best cultivated.' On the way to Upton they passed through the Pershore Vale, always renowned for its fertility and abundance of fruit trees. If by 'Newport in Gloucestershire' the Countess meant Newport, Monmouthshire as their next stop, then they presumably intended to enter Wales. Perhaps they were again deterred by the rain, for after remarking that the church was Gothic and fairly pretty they retraced their steps to Gloucester. The cathedral and the new prison were inspected. It must be conceded that her curiosity was catholic enough. This town 'is crawling with sheep and horned beasts.' Thence through the Berkeley vale to Bristol.

The busy sea port had a very wealthy look but was dismissed as 'vile and sad.' Nevertheless the suburbs and surrounding country were charming, 'dotted with country houses in very picturesque situations.' They stayed the night of the 30th and possibly the 31st, for they had time to take the famous waters of Hotwell springs below Clifton, 'at the seat of Lord Clifford which is three miles' from Bristol, and was one of the most agreeable sites of all. Edward Southwell, the 21st Lord Clifford, a young man of twenty-four, was the owner of Kings Weston, then enjoying an open view westwards across the waters of the Bristol channel, crammed with the masts of sailing vessels. The house is one of the masterpieces of Vanbrugh, the architect whose works the Countess found deplorable.

On 1 August the couple set off for Bath where they stayed. Louise considered that 'this town is the best built in England. It is all of cut stone,' which was not the case in the other English towns they had visited. 'There are some beautiful squares, in circles and semi-circles. The corporation constantly endeavours to improve and embellish this place in order to attract visitors' – which is surely more than can be claimed by the city council today.

The Countess states that the rich English are driven to Bath by the boredom which consumes them. And now she waxes very critical of the English in general. No nation, she says, seeks so much pleasure and amusement, or derives less contentment from its distractions. Smart London women in particular are excessively dissipated and addicted to gaming. When in the country, which is eight months of the year, they strive to lead the same existence as in London. They can seldom get up before midday, or go to bed before four in the morning. When they are up they can never be alone. Yet she acknowledges that English women make good wives and mothers. They spend most of their time with their husbands and children, but pay no attention to their ageing parents. They are more cunning than women in other countries for the following reason. They have more at stake. Their houses are so planned that their husbands and servants must always find out whom they are entertaining. In other words their superior quick-wittedness amounts to great dexterity in deceiving their stupid spouses. English husbands are very exacting and severe. They only love women for the satisfaction of their physical appetites and have no use for their society. These dull, brutish creatures in spite of their hunting, shooting and dedication to exercise, spend months, no, sometimes years of their middle life in bed suffering from gout. This complaint is brought about by their gross intemperance, of which of course the Countess has had some experience. Consequently there are more cuckolds in England than are to be found in other European countries. Nothing, she opines, exceeds the dullness of English society. And those dreadful, interminable walks!

The 2nd, 3rd and 4th of August were spent in the neighbourhood of Bath. Unfortunately no names of places visited were given. One wonders if they stayed a night in that stronghold of Jacobitism, Badminton, where the portrait of the young Princess of Stolberg still hangs. The night of 5 August they slept in Marlborough. Louise noticed that although few really poor people were to be seen in

England, yet in Marlborough the children went naked or in rags, begging passers-by for money, an experience she came upon nowhere else this side of the Channel. On the 6th they continued their journey eastwards, 'not without regret at leaving the most lovely inn imaginable,* which really resembled a country house, and in fact once was one, belonging to the Duke of Somerset. I went to spend the night at Reading,' which was a different matter altogether. They passed more country houses off the London road, 'but always melancholy.' And they drove through Windsor Forest which had been so much praised by Pope.

On the 7th they were at Windsor. With what interest must the Countess of Albany have looked over the Castle, of which by rights she should once have been the châtelaine. From the terrace she admired the view of the Thames and Eton College beyond, although it was not as extensive, she noticed, as the view of the Seine from Saint-Germain. In the royal collections what interested her most were the Rubens, Van Dyck and Lely portraits of her predecessors, and the Raphael cartoons. Curiously enough she much admired the paintings by the American Benjamin West, a great favourite of George III. Charles II kept a brilliant court at Windsor, she observed wistfully. And she was indignant that there was no mausoleum or even epitaph over Charles I's remains which were buried in St George's Chapel. The whole castle was enormous, and impressive.

One wonders whether she and Alfieri stayed at the inn in Windsor like any ordinary travellers. On the 8th they left. They slept at Salt Hill not very far away where the Eton Montem ceremony used to take place, in order to call upon the man whom Louise thought really worth while meeting, William Herschel the astronomer, then resident in Slough. He told her that he could see the rings round Saturn and the volcanoes on the moon through his telescope which was fifty foot high and large enough to contain a man. In fact before the tube was fitted with lenses George III had walked through it, lending a hand to the Archbishop of Canterbury with the words, 'Come, my lord Bishop, I will show you the way to heaven!' Louise was vastly

* A famous coaching inn, now part of Marlborough College. The house was acquired by the 1st Duke of Northumberland in 1766 by marriage to Elizabeth Percy, heiress of the 7th Duke of Somerset, before it was converted to the Castle Inn. William Beckford describes it in a letter to G. Franchi of 11 January 1819.

impressed by Herschel's genius in spite of his being by birth and inclination a Hanoverian. The reservation is interesting in denoting the persistence of an ingrained resentment of all things Hanoverian even at this terminal stage of the Jacobite fortunes. Yet she seemed not to have minded staying with General Conway, who had actually fought for Butcher Cumberland. Notwithstanding Herschel's alleged political sympathies, his genius, modesty and simplicity appealed to her. She was in any case fascinated by scientists, and was to become a close friend of Sir Humphrey Davy, taking an intelligent interest in his invention of the famous safety lamp.

On 9 August Louise visited Hampton Court, the greater part of which had been built by Sir Christopher Wren for her grandfather-in-law's supplanter, William of Orange. It is hardly surprising that she, who was acquainted with several of the greatest palaces of the continent, thought little of this one. She found the enfilades of low and poky rooms monotonous and silly. The Mantegna cartoons, which had been collected by Charles I, received her commendation. The gardens on the other hand were, after those of Versailles, derisory, and badly kept. From Hampton Louise and Vittorio returned to London where, with the exception of one subsequent visit to Lord Tilney's vast seat of Wanstead by the architect Colen Campbell, which she pronounced the best built house in England, they remained until 20 August.

Louise's opinion of London was unfavourable. She deplored the dirt. The air was rendered so sooty with smoke from coal fires even in the summer months that the sun could seldom penetrate it. Because of the window tax too the grandest town houses had little light and fresh air. Consequently they smelled atrociously. In any case London houses were narrow, tall and inconvenient. She attributed their verticality to the exorbitant value of ground sites in the capital. As for London food, it was as heavy as the atmosphere.

Alas! England and the English do not come very well out of Louise's candid and thoroughly sincere memoranda which were recorded for no eyes but her own, and possibly Alfieri's. She deemed the inhabitants devoid of imagination and spirit. They were not truly susceptible to the arts, and they were not creative (she ignored their achievements in literature). They bought expensive pictures without understanding them. She visited the principal private collections in

London and found that of 'Mr Egard' the best, not merely in London, but outside Italy.* She enumerated some of the most famous old masters represented, and made shrewd comments on them. She concluded that the dominant interest of English men, whether rich or poor, was money. In other words England was in her eyes, as in most continental eyes of the time, the proverbial nation of shopkeepers. There was nothing, absolutely nothing that could not be bought in this country, which was the most corrupt and the most class conscious in the world. The only meed of praise – and even that was qualified – which she handed out was to the British constitutional system. 'The only good thing which England enjoys, and which is invaluable, is political liberty,' she wrote. Every man in England knew that before the law he was theoretically the equal of his most exalted and powerful neighbour. It was only good government which made life in this country tolerable. But, unfortunately, the exalted and powerful too often had the means of purchasing justice! In the same way, although English taxes were very high for the ostensible and laudable purpose of relieving the poor, the abuses in the tax collecting system were such that the poor did not benefit as much as they should have done.

It is to be feared that had Queen Louise ever worn the crown of Great Britain she might not have been very popular with her subjects.

Louise and Alfieri's actual departure from England was marked by an odd coincidence. They were about to board the packet at Dover to take them across the Channel. A crowd of sightseers assembled upon the pier. Among them Alfieri spied his former love, Penelope, on whose behalf he had fought the duel in the Green Park twenty years ago. No longer Lady Ligonier, she was now plain Mrs Smith. 'She was still very beautiful,' Alfieri wrote. 'At first I thought I was

---

* Mr Frank Simpson has informed me that by 'Mr Egard' the Countess of Albany was referring to Mr Welbore Ellis Agar (1736–1805), the second son of Henry Agar and Anne, daughter of the Rt. Rev. Welbore Ellis, Bishop of Meath. His elder brother was the 1st Viscount Clifden and his younger brother Archbishop of Dublin and Earl of Normanton. W. E. Agar was a commissioner of the customs, and deputy-commissary general. 'He formed over the years a highly important collection of sixty-five pictures at a cost of over £20,000. It contained several Rembrandts, Claudes, Poussins, Rubenses, etc. (listed in George Redford's *Art Sales: A History of Sales* . . . vol. 1. 1888). After Agar's death the whole collection was bought in 1806 for 30,000 guineas by the 2nd Earl Grosvenor, later 1st Marquess of Westminster.'

dreaming; I looked more closely, and her faint smile when she caught sight of me convinced me I was right . . . However I did not utter a word to her. I boarded the ship, and did not leave it again.' Had Louise also caught that smile and hustled her lover below deck? She already knew about this old affair with Penelope because they concealed no incidents of the past from one another. At all events Alfieri was much moved by this reminder of spent passion and folly. He was incurably romantic. When he reached Calais he sent Penelope a long letter, not devoid of tenderness but fraught with guilt, enquiring how she fared. Penelope replied that although irretrievably *déclassée*, cut off from her family (she was a daughter of Lord Rivers) and the society to which she had been accustomed, she was now married to an ex-trooper in the Blues and living amongst humble folk. She was as happy as the days were long. She did not regret the step she had taken and her new life one jot. It is a strange commentary on the stringent conventions of the age that Alfieri, whose own life departed from most of the recognized canons of propriety, was shocked by Penelope's letter. He called it perverse and obstinate.

Before returning to Paris the couple visited Louise's mother and two younger sisters in Brussels. At the end of October they were back in the French capital to witness very disturbing developments. By now the Revolution was well under way. Louis XVI and Marie Antoinette had been arrested at Varennes on 21 June and brought back to Paris in ignominy. Louis, virtually a prisoner, was obliged to sanction the National Constitution of the People in September. This was the moment when the Stuart Queen and Count Alfieri resolved to set up a joint establishment in the Hotel Thelluson, rue de Provence, which was a less smart quarter admittedly than that of the Hôtel de Bourgogne. Wiser aristocrats than they were clearing out of Paris while they could. True, these two were foreigners, but foreigners known to be critical of the way affairs were moving in France. The Paris mob was rapidly reaching a stage when it made no distinction between royal and noble persons, French or alien. Louise and Vittorio's situation was not made more comfortable by the coalition of Austria and Prussia against France and a declaration of war in June 1792. All foreigners were regarded by the French as foes of the Revolution. On the 20th of that month the mob, bearing the red bonnet of liberty, stormed the Tuileries. On 10 August the royal guards were cut to pieces. The Countess and the poet at last decided that they ought to quit the capital. They had left their decision to the very last minute. Hurriedly Alfieri obtained the necessary passports for their departure on the 25th. A premonition warned him that the date might be too late. Instead, on the 18th they piled high their coach with luggage and drove from their *hôtel*. At the city barrier they were greeted with extreme hostility by a crowd of drunken, yelling proletarians. At first the guards refused to let the coach pass through the gates. The crowd threatened to overturn it and lynch the occupants. Alfieri in desperation reacted with a fury which surpassed that of the French scum, whom he abominated. He lost his temper. He stormed at them; he yelled at them, brandishing the passports above his head. 'Listen, you apes, my name is Alfieri. I am a famous Italian poet. I am *not* a Frenchman. Can't you see? I am what my passport describes, a tall, thin man with red hair. Look at me! Read my passport!' And he cursed them into heaps. Solely by dint of giving them in their own coin more than they gave him, which is the only way of dealing with curs, he saved the situation. They were completely taken aback. Amidst mutual imprecations and insults, spitting and the waving of fists the coach containing the Countess and the poet literally forced a way through the barrier to eventual safety. It was a narrow escape, because on the 20th a posse of national guards went to the Hôtel Thelluson to arrest Louise. The murder of the Princesse de Lamballe and the appalling September massacres to which they would doubtless have fallen victims, followed within a matter of days. As it was, they lost all their possessions, including at least 3,000 books, apart from the few objects which they just had time to cram into their travelling trunks.

Alfieri's dislike of the French, which had been seething for years, was turned into almost pathological loathing by the experiences of 1792. They finally and completely dissipated the last liberal sentiments of his youth. Henceforth Alfieri was quite intemperate in his expressions of hatred, not only against the revolutionaries, which was understandable, but against Bonaparte and everyone who supported him. Louise naturally adopted Alfieri's attitude. The course of the French Revolution also thoroughly disabused her of the democratic sympathies which she formerly entertained. 'I used to be silly enough,' she wrote, 'to pity the fate of the rabble; but now I realize that the rabble is a beast to be beaten and given bread or little more, until it can make itself worthy of becoming part of the state.' Although strongly in favour of a royal restoration she did not, according to Lady Holland who saw her in Florence in 1793 and found her 'lively and good humoured . . . fall into the violent strain of invective she might be allowed to feel.' She was not quite as vociferous as Alfieri. Nevertheless she was very outspoken in her condemnation of Napoleon's régime, and rash in openly deploring her sister, Madame d'Arberg's appointment as Dame du Palais to Josephine. Her sister's acceptance of the post did not however prevent Louise writing to Josephine begging for the pension she had received from Marie Antoinette to be resumed!

In their extremity the couple landed up in Italy, which although Louise disliked it, was Vittorio's land. The question arose in which part of Italy should they settle. Piedmont, whence Alfieri had disfranchised himself, was out of the question. So too was Rome, where the Cardinal Duke and the Pope's interference would be encountered. For the same reason the Papal States were best avoided altogether. Tuscany seemed the most suitable principality. Florence was the city selected. For a month or two they lived in lodgings with their French servants, in much discomfort. Finally they acquired in 1793 the Palazzo Masetti on the Lungarno Corsini. This house was one third part of a block of palaces – which formerly belonged to the rich Gianfigliazzi family of medieval origin – lying to the west of the junction of the via Tornabuoni with the Lungarno at the Ponte Santa Trinità. During their residence the Casa Alfieri, as it eventually was called, had above the ground floor two storeys. Alfieri added a top storey for his own study. Here he worked and ruminated undisturbed. And from here he enjoyed an uninterrupted view south across the Arno, over the russet brown roofs of the houses built as it were on stilts like giant storks' legs in the river bed, to the umbrella pines and the castellated towers of Bellosguardo.

In this palace on the bank of the Arno Count Alfieri and the Countess of Albany were to pass the remainder of their days. It became famous as the shrine of one of Italy's greatest poets and the setting of the Queen Countess's *salon*. To the palace distinguished writers and artists, musicians and scientists flocked over a period of thirty years. The only people who were not welcome were politicians, whom the couple found uninteresting. It is a pity that a later owner, in linking the Palazzo Masetti with its neighbours on either side, altered the character of the façade, which subsequent modernization has helped further to destroy. Nevertheless the rooms of the Alfieri section, or third *palazzetta*, still retain some of their eighteenth-century painted decoration and ceilings. With the assistance of the inventory taken on the Countess's death in 1824 we are able to identify several of the rooms and from the description of their contents to imagine what the others looked like. Without detailing every room we may refer to the first floor *salotto* wherein so many of the Countess's receptions were held. It was sparsely furnished. Indeed where walls of Italian drawing-rooms are profusely frescoed, few furnishings are called for. The sole picture mentioned as being in the *salotto* is Fabre's famous *Saul*, which was the cause of this painter's introduction to the family circle, and will be referred to shortly. A brown varnished sofa with red leather cushions and brass nails, and twelve chairs *en suite* provided the only seating, apart from a single-backed chair, also of brown polished wood with brass studs to the upholstery. This was Louise's customary throne on which she would sit beside the great marble chimneypiece facing the windows. There were two mahogany side tables, not a pair but similar, one painted white with a marble top and metal border. They do not seem to have been very elegant pieces in a room painted with delicate and colourful arabesques. The other contents were a fire screen in four folding panels of green silk, and four candelabra of English plate. We have to remember that Louise and Alfieri lost all their valuable belongings, including Mary Beatrice's tables and chairs, in the French Revolution. What we have described were doubtless a job lot picked up in Florence. In any case the couple were by now indifferent to splendour and fine belongings.

The ante-room contained one of Canova's designs for Alfieri's monument and a column of painted wood carrying Alfieri's bust in marble. Was it the striking bust by Barthélemy Corneille – now in the Fabre musuem, Montpellier – taken in the sitter's early middle age, showing an oval face, firm chin and slightly hooked, arrogant nose? Louise's bedroom was scarcely less sparsely furnished than the living rooms. She had a bed with yellow silk hangings and a mosquito net, one large and three small bookcases, two *intarsia* chests of drawers, a night commode of mahogany and white marble, and an ormolu clock. On Alfieri's bedroom walls hung nine drawings of divers philosophers done by Louise. Otherwise apart from chests of drawers and a small bed, there were bookcases. I suspect that books occupied most of the spare space in the house. The upstairs library which the poet added was of course lined with shelves. It contained, beside the necessary writing table of walnut, and some brown varnished and red leather chairs, a barometer and a terrestrial globe. The library was never used after his death, but was shown to favoured pilgrims of unqestionable piety as a holy of holies.

In Florence the couple lived comfortably but unostentatiously. Since the Revolution both of them were far poorer than they had been. Alfieri lost the revenues he had indirectly been receiving from French property; Louise had lost her French pension. At first they had few friends because Alfieri, embittered by their misfortune and in much pain from gout, became withdrawn and unsociable. At the best of times he had abominated parties. He could never endure with patience the artificiality of social intercourse. He disliked the company of more than a handful of people simultaneously. In truth he was now so bad tempered that acquaintances were afraid of coming to the house. When he did deign to meet them downstairs his manners were savage and repulsive, unless he was in one of his rare good moods. He would sit on a sofa, refuse to mingle with the guests and frown at everybody. He made no attempt to conceal his intense dislike of certain individuals. The poor Countess, wearing an ordinary apron over her dress and a *fichu* à la Marie Antoinette round her neck, would smile as though nothing were the matter, and dispense the tea. Lady Holland who was a privileged guest admitted that Alfieri could be good company 'when he condescended to unbend.' In the absence of the host the Countess's small gatherings were held to be extremely relaxed compared with the formality of most Italian receptions in Florence.

Louise was quick to recognize that each of them must lead his and her own existence independently. So while Alfieri either rode desperately round and round the Cascine like a madman, when he was well enough, or worked and sulked upstairs like a bear with a sore head when he was indisposed, she read voraciously and wrote interminable letters in her apartment. For exercise she took rapid walks by herself along the Arno to the Cascine and back, or drove in her carriage round the city. The horses would trot to the famous Caffè del Bottegone at the junction of the via de Martelli with the piazza del Duomo. Here on hot evenings the waiters would bring tea, cake or pistacchio, which she consumed without getting out of the carriage. The beggars from the steps of the Duomo, attracted by the elegant equipage, would congregate around it. Occasionally they would be tossed a coin and told to enter the west door of the Duomo and offer a prayer for their benefactress.

From 1797 until 1802 Louise's chief correspondent and most intimate friend was Teresa Mocenni. The two women were exactly the same age. They originally met through Mario Bianchi, a close friend of Alfieri's who had died in 1796. Teresa had been Bianchi's mistress. She belonged to a very different world from Louise's. She was the wife of a Sienese shopkeeper. Although she was a remarkably cultivated and superior woman who presided over that Sienese intellectual society wherein Gori Gandellini had shone and the Abbate Caluso was still shining, her husband Asano was a philistine. He was jealous of his wife, with some reason, and brutal and lustful. He was also a religious maniac. 'These bigots never cease wishing to people the world with more imbeciles like themselves,' Louise observed tartly. She detested this middle-class business man, referring to him in her letters to the wife as 'il brontolone' (the grumbler), 'lo zanzaro' (the mosquito) and as someone she could gladly strangle with both hands. 'What a tragedy that certain individuals exist and are the husbands of people like our Saint Thérèse.' Saint Teresa disliked her spouse as much as her friend did, and did not scruple to admit it.

Louise's weekly letters to Teresa Mocenni disclose that in her first years at the Palazzo Masetti she was rather lonely; that her relations with Alfieri were no longer romantic. After all they had known each other for twenty years; and it is hardly surprising that they now talked, when they did meet, more about world affairs, literature and life, than love. Besides if Vittorio was as thin as a skeleton – he scarcely ate a thing – with scrawny legs and thighs, his noble face lined like corrugated parchment, his brow deeply furrowed, and his temper most uncertain, Louise too had changed. Chateaubriand noted that middle age had produced an effect upon her different from that of most women. It had ennobled her face. It had imprinted an antique beauty upon her forehead. Her figure, it is true, had thickened, he said. Her body was almost gross like those of Rubens's women, all bulges and pendulous wodges of fat. Stendhal however was not flattering about her features. He saw in her no remnants of a pretty face, but simply the lineaments of 'a cook who happens to have pretty hands'. Gino Capponi, the historian and Dante scholar, called her 'plump in body and somewhat material'.* For all her education and intelligence she was 'a little coarse, not the least poetical; dressed like a servant, keeping the establishment of a princess'. In other words she had entirely lost her physical allure. There is some poignancy in the fact that by the time these illustrious lovers attained the freedom to indulge their passion, it was too late. Nonetheless they were bound by indissoluble ties of affection and respect. Neither could flourish without the other's inspiration and support. Alfieri was emphatic that without Louise he would never have produced anything great or good. And after Alfieri's death Louise wilted and existed as though in a vacuum. Stendhal's assumption that he 'bored her to death', and Capponi's assertion that he 'had ceased to care for her for years' were quite without substance. They were too hastily based on the curmudgeonly front which Alfieri often presented to his mistress's guests.

Louise's fondness for Teresa was matched by admiration of her friend's gaiety in the face of a wretched home life, and of her goodness of heart. She basked too in the affection, tinged with reverence, which Teresa returned. When Teresa died suddenly in 1802 she was heartbroken.

Louise's letters make it abundantly clear that she despised all Italian women – with the single exception, of course, of Teresa – for their stupidity and hearts of bronze. And doubtless she made little effort to conceal these views when she was in their company.

She professed to be quite indifferent to religion. Had she been

---

* Compton Mackenzie (*Prince Charlie and His Ladies*, 1934) quotes in this context a very gross epigram relating to the Countess of Albany which circulated in Florence during her widowhood:

> Lung Arn ammiravano i fuorestieri
> Una reliquia del Cont' Alfieri;
> Si crede il fodero del pugnale
> Secondo i fisici e l'orinale!

devout, she told Teresa, her faith would long ago have evaporated when she learned how invariably the wicked triumphed over the good. Nevertheless she counselled her friend's son, and Alfieri's godson, Vittorio Mocenni, not to reject the New Testament teaching, declaring that 'morality is more readily enforceable when based on religion,' and that religion consists above all 'in not doing to others what one does not wish them to do to us.' Her cynicism was not unmixed with cruelty. 'Your stepson will never be cured of epilepsy,' she wrote to Teresa in answer to a distracted letter about the child's condition. 'His father is the cause.' She told Vittorio, when he was nineteen, that his sister Quirina had married a half-wit and that, since her father-in-law was in love with her he would, if he had any sense, beget himself a grandson by her.

She informed Teresa that she had read nearly all the epics in every tongue, even Voltaire's *Henriade*, which was pretty stiff going. She kept lists of her reading which was immense, most of it in French and English, less in Italian and German. Her books were her most cherished possessions. She became so attached to them that she could not bear to part with them when read, believing that the spirit of the author mysteriously abided in them on the shelf, to be released as soon as the pages were re-opened. She was deeply immersed in Kant when she was only twenty-four. Montaigne was her breviary, and would be her desert island book. She read several pages from the *Essais* daily. In the evenings when she and Alfieri were alone they met to read aloud to each other and discuss what they had been studying independently during the course of the day. This conjures up the picture of a happy middle-aged Darby and Joan. But Louise preferred whenever possible, to see people at the end of the day, which explains why she disliked the country where visitors were hard to come by.

Next to Teresa Mocenni Louise's most favoured correspondent was the Archpriest Ansano Luti. After Teresa's death he was advanced to chief confidant until his death in 1807. Unfortunately he suffered a stroke in 1802 which restricted his letter writing. Luti was Professor of Canon Law at Siena University and another prominent member of the intellectual circle in that city. He was theologian, philosopher and man of liberal views and few prejudices. He too was socially undistinguished, coming from bourgeois stock. He had been the platonic lover of Teresa, and her greatest ally in the warfare against her husband.

In her correspondence with Luti Louise rather naturally wrote less about personal and domestic matters and concentrated upon world affairs and literature. Consequently her letters to him made greater demands upon her intellect. They often manifested considerable shrewdness, and even wisdom in spite of her unrestrained cynicism. In 1803 she gave Luti the résumé of a day of her life which probably resembled most future days in Florence up to her last illness and death. Here it is. She woke at 5 in the morning, and read metaphysical and other works while her mind was fresh. She wrote letters in bed – an awkward accomplishment when ink pot, quills and sand for blotting were essential accessories. At 9 she rose and dressed. At 10 she lunched – her first meal of the day – presumably alone. From 11 to 12 she read again, carefully keeping a list of every book perused throughout the year, and often composing for her own edification essays on the authors. At midday she either took a walk, or visited a shop. Actually she seldom went to other people's houses, her superior station prohibiting such condescension. Lady Morgan tells how she heard with amazement her servant announce one day that the Countess of Albany was at the door. 'Here was an honour which none but a Florentine could appreciate! . . . Madame d'Albany never paid visits to private individuals, never left her palace on the Arno, except for the English Ambassador's or the Grand Duke's.' At 2 o'clock she went to Fabre's studio to watch him painting, discuss art or chat with him. By 4 o'clock she was home again. At 6 she dined with Alfieri. She slept afterwards for an hour. If people visited her at 7, which was often the case, they might stay for two hours. At 9, if the pair were without company, they sometimes went to the theatre. After the theatre she and Alfieri would read together. Otherwise at half past 10 she went to bed.

And now it is high time that we should be introduced to Fabre who was to play such a prominent role in the joint lives of Alfieri and the Countess of Albany in Florence, and to become the Countess's inseparable companion until her death.

François-Xavier Fabre was born in 1766, the second son of a poor painter of faience in Montpellier. He began life as an under-scullion in the kitchen of the Marquis de Montferrier. The village curé was the first person to notice the boy's skill at drawing. The Marquis on being informed gave Fabre every encouragement and finally sent him at his expense to the École des Beaux Arts in Paris. Fabre continued his training as an apprentice in the studios of J. M. Vien, who was also a native of Montpellier, and J-L. David. At the age of eighteen the young Fabre received a subsidy to visit Italy. He was a grave, intensely serious youth. In Rome he attended the French Academy, and was patronised by the French Ambassador the Cardinal de Bernis, and the English Earl of Bristol, Bishop of Derry. Fabre's painting of 'Nebuchadnezar killing the sons of Sedecias under the eyes of their Father', a typical neo-classical subject, won him the Prix de Rome and brought him acclaim. In 1791 he was joined in Rome by his elder brother Henri who was a doctor, accompanied by their father and mother who had fled the French Revolution. The closely united Fabre family were old-fashioned legitimists. Together they lived for a time in great poverty in Rome. In 1793 François-Xavier, after a year's sojourn in Naples, drifted to Florence where he became a professor of fine arts at the university. One evening he happened to attend a performance of Alfieri's *Saul*. He was so impressed that on returning home he made a sketch of 'Saul tormented by remorse and believing he sees the ghost of Abimelech'. Alfieri on being informed of this work was flattered by the compliment. Within a few days the Earl-Bishop introduced his young protégé to the Casa Alfieri. The painter soon became a daily visitor. It was Alfieri who was the first attraction of the Lungarno, and Fabre sat at the poet's feet in a state of near adoration. His earnestness, intelligence and views on politics, art and life instantly appealed to the poet, who was usually churlish with admirers. His total dedication to painting which he believed to be the supreme art, transcending all other media leading to man's redemption, equally impressed the Countess, who was herself an amateur painter of some merit. She was also drawn to him by his infectious animation, idealism, and his good looks. For in his twenties Fabre's appearance was romantic. He had high cheek bones, large questioning yet dreamy eyes, and the melancholy mouth of a thinker. His sloping forehead and inordinately long nose had not yet grown out of all proportion to the finer features of his prepossessing face. Soon Fabre was joined in Florence by the rest of his family. The four of them lived together in perfect amity in a neighbouring street.

Henri became Alfieri's doctor upon whom the ailing patient became increasingly reliant.

Immediately after his introduction to the Casa Alfieri Fabre painted the pair of portraits of the Countess and the poet which now hang in the Uffizi Gallery. Louise is seated in an Empire bucket chair upholstered in red, her plump arms crossed and her hands holding a pair of gloves. She wears a striped skirt of heavy silk, a white linen blouse with fichu crossed over her breast. Round her shoulders is draped a yellow silk shawl with floral galloon border. Her greyish curly hair is tied with a thick blue bandeau. Under dark pencilled brows her eyes appear to be deep blue with black pupils. Her chin is firm and her jowl pronounced. She has smooth, fair skin and a small, delicate nose, which Henry Swinburne once described as 'pug-like'. Her mouth is disdainful and determined; the lips are slightly parted. On the back of the portrait is pasted a holograph sonnet addressed to Louise by Alfieri in which he praises her virtues undimmed since their first meeting. Below the sonnet he appended the words, 'Completed today, precisely two years after I saved her from the slaves, cannibals and assassins' of Paris, and the date 18 August 1794.

Alfieri is seated in a similar armchair. His open face is somewhat rugged, and his forehead puckered. He has thick, crinkly, red hair, grey at the roots and swept off the forehead. His eyebrows are red. The staring blue eyes protrude and the whites are very prominent. The long nose is well fashioned. There is a slight weakness about the corners of the mouth. The open neck is a little distended. The condition of eyes and neck suggest that he was suffering from thyroidal goitre. He wears a plain white linen shirt with pleated collar loose at the throat; and over the shirt an old blue coat with brass buttons. A brown cloak with scarlet lining is slung casually over one shoulder. A huge cameo ring is worn on the wedding finger of his left hand. The nails are cut square.

The pair of portraits were taken of the sitters, not dressed up in party clothes, but in everyday wear. And the sitters were delighted with the likenesses. Alfieri was also moved to address a sonnet to his portrait, to which it is appended. It begins: 'Sublime specchio di veraci detti' – sublime mirror of spoken truths, which shows me what I am bodily and spiritually. The poet lauds his fair complexion, azure eyes, frank countenance, straight nose, fine lips and faultless teeth, which incidentally are not shown, and his face paler than that of an enthroned king. He has the humour to refer to himself as constantly angry but never malignant, and to his mind and heart as being in perpetual conflict with each other. He ends with an invocation: 'Man, are you great or vile?' and the response, 'When you are dead, it will be known.' The looked-for postscript runs, 'Delivered two years ago today from the tyrannical French butchers,' and the date, 18 August 1794.

While Alfieri grew angrier and angrier with European events, more and more misanthropic, and more withdrawn in desperate endeavour to finish his autobiography, Fabre and the Countess were thrown more and more together.

There can be little doubt that as Alfieri's companionship receded from her, Fabre's to a certain extent took its place. Companionship turned to deep friendship and ended in a devotion between the couple of disparate ages, which has seldom been paralleled. Each loved the other most dearly, but all the evidence demonstrates that their liaison was platonic, and not physical. Whatever its nature, it was conducted with the utmost propriety. The story of Massimo d'Azeglio's aunt at a party in the Palazzo Masetti watching Fabre cast tender glances across the room at the Countess and kiss a ring on his finger, is probably a fabrication. Fabre was an exceedingly reserved young man and Louise hedged by circumspections. Certainly Fabre was inspired by Louise to work assiduously on the commissions which his friends in the Palazzo Masetti brought him. It is significant that neither after Alfieri's death nor after his brother Henry's in 1816, when both his parents were also dead, did Fabre leave his apartments on the *piano nobile* of no. 2117 via del Moro to move into Louise's house. He visited or was visited by her every evening. But he never presided at her *conversazioni* or table. He always treated her with a distant respect, at least when other persons were present.

The satisfactory tripartite relationship was temporarily interrupted by the events of 1799 when Alfieri and Louise were obliged to leave Florence on the approach of the French army. Just before Bonaparte's troops occupied the city in March the inhabitants of the Casa Alfieri moved to a villa outside the Porta San Gallo on the slopes of Montughi. There they remained until August, Alfieri fuming with rage against the French, Louise reading everything she could lay her hands on and sending presents of chocolate and gingerbread to Teresa in return for books. The Fabre family who were French and whose anti-Bonapartist views were well known, were obliged to go into hiding during these summer months. When the troops withdrew, the palace on the Lungarno was occupied once more, and the charmed circle reassembled.

Massimo d'Azeglio, artist, patriot and statesman provides an amusing glimpse of Alfieri's last years as seen through the eyes of a child. Born a Piedmontese aristocrat in 1798 Massimo was only four when he was painted by Fabre as the child Jesus seated naked on his mother's lap. The sitting took place in Fabre's studio where a terrible man in black with flaming red hair scooped back from the temples and forehead, with great clear eyes, knitted brows and a pallid face kept shouting at him, 'Ehi, Mammolino, stai fermo!' Keep still! He remembered being taken to the Casa Alfieri where Louise would listen to the child's recitations learned the previous week, and reward him with sweets according to his deserts. She remained in his memory a stout grey lady wearing a white fichu, who gave parties for children every Saturday evening. As an elderly man, Azeglio still recalled the round arched windows overlooking the Arno with steps leading to them, on which he sat eating an ice; and the two great canopies of white and gold suspended over Fabre's portraits of the couple, and the red morocco chairs in the *salotto*. The solitary Alfieri dwelt upstairs like an anchorite in his cell; and his descent was dreaded by the child. Azeglio affirmed that every evening at 9 o'clock Alfieri went out visiting an unknown French lady; that on returning from his nocturnal visit he would slam the front door loudly behind him. André Maurois believed that Alfieri was unfaithful to Louise towards the end of his life. He probably was – carnally.

With the turn of the century it was clear that Alfieri's health was failing. Louise wrote to Teresa Mocenni that she was haunted by the dread of losing him. 'I think with horror of the ultimate occasion. I do not pray to be the last, yet how can I wish the better half of myself to accept what I should never have the courage to bear? These are dreadful thoughts. I often have them in my mind. I even write verses on the subject in order to gain some relief in thus easing my soul.' Then came the day when the sick man said to her, 'My dear friend, if they do not make me well, we shall have to part.' By now there was no

Teresa on whom the unhappy Countess could unburden her fears. By 1803 Alfieri prepared himself, apparently willingly, for death. He told his friends he was going to die; he sent a message to the Abbate Caluso begging him to come to Louise's assistance. He rejected the remedies for his gout which Henri Fabre and the other doctors prescribed for him. Azeglio believed that just before his death he wished to be reconciled to the Church which all his life he had spurned. Who knows? At any rate there was no spoken reconciliation. A priest was sent for too late. He arrived in time to see Alfieri incline his head, which he mistook at first for a salutation. In fact it was the end. For sitting in his chair he expired, 'like a bird, without a sound . . . like a lamp which has run out of oil,' Louise wrote. He was fifty-four.

Chateaubriand had long cherished the wish to see Alfieri whom he, like many other contemporary writers, held in high esteem. His wish was to be gratified – once only. He was admitted to the death chamber, and gazed upon the face of his hero. He remarked afterwards that the dead man's head was crushed upon his breast because the coffin, in which he was laid, was too short for the corpse. The attitude gave him a stunted and macabre appearance. Chateaubriand turned away, sad and disenchanted.

VII

ROYAL BLUE-STOCKING

The faithful Fabre, who in 1803 was aged twenty-nine, stood at Louise's side throughout the whole agonizing experience. And he alone was able to provide comfort. He was never to leave her for the remaining twenty-one years of her life. Louise was overwhelmed by grief. There can be no question of that whatever. Her letters to Luti leave no room for doubt, even though she did tend to dramatize her sufferings in a manner which we, who have learned from a non-stop concatenation of wars, slaughters and disasters that others quickly tire of our wailings, no longer give rein to. In her day people of social standing could presumably spare the time to enlist and enjoy a prescriptive sympathy. Louise wished she had the courage to commit suicide. She was absolutely certain that life had no compensations in store for her. The good Abbate Caluso, who was Alfieri's best surviving friend, hastened from Turin, as the poet had bidden him, to fortify the bereaved Countess and to put the deceased's papers in order. When Caluso's job was done Alfieri's keys were handed over to Fabre.

Vernon Lee's assumption which, derived from Stendhal and Capponi, has been reiterated by subsequent biographers, that at the end of the poet's life the two old lovers were indifferent to each other, is rubbish. As for Fabre, he was so upset by the loss of his friend that for six months he could not settle down to work. No one knew better than he what the exact relation of the lovers had been. It was that of man and mistress. He strenuously denied that they had ever been married. 'I have their wills,' he said succinctly years later.

Louise, with Fabre's active assistance lost no time in making arrangements for a memorial to Alfieri in the church of Santa Croce.

In this Tuscan pantheon many of Italy's illustrious dead already lay. First of all Louise had to battle with the clergy, who were opposed to any commemoration within its sanctified walls of a well-known scoffer of Holy Church. But she triumphed to the extent of acquiring a site for her poet's monument between those of Dante and Macchiavelli, and one away from Michelangelo's. Next she approached Canova, the most renowed sculptor in Italy, and probably in Europe at that time. Canova's accounts show that in 1804 the Countess pledged herself to pay him 8,000 écus for the execution in marble of a monument after a model to be submitted. Thereafter several letters passed between Canova and Fabre on the subject. It was not until the winter of 1811 that Louise saw the completed tomb. 'It is very grandiose within being gigantic,' she wrote. It certainly is. The sarcophagus stands on solid legs. A cornucopia is thrown at the feet of mourning Italy. The acroteria of the sarcophagus are formed of the masks of tragedy. The poet's handsome bas-relief profile with curls falling down the nape of the neck, the floral swags of the podium, and the laurel wreaths of the socle are finely carved. So too at either end of the sarcophagus is the unstrung harp in relief. The long and laudatory epitaph which Louise composed was not inscribed. Instead the words, 'Victorio Alferio Astensi Alisa e Principibus Stolbergis Albaniae Comitissa MPC An MDCCCX' indissolubly link their names together for all posterity to read.

Louise's attitude to Canova in regard to his art and personality was equivocal. She must have regarded him as the greatest sculptor available or she would not have chosen him, for she certainly did not stint herself in raising the most extravagant monument to the poet which her limited means allowed. When she and Fabre were in Rome in 1811 they went to St Peter's early one morning, 'to pay tribute to that beautiful residence of the Almighty,' as she expressed it. She was not enchanted with Canova's enormous monument to Clement XIII, in which the Rezzonico pope is made to kneel upon a sarcophagus flanked by allegorical figures of Religion and Death, each poised over a growling and a sleeping lion. She complained that the figure of Religion was 'foreshortened without dignity', and that the lions wore the same expressions as the pope. It is true that the docile beast does somewhat resemble the praying pontiff. They also visited the sculptor's studio, where she found that he had greatly increased his forest of statues since she was last there. He had done too many, she opined, so that his style had become mannered. She thought Canova was too pleased with himself. He was so accustomed to praise that he would brook no criticism. He resembled a king who must receive homage. She remarked, 'I have also seen the tomb of my husband and my brother-in-law which are put in the subterranean church.' There is no further comment. We can imagine what memories were stirred as she gazed upon their simple sarcophagus in the crypt, for Canova's masterpiece to the memory of the three uncrowned Stuart kings in the south aisle of the church above had not yet been set up. Louise was not given to sentiment, but she was a woman of sensibility. Were feelings of revulsion or pity aroused as she stood before the gathered remains of the husband who had ruined her youth, altered her character from one of carefree enjoyment to crabbed cynicism, and the brother-in-law who, by virtue of his elevated position in the hierarchy, so harassed her that she was prevented from living openly with the only man in the world whom she adored?

Alfieri's death aged Louise. She was over fifty at the time. For the remainder of the year 1803 she rarely went out and saw few friends. Only Fabre was in regular attendance. But shut up in her library she read more than ever before. She discovered 'Scheasper' as she called him, and was transported. The sudden revelation of Shakespeare to a widely read and intelligent person of middle age is not without interest. 'He is extraordinary . . . This author is one of the prodigies of nature,' she exclaimed delightedly. Whereas 'with Milton you have to pick your way through the thorns to reach the roses,' with Shakespeare it is roses all the way. 'His situations are always true and his characters sustained; the more I read, the more I am astonished.' Yet even roses are prone to greenfly and blackspot. 'Besides faults of the most blatant sort [Shakespeare] has beauties comparable with Homer.' He struck her like most French-educated foreigners brought up on the polished prosody of Racine, as slightly barbarous. His genius lacked art. Every rift was not sufficiently loaded with ore. And again she said, 'The style is very singular. He often plays on words with different meanings.' The English writer's addiction to punning is after all a national conceit. Nevertheless Shakespeare came to the Countess as an unsolicited solace in her mourning.

She did not have the same regard for Byron's verse. Cornelia

Knight, that 'vieille miss authoress et déja touriste-Cook' as one writer described her, had recommended her notorious countryman as a 'poet, truly a poet. His principles are perhaps less bad than his manner of expressing them is shocking. It is a pity that his writings lack design; that everything is in disorder.' How Byron would have resented Miss Knight's criticism! And how he would have enjoyed snubbing her! Louise however, less readily shocked by an author's principles, agreed that Byron was wicked right enough. But what displeased her more was the ambiguity of his poetical style. She failed to appreciate or understand his breathless, slapdash phrases, his topical allusions and his slang. His message for her was far from clear. Besides he revived archaic words and expressions used by Spenser and the Elizabethans. In other words the Countess of Albany's grasp of the English language was none too good. As for Sir Walter Scott's prose, it was easy enough to understand. But what she called the sentimental twaddle of the novels infuriated her.

Madame de Staël was the first person to take Louise out of herself after the bereavement of 1803. Rather she descended upon the Casa Alfieri like a tornado, burst open the windows and doors of the fusty house of mourning, thoroughly aired it with the sirocco wind of her overheated presence, and, in the way of tornadoes dragged the Countess up by the roots and deposited her on the pavement. Thence Louise was fairly obliged to look upon the outside world and take note of its inhabitants. One of these was her old beau Bonstetten who had actually introduced the two women by letter. Less ridiculous than formerly the gilded lad was now an obese elder statesman and widower, still vain, still on the crest of every wave, still bubbling with chat about the great personages all over Europe with whom he corresponded or hobnobbed. Lady Morgan described him in his old age as 'an old darling, fresh, frisky and full of agreeable conversation'. He wrote to Louise on intimate terms, now that Alfieri was out of the way: 'If pleasure has rejuvenated my person as it has rejuvenated my heart, you will find me just as I was in days gone by, so eagerly am I running to see you again.' In due course he called at the Casa Alfieri. It was 1807. Alas! 'I saw the one whom I had left like an opening rosebud,' he wrote, 'now scarcely recognizable.'

'How thankful I was the twilight darkened the room, for though it was still her voice and, in some degrees, her expression, all that remained of her beyond this was an old woman, whom in my heart I accused of having taken the place by magic of the one I had left in Rome. My first thought on reaching home was to look in the glass to see to what extent I myself had changed.'

He would of course do just that. And his reaction was just what one would expect. 'I was surprised to find I did not look horrible at all.' The Countess has left no record of the impression Bonstetten made upon her. But she did write on another occasion, 'Les revenants font de grand bêtises!' In spite of his disillusion Bonstetten continued to send her affectionate letters and even protested that if only he were rich enough he would take a house in her street so as to be able to see her every day.

Germaine de Staël may have been right in supposing that Fabre's excessive solicitude fostered the Countess's grief, which she interpreted as remorse. Louise did not relish the supposition when she got to hear of it. Indeed she never relished Madame de Staël, in whom the only thing she easily tolerated was her genuine reverence for Alfieri.

In all respects Madame d'Albany and Madame de Staël were opposites. Louise, who was the elder, was reactionary, cautious, circumspect and cynical. Germaine, the younger, was advanced, imprudent, indiscreet and starry-eyed. Louise favoured autocracy, and Germaine professed to be a radical in politics. Yet they shared a common detestation of Napoleon for different reasons. Louise's disapproval was directed against the tyrant who had supplanted the legitimist line of Bourbon kings; Germaine's disenchantment was brought about by his failure to maintain the democratic constitution introduced by the revolutionaries. Yet she was wildly inconsistent. Her professed republicanism did not prevent her addressing her friend as 'dear Majesty', 'dear Queen', or 'my dear Sovereign'. She fairly gushed over her royal status. In 1816 she told the Countess, 'The Duchess of Devonshire writes to me that she prefers you to Princess Charlotte [the daughter of England's Prince Regent]. At this moment of legitimism, couldn't you get yourself re-made Queen of England? I kiss your hands in sign of loyalty.' And in 1817 she wrote from Paris that she had discussed with the British Ambassador whether Louise ought to become a British subject in order to apply for a pension from the state! On the whole she counselled her friend against doing so on the grounds that she was too great a lady and would thereby be demeaning herself. Her intentions were perhaps well meant, but her interference was officious.

As it happened Louise was by now enjoying a pension from George III. Perhaps she had not disclosed this fact to her inquisitive friend. Louise was never one to scruple to ask for what she wanted. As long ago as 30 January 1805 she had boldly written to Sir John Coxe Hippisley, whom she knew to have been responsible for obtaining a pension for the Cardinal of York in 1800. She told him unequivocally that she too was in financial straits. Her allowance from her brother-in-law was not to be depended upon, 'because this prince who is good, and incapable of suspicion, lets himself be governed by priests whose interest it is to deceive him.' In any case he was now a very old man who must soon die. In which event her allowance from him would cease. And where would she be then? She implored Sir John to put her needs before George III and ask the Prince of Wales for his intercession. The callous tenor of the letter was hardly calculated to appeal to an admirer of the old Cardinal. But Hippisley who was a kindly man and sympathetic to the whole Stuart family, did as she requested. He did not meet with an immediate response. Louise then wrote a begging letter direct to George III. She complained that her brother-in-law's attendants in order to better their own fortunes were alienating the Cardinal's affections from her. Still no response. She also wrote to the Prince of Wales.

On 7 March 1807 she returned to the attack on Hippisley. She pretended that she was sixty. She was in fact fifty-five. She said that the Cardinal was now in his second childhood, and surrounded by people 'qui le dévorent'. She pointed out her kinship with Hippisley through his first wife who was now dead. She confided in him that her total income amounted to the equivalent of £800 sterling a year. Hippisley conscientiously forwarded this letter through the proper channel to the British government. The Foreign Secretary wrote back that he was not prepared to recommend further demands upon His Majesty's generosity to the Stuarts. But George III on learning of the Cardinal's death a few months later agreed to let the Countess of Albany have £1600 a year for life.

By 1807 Louise actually admitted to having cast off mourning, to being free from financial anxieties and content with her lot, which was that of a widow who has come to terms with what remains of her span. In 1809 the smooth course of intellectual exchanges on the Lungarno was rudely interrupted. From Napoleon, that storm cloud brooding over the European scene and threatening to burst at any moment, came a warning. The Countess of Albany's *salon* in Florence was a hotbed of disaffected anti-Bonapartist agents. The Emperor was aware in which direction the Countess's political sympathies lay. The lightning flickered. Let her check her enthusiasms which were disobliging to him, and learn to control her tongue. The Countess paid no heed. So, like Zeus the Emperor struck. He commanded her to come to Paris. And she duly went to that 'cloaca maxima', as Alfieri called it, accompanied by Fabre. Lest it be asked why she obeyed the summons, we must bear in mind that two years previously Tuscany had been ceded to France, and was now ruled by Napoleon's sister, Elisa, as Grand Duchess. Louise therefore had no option but to obey. In Paris she had an interview with the Emperor; and it seems that the Countess came out of the encounter unscathed. Napoleon began by accusing her of making bad blood in Florence, but was left satisfied that she had no taste for serious political intrigue and could be of little menace on the distant Arno. She behaved throughout the interview with dignity and good humour. Napoleon asked her outright whether she had ever had a son by Princes Charles. On being assured that she had not, he said it was a pity. If there had been a young Stuart prince he would have put him on the throne of Britain. Evidently 120 years after James II's expulsion from Whitehall the Stuarts were still a dynasty to be reckoned with. Louise may on this sole occasion have regretted that she had not produced an heir. Only ten years previously she had told Teresa Mocenni she rejoiced that she was childless: 'Si j'avais des enfans, j'en deviendrois folle; hereusement de ce côté; j'ai été heureuse.' She was obliged to dawdle in Paris a year. In October 1810 Napoleon allowed her to return to Florence. That Louise had aroused an interest in him is suggested by Napoleon asking Madame de Souza the following year to press for her voluntary return to Paris.

She was forced to admit to Sismondi that the Emperor had treated her affably. With Jean Charles Léonard de Sismondi the Countess was now carrying on a lengthy correspondence which was to continue right up to her death. She had first met this stocky, middle-class, old-young Swiss with an incisive mind, when he was travelling in the suite of Madame de Staël on her famous Italian journey. Sismondi quickly transferred his somewhat equivocal affection for Madame de Staël to her friend. Publication in 1807 of his first volume of the *Italian Republics of the Middle Ages* placed Sismondi in the front rank of European historians. The Countess entered into her new friend's literary and domestic problems with zest. He had a doting and possessive mother; and when she was dead and buried a doting but submissive English wife, Jessie. Historian and ex-Queen enjoyed exchanging opinions on peoples and personalities. Thus Louise wrote to Sismondi that the Italian upper classes, 'think only of love or foolishness, and have no sensible ideas about anything'. The correspondents analysed each other's character. Of herself Louise confided to Sismondi, 'My only merit is to have judgment and good sense. I do not flatter myself by claiming to have wit and the sparkle which goes with it.' Sismondi told her that his loyalties were to principles, hers were to persons; that whereas she was always looking back at the past he was looking forward to the future. Indeed this difference was to be an ultimate cause of disagreement between them.

Their letters are however mostly concerned with the political events of the day. Louise renewed her detestation of Bonapartism, notwithstanding the manner of her reception by the tyrant in Paris. It was not shared by Sismondi, who would not subscribe to his friend's reactionary views. 'You always look the world up and down when you pass judgment,' he scolded her. His own views were frankly radical. And when in 1816 he dared to be reconciled to Bonapartism she was extremely angry. Nevertheless she forgave him because his motives, unlike those of some of her friends, such as Ugo Foscolo, were genuine. The correspondence was resumed amicably, although on a lower key than hitherto.

Her friendship with Ugo Foscolo ran less smoothly. But then it was founded on an emotional basis. This young Dalmatian poet first swam into her orbit in 1812 when he was thirty-four. As a boy he had moved with his parents to Venetia which henceforth he regarded as his country. He supported Venice's political struggle against Austria, to which Napoleon had handed over the city and province in 1797, in the light of a holy crusade. He even fought with the French against the Austrians at the battle of Trebbia and in the siege of Genoa, where he was wounded and taken prisoner. He cherished the belief that Napoleon might see the error of his ways and help to retrieve Venice's independence. Disillusioned with the conqueror of Europe he wrote a tragedy, *Ajax* in which he made unfavourable allusions to Napoleon. After the play's unsuccessful performance in Milan Foscolo was obliged to leave for Tuscany. In Florence he composed another tragedy, *Ricciarda*, and made the acquaintance of the Countess of Albany.

Whereas Sismondi was a straightforward liberal, Foscolo was a revolutionary. As such it might be supposed that he would not appeal to the Countess. It is true that that side of him did not. But he was also a romantic. He saw himself as a Yorick who at every turn meets with adventure and love; he actually began a translation into Italian of Sterne's *Sentimental Journey*. Furthermore he was endowed with physical attraction, at any rate before he reached middle age. He had a thick hedge of curly hair, a slightly retroussé nose, a puckered brow, deep-set fiery eyes under flame-like brows, and the most ridiculous cupid-bow mouth several sizes too large for his face. He was very well satisfied with his appearance, judging from the sonnet which like Alfieri he addressed to his portrait – 'Capo chino, bel collo e largo petto / Giuste membra, vestir semplice eletto,' and so forth. He was perpetually in love, and women found him irresistible. In spite of her disclaimers Louise was in her old age susceptible to youth and fervour. Besides in a way Foscolo reminded her of Alfieri, whom he affected to resemble in his air if not appearance, in his temperament and addiction to tragedies. Soon however Louise found his resemblance to Alfieri counterfeit. His inordinate vanity and courtship of notoriety amused before it irritated her. Quite soon after their first meeting she was addressing him as 'Cher Ugo', a familiarity which might suggest very close intimacy. In this case it meant no more than what it was, the unrequited infatuation of an older woman for a provocative younger member of her circle. And the Countess's cosmopolitan circle was, contrasted with the narrow Florentine society, unconventional and *avant garde*.

When Foscolo returned to Milan in 1813 he was showered with letters from the Countess which he countered with his own. A tender correspondence ensued until Napoleon escaped from Elba in 1815. Whereupon Foscolo, declaring political inconsistency to be the better part of valour, fled to Switzerland rather than fight with his old foes the Austrians against the tyrant of Europe. Louise was infuriated. She wrote him a scathing letter about his dishonourable conduct. He replied lamely. The Countess read 'cher Ugo's' letter to all and sundry, making mock of his excuses. In 1816 Foscolo moved to England, where he lived and died eleven years later.

Louise's attitude to Napoleon was more than a legacy from Alfieri. If his loathing of the French people had been partly attributable to their indifference to his poetic fame, hers of Bonaparte was motivated by royalty's engrained fear of the demagogue. Not for nothing was she the dowager of a rightful King of England. Her short and inglorious marriage to Prince Charles coincided with the most impressionable years of her youth. During this period she imbibed her husband's implicit faith in the divine right of kings, however much she may at the time have proclaimed the doctrine absurdly out of date. It often happens that old people grow to accept the beliefs which, when formerly expounded by their seniors in age, they spurned. Louise also developed the ineradicable prejudices of the exile. In her later years she certainly saw herself first and foremost as the holder of an intellectual *salon* at which the greatest minds of Europe gathered. She despised the empty heads of society good-timers. But she remained queen enough to despise even more, and hate as well with all the depth of her being, the parvenu usurper. Her instincts being conservative her sympathies were with the old established orders that had stood the test of time, the monarchical constitutions of Bourbon and Stuart, under which the arts, literature and civilized living sheltered and flourished.

What the Countess of Albany in her old age enjoyed most of all was corresponding with younger people who shared her old-fashioned views. And after the death of Teresa Mocenni the woman who took her supreme place was Adelaide-Marie, Marquise de Souza. She was born in 1761, and was said to have been fathered by Louis XV. She first met Louise in Paris with Alfieri between 1787 and 1790. In those years she was married to the Comte de Flahaut, a man considerably her senior in years. She established in Paris a *salon* of which the brightest ornament was Talleyrand. Madame de Flahaut's tribulations during the Terror helped to forge a strong bond with Louise. When the Revolution broke out she fled with her young son Charles (who incidentally was Talleyrand's son also), to Germany and England. Her husband was captured and guillotined. Madame de Flahaut was obliged to earn a living. In Hamburg she worked as a milliner. She then turned to writing, and her first novel, *Adèle de Sénage* was published in 1794. In 1802 she married the Portuguese Minister in Paris, the Marquis de Souza-Botelho, a highly cultivated man and a devoted husband. Later novels followed – *Émilie et Alphonse, Charles et Marie, Eugène de Rothelin* and *La Comtesse de Fargy*. They were extremely popular and brought Adelaide-Marie wide acclaim.

By 1805 the Souzas were permanently settled in Paris where they had a host of friends, including Sismondi. After Alfieri's death when the Countess of Albany was in Paris with Fabre in 1809, the old friendship was renewed after seventeen years. It quickly ripened into deep affection. The younger woman looked upon the elder almost as a mother to whom she turned for advice. Probably no one understood Louise's contradictory nature better than she. Madame de Souza made allowances for Madame d'Albany's uncertain temper because of the trials and disappointments which her married life had brought upon her. Her humours, she said, fell from her at a shrug of the shoulders, and were not to be heeded. The elder sought and received sympathy from the younger who urged her to return to Paris and even live in her house. As for Charles de Flahaut, Louise treated him as though he were her son, and was unsparing with her advice. This extremely handsome and engaging young man, spoilt and adored by the two women, was often in need of it. He got it whether he wanted it or not. Before Charles came of age he was involved in a passionate affair with the Countess Potocka in Warsaw. The affair was followed by another with Queen Hortense of Holland by whom he became the father of the Duc de Morny. But what caused Louise greater concern and displeasure was the young man's consenting to serve under Napoleon. In the circumstances a junior French officer with ambitions could hardly be expected to do anything else. The imputations which Louise levelled against Charles's honour were resented by the young Comte de Flahaut and his mother, and were the cause of a temporary coldness between the two women. 'How can you, how can you tell me,' Madame de Souza expostulated with her friend in 1815, 'that I have overlooked the conquests [of Napoleon] because I see in them the means of promotion and money for my son?'

But there was no permanent estrangement. Charles de Flahaut not only continued to write to but visited Louise when he was in Florence. Adelaide-Marie remained on most loving terms with her. She was also genuinely attached to Fabre, whom she frequently addressed by postscript in her letters to Louise. In 1811 she had begged him to paint for her a picture of the Countess visiting the tomb of Alfieri by torchlight. The idea did not materialize. Next she asked for a straightforward portrait of Louise; she insisted that she must be wearing a respectable hat, and not the dreadful old bonnet which she was accustomed to clamp on her head in the mornings. Did not Fabre agree that the Countess paid too little attention to her clothes? The portrait was evidently done and sent to Adelaide-Marie. After the couple's visit to Paris in 1809–10 the friends met only once again. For thirteen years Madame de Souza kept pressing her to come and live in Paris for good. She longed to show her friend her pictures and her beloved roses in the garden. 'Leave!' she enjoined her. 'Have you left? Come! Arrive!' In May of 1822 Fabre took her to Paris on a flying visit. The main objective was to extract a pension from the new French government of Louis XVIII. In this endeavour she was to be disappointed. She was treated by the court with deference, but granted no money. Madame de Souza however welcomed her with wide open arms, and was miserable when she left. Only a month before Louise's death she wrote, 'I would far rather see come into my room that serene face, those laughing eyes than all the pictures of Raphael.'

Towards the end of her life the Countess of Albany was a legend. As an historic link with the past she was revered. Bonnie Prince Charlie's widow, the daughter-in-law of the Old Chevalier who had been born Prince of Wales in St James's Palace in 1688, was still living in Florence in the 1820s. She was to survive Keats and Shelley and to die a few months only before Byron. Her house on the Lungarno, the last home of the famous Vittorio Alfieri, was a place of pilgrimage. Now that he was dead Alfieri's tragedies were having a tremendous posthumous success. And the woman, a queen of sorts, who had inspired the best of them could still be seen and actually spoken to. Curiously enough, it was the French who now appreciated her most. Lamartine was among those who found her enchanting. He was fascinated by her conversational powers, the asperity of her wit – a trait preeminently appreciated by his compatriots, an attribute be it remembered which she had denied to herself – and her reminiscences. He remarked that talk in the Casa Alfieri was like a dialogue with the dead rather than the living. He was no less critical of her physical appearance than Stendhal and Chateaubriand had been. 'A little woman, whose figure, collapsed under her weight, had lost all lightness and all elegance,' he wrote. Nevertheless, although she retained no traces of beauty, or even majesty – this was in 1810 – 'her eyes had a sparkle, her grey hairs a freshness, her mouth a welcome, her whole countenance an intelligence and a graceful expression' which put people in mind of the time when she was so greatly admired. Her gentle voice, her unaffected manners, her reassuring friendliness immediately raised those who came in contact with her to her own level. One really did not know whether she descended to yours, or if you were raised to hers, her whole personality was so natural.'

To be sure very many English travellers attended her *salon* out of curiosity. On the whole they did not write about her with enthusiasm. Most of them were Whigs, or partisan to the old Whig prejudice against the Stuarts. And nearly all of them were frightened of her learning and her tongue. For her part she found few English people likeable. Lady Holland, for instance, was embarrassingly egotistical. Elizabeth Duchess of Devonshire considered herself more of an antiquarian than she was. Louise enjoyed the company of Sir Humphrey Davy and his lady because she could admire him for his genius in chemistry, and her for her cosmopolitanism. Cornelia Knight she also liked, for 'Miss' had been brought up in French-speaking society. She complained that the English did not shine in society like the French. When abroad they consorted with each other, dined late and drank to excess. They might just as well have stayed at home for all the advantages they derived from foreign travel. They had no graces and little gaiety. Worst of all, they despised foreigners who possessed the superior qualities which they lacked. In short she preferred reading English books to listening to English people, except in Parliament, where, she conceded, they deployed their rhetorical talent skilfully.

For their part the English found her haughty and moody. They commented upon her bold, outspoken manner. For she did not care what she said in company, and often did not stop to think before she spoke. She might flatly contradict what she had maintained with emphasis only a minute before. Certainly she could be formidable, and caustic at the expense of ill-bred people. Azeglio related how, on two of his student companions following him to her house after the theatre late one evening, and being presented to her, she turned to a neighbour and remarked loudly in their hearing, 'What a time for these young men to arrive!' Azeglio then himself a young man, feeling in some way responsible for their behaviour, was covered with confusion. In his shyness he proceeded to blot his own copybook. Rashly he took from the footman a 'mattonella', which was a species of ice, round like a cricket ball and just as hard. Holding the object in a saucer in one hand, he attacked it, while standing up, with a spoon in the other. The 'mattonella' shot across the room, hit the Sardinian Minister a blow on his cordoned chest, and ricocheted to the feet of his hostess. She was not amused, and made no comment. Her silence was as glacial as the 'mattonella'. Azeglio was not invited to the house again.

Henry Matthews happening to be in Florence when news of Princess Charlotte of Wales's death reached the English colony was shocked that Louise gave a party the very next day. 'She was almost the only person out of mourning,' he wrote. 'This was to say the least of it, bad taste. If there is no alliance of blood, there is a pecuniary relationship.' Here the diarist hit the nail on the head. He was of course referring to the £1600 a year pension, half of what the Cardinal King had been paid, which she was now receiving from Princess Charlotte's grandfather. Lord William Russell, having attended one of her weekly *salons*, called her 'a cross, ill-natured old cat, speaking ill of everybody. Her house was crowded with vulgar English, and the rooms so small that it was very disagreeable.' It is true that the apartments of the Casa Alfieri must have seemed poky after the reception rooms at Woburn. And there would have been something preposterous to Lord William in the elderly, frumpily clad blue-stocking seated bolt upright in a chair of state like a sovereign, greeting her guests with a slight bow, and only half rising to women of equal rank to her own.

Apart from spending the summer of 1811 at the Baths of Lucca for the benefit of Fabre's gout of which he was a chronic sufferer, the ensuing winter in Rome, and the spring of 1812 in Naples with her sister, the Contessa di Castelfranco (with a visit to St Peter's in Rome on the way south) Louise scarcely left Florence for ten years running. At the height of the summer heats she might go to Leghorn for a week or two at most. The 1822 excursion to Paris was undertaken with much reluctance for what may be termed business reasons. 'Old Madame d'Albany is gone to Paris,' wrote Lord William Russell. 'She is grown so cross that every body was glad to get rid of her.' In 1823 she returned to Florence by way of Montpellier. The purpose of a week's stop at Fabre's birthplace was to ascertain whether Louise should leave Alfieri's manuscripts and books, and Fabre his collection of pictures and other works of art, including many of his own paintings, to the city of his origin.

Louise's letters of 1823 indicate that her health was failing. She was by now over seventy. Those rapid summer walks along the Arno before 7 in the morning, her floppy straw-hat tied under the chin with a broad ribbon, and a shawl thrown carelessly over the shoulders, were activities of the past. She was far too bronchial and breathless nowadays. Madame de Souza wrote recommending snuff to relieve her catarrh. But this was the least of her afflictions. She was assailed by dropsy, by revulsion from food, by unquenchable thirst, by fevers and numerous symptoms of mortality. In her last illness she turned, as people are wont to do, to her nearest of kin. She wrote piteous letters to her unmarried sister Gustavine who was living with their mother, still alive at ninety, and who detested the Princess Stolberg-Gedern as heartily as Louise did. Gustavine replied full of solicitude. She declared that Louise, whom she had barely seen these fifty years past, was her virtual mother, whereas her real mother was an old intriguer whose sole interest was ordering new dresses and trying them on before a looking-glass. The 'old intriguer' was to survive her eldest daughter by four years.

Attended by the ever faithful Fabre the Countess of Albany died, fortified it is said by the rites of the Church which all her life she had ignored. At any rate having prefaced her will (drawn up in Florence in

1817) in surrendering her soul to 'the omnipotence of the Almighty and St Louis of France [and] beseeching them to assist me in my last dwelling place,' she arranged for fifty Masses to be said for her salvation. She was buried in the Cappella Castellani in Santa Croce church as near as could be to Alfieri's monument, in accordance with her expressed wishes. Either to avoid scandal or, which is more probable, in deference to her poet-lover's solitary genius, she did not give directions for her corpse to lie with his in the same vault.

So great was the crowd assembled to witness the Countess of Albany's funeral obsequies that the police had to be called to control it. Fabre took immense pains to raise a worthy monument over her remains. He consulted the Florentine painter Pietro Benvenuti, who sent him an outline sketch for a tomb, and corresponded with the Comte de Cambray-Digny* before deciding what exact form the memorial should take. He decided that the laudatory epitaph which Alfieri had composed for her was too long, and had an abbreviated version inscribed: 'Genere. Forma. Moribus. Incomparabili. Animi. Candore Praeclarissima . . .' The words of the glowing, loving tribute are the poet's own. Finally at a cost to himself of 10,980 lire Fabre had a monument erected by the French architect, Charles Percier. The design of a tabernacle harking back to the Renaissance is over-contrived and uninspired, although the opulent detail is finely executed. Louise had just outlived the age of Neo-classical purity of which Canova was the master, and reached that of the halting nineteenth-century eclecticism. The sculptors employed upon the tomb were the Florentines Luigi Giovanozzi and Emilio Santarelli, who carved the two *putti* and the bas-relief of Charity and Hope attending Religion. Santarelli was at the time a young man of twenty-three, and may well have been Fabre's son. Fabre almost certainly kept a mistress in Florence; and he bequeathed his free fortune to Santarelli, including a portrait of Prince Charles and his seal.

In her will Louise bequeathed a porcelain breakfast service and a silver coffee service to each of her married sisters, Caroline di Castelfranco and Françoise d'Arberg; and to her unmarried sister Gustavine Stolberg 15,000 écus. To her nephew the 6th Duke of

* The son of a French financier he gave his life to the study of the arts and architecture. He was made Director-General of Historic Buildings in Tuscany.

Berwick, who also happened to be a descendant of James II, she left a cameo portrait of her husband and a miniature of Mary Queen of Scots; to the Conte di Marino the bust by Bartolini of his uncle the Abbate Caluso, whom she called her 'father by adoption', having known him as the valued friend of Alfieri since he first stayed with her in the Palazzo Guadagni in 1779; and to Cardinal Consalvi a picture by Fabre of St Jerome at prayer. In the will she bequeathed to the grand ducal palace in Florence the pair of portraits which Fabre had painted of Alfieri and herself as well as Fabre's large landscape of the death of Marius. For some unexplained reason – perhaps resulting from the visit to Montpellier in 1823 – a codicil cancelled this last direction. Finally, she generously pensioned her servants according to the years of their employment in her household.

To Fabre she bequeathed absolutely her houses,* furniture, pictures, statuary, silver, jewelry, manuscripts and all curiosities collected by Alfieri and herself. In a clause of the will she recorded her deep gratitude to Fabre for his unfailing attachment of twenty-four years and his unwearied attentions, whatever her circumstances, ever since she was deprived of her incomparable Alfieri. In case of any ambiguity in the drafting of her will she wished it to be clearly understood that the interpretation of her wishes must be left for him to determine. Needless to say Fabre took infinite pains to fulfil his dear friend's every wish. He committed all Alfieri's manuscripts to the Laurentian Library. He informed the director of the Uffizi that he felt bound in honour to offer the pair of portraits of Louise and Alfieri to the gallery in spite of the unexplained codicil, but not the landscape which he would take to Montpellier. In his home town, whither he repaired at the end of a ten months' period of packing the treasures and disposing of the Countess's palace and surplus furniture, Fabre lived, painted and went on collecting for the rest of his days. He was a discerning connoisseur and managed to acquire paintings by Poussin, whose landscapes he copied, Gaspard Dughet, Carlo Dolci, Guido Reni, and his contemporaries, including David and Géricault. He became a highly respected citizen of the town. His offer of Louise's treasures and his own was accepted in 1825 by the municipality which bought the Maison Massilian in which to house them. In 1828

* By which presumably the two palazzine Masetti and Gianfigliazzi, joined together, are meant.

Fabre was created a baron by Charles X. The same year the museum in Montpellier was officially opened and Fabre was made the first director. He died full of honours in 1837, denying to the day of his death that either Alfieri or he had been married to the Countess.

Notwithstanding Fabre's determination faithfully to preserve Alfieri and Louise's papers, he was indirectly responsible for the loss of the most important of them. It happened that when the Museum was opened in 1828 a certain Monsieur L. A. Gache saluted the city's benefactor with a highly commendatory poem in Latin. The recipient of these unsolicited verses was not unnaturally flattered. Monsieur Gache proceeded to ingratiate himself with the director to the extent of being nominated Fabre's sole literary executor. The man was a deep dyed Jansenist of narrow views. He took it upon himself to destroy all the intimate correspondence of Alfieri, Louise and Fabre. Years later he boasted to Saint-René Taillandier, the Countess of Albany's French biographer, that he had burnt all 'les lettres passionées' in the collection, as well as all letters from Madame de Staël, Madame de Genlis, Ugo Foscolo and others which had the smallest bearing upon their private lives. On the contrary he spared the briefest and least interesting notes conveying polite acceptances or refusals of invitations which were autographed by distinguished persons. In consequence not a single love letter to and from Alfieri and Louise, so deeply cherished by the recipients, or a letter of any character whatever between Fabre and Louise has survived to enable us to assess their exact relations one with another. This is a matter for deep regret, for whatever our opinion of the Countess of Albany's character may be, she inspired love and stoked the fires of creation in two outstanding men, besides fanning the flames in several others. 'You, madame,' wrote Sismondi, 'who have experienced all the storms of passion.' Yes indeed, she must have agreed, for did she not confess to another friend, Alessandro Cerretani,* that she knew no torments worse than love? The officious service which Monsieur Gache (he could not possibly be more appropriately named) had the effrontery to render to the memory of these famous figures in history, has deprived posterity of the complete story of a fascinating triad.

* Styled Il Cavaliere Cerretani, Treasurer of Siena University, an intimate friend of the Archpriest Luti and a member of the Siena circle. He first came into the Countess of Albany's life in 1804.

Monsieur Gache's holocaust went far beyond Fabre's expressed conviction that 'certain secrets of the heart should not be given to the public'.

The Countess of Albany's death took place on 29 January, a month which had closed the eyes of Prince Charles and his father, the Chevalier of St George. It was the eve of the anniversary of King Charles I's execution, which had happened precisely 175 years previously. That event deeply coloured the destinies of his legitimate descendants. In a sense it may have determined them, for there is little doubt that bad luck, or rather a tendency to it, can like drink and venereal disease be transmitted through families. The legendary evil fate which attaches itself mercilessly to fathers, sons, and grandsons will develop its particular tribulations for each in turn. The exiled Stuarts reacted in different ways to their successive misfortune. Unhappily misfortune seldom improves a person's character. Only that rare phenomenon a saint positively thrives upon it. The near-saint may be driven to seek solace in the periphery of God's communion without necessarily penetrating the inner sanctum. The off-saint may be driven to the bottle. The sombre mantle of the dynasty fell upon the Countess of Albany although she was not a Stuart by blood. She accepted it in her own uncompromising fashion. She chose to triumph over her lot by cultivating the society of men who were her intellectual superiors, and devoting her gifts to fostering the genius of others. Of the members of this sad family, who since 1688 were destined to eke out their long lives in exile, she alone would have earned a niche, for what that is worth, in the temple of fame, not by virtue of rank but of mind.

APPENDIX

As I have already indicated nothing is known about the two daughters, Algae born in 1780 or 1781, and Marie born a year or two later to the tragi-comic Duchess of Albany by her lover Prince Ferdinand, Archbishop of Bordeaux. But the history of their son Charles Edward, who was born in 1784 has recently been laid bare.* He was a picaresque, Walter Mitty character brought up by Clementina Albestroff, whom he knew to be his grandmother, and for whom he endeavoured to enlist financial help from various sources and by devious means. It is uncertain whether he actually knew who his father was although our supposition is that he did. He pretended to be the legitimate son of an entirely fictitious Swedish count, and took to himself the title of Count Roehenstart – a portmanteau combination of Rohan and Stuart which at once contradicted his claim. From the age of seventeen to twenty-one he lived in the household of a famous Prussian cavalry commander, Prince Alexander of Württemburg, whose major-domo he became. He was an excellent linguist, speaking and writing perfect French, English and German. He fought in the Napoleonic wars. He was in the United States from 1812 to 1814 in pursuit of money which he believed to be owing to him, but was such a compulsive liar that nothing he wrote can be accepted without question. In the latter year he was in Florence and forced his presence upon the Countess of Albany who was then living there, hoping to obtain from her the Stuart family jewels. The visit was not a success. The Countess resented being referred to as 'grand'maman' and said so in no measured terms. Her dislike of him was recipro-

* George Sherburn – *Roehenstart, A late Stuart Pretender*, 1960

229

cated. Roehenstart wrote, 'I have to agree that she is a woman of great intelligence; but she is malicious and vindictive to a superlative degree.'

Roehenstart's life-long pursuit of phantom fortunes was totally nugatory. He landed up in Scotland, was killed in a coach accident, and buried in the ruined nave of Dunkeld Cathedral in 1854. Although twice married he left no offspring.

The preposterous claims of the brothers 'John Sobieski Stolberg Stuart' (?1795–1872) and 'Charles Edward Stuart' (?1799–1880) to be legitimate grandsons of Prince Charles and the Countess of Albany, were disproved as soon as they were hatched in 1847.* After all, the sole purpose of the Albany's marriage was to produce a son and heir. Had they done so there would have been few valid reasons for concealing him. The brothers pretended that a son was born to the Albanys; and that for fear lest the Hanoverians might have him assassinated, the parents had him immediately adopted by an Admiral John Carter Allen, and baptized Thomas. The only evidence of this story which they could rake up was the fact that the Admiral on his death left a mere £200 to Thomas and £2,200 to a younger son! At all events the 'Sobieski' brothers succeeded in fabricating around them an aura of bogus royalty which attracted the allegiance of a few romantic Jacobites in Victorian times. Sir Charles Petrie is the only reputable historian not totally to reject the possibility, while discounting the probability that their father was an illegitimate son of Prince Charles during his marriage, and that the birth had to be hushed up in order to avoid scandalising his supporters. While Sir Charles was writing *The Jacobite Movement* in 1932 a grandson of 'Charles Edward Stuart', by name Alfred Edward von Platt, was still living.

---

* *Tales of the Century* by the two brothers was refuted by Professor George Skene in the *Quarterly Review* of June 1847. As early as 1829 Sir Walter Scott pronounced the brothers' alleged discovery of a manuscript entitled *Vestiarium Scotiae*, to be fraudulent.

BIBLIOGRAPHY

Those entries marked with an asterisk (*) are articles; those marked with a dagger (†) are manuscripts.

GENERAL

*Anon, 'The Stuarts in Italy', *Quarterly Review*, Vol. 107, 1846
Arnold, Ralph, *Northern Lights, The Story of Lord Derwentwater*, 1959
Ashley, Maurice, *The Stuarts in Love*, 1963
Bloch, Marc, *The Royal Touch*, 1973
Bolingbroke, Henry, Viscount, *A Letter to Sir William Windham*, 1717
Boswell, James, *A Tour in the Hebrides with Dr. Johnson in 1773*
Carlyle, R. W. and A. J., *A History of Medieval Political Theory*, vol. 1, 1903
Charteris, Evan, *William Augustus, Duke of Cumberland: Early Life*, 1913.
Crawfurd, Raymond, *The King's Evil*, 1911
Dickinson, H. T., *Bolingbroke*, 1970
Edwards, William, *Notes on British History*, 1923.
Figgis, John Neville, *The Divine Right of Kings*, 1922.
Green, David, *Queen Anne*, 1970
Jones, G. H., *The Main Stream of Jacobitism*, 1954
Kenyon, J. P., *The Stuarts*, 1958
Krammick, Isaac, *Bolingbroke and His Circle*, 1968
Kroll, Maria (editor and translator), *Letters from Liselotte* (Duchesse d'Orleans), 1970
Luddy, J. Ailbe, *The Real Rancé*, 1931
Luttrell, Narcissus, *A Brief Historicall Relation of State Affairs*, Vols. 4 and 5 (1690–1702)
Macpherson, James, *Original Papers, containing the Secret History of Great Britain, etc.*, 1775
Macky, John, *Memoirs of Secret Services of, during the reigns of King William, Queen Anne and King George I*, 1733
*Oman, Carola, 'The Exiled Stuarts in Rome', *Parsons Journal*, Vol. 9, Nos. 53 and 54, 1961–2
Petrie, Sir Charles, *The Jacobite Movement*, 1959

Prebble, John, *The Highland Clearances*, 1963
Ruvigny and Raineval, Marquis of, *The Jacobite Peerage*, 1904
Skeet, F. J. A., *Stuart Papers, Pictures, Relics, etc., in the Widdrington Collection*, 1930
Stuart Papers to 1719 from Windsor Castle, Royal Historical MSS. Commission, (seven vols), 1902–1923
Stuart, John Sobieski and Charles Edward, *Tales of the Century*, 1847
Tayler, A. and H., Introduction to *The Stuart Papers at Windsor Castle*, 1939
Tayler, H. (editor), *Jacobite Miscellany*, (eight original papers on the Rising of 1745–1746, including Lord Elcho's Private Diary), Roxburghe Club, 1948
Walcott, Robert, *English Politics in the Early Eighteenth Century*, 1956
Walpole, Horace, *Correspondence*

JAMES II
Acton, Lord, *Lectures on Modern History*, 1906
Ailesbury, Thomas Bruce, 2nd Earl of, *Memoirs*, Roxburghe Club, (2 Vols), 1890
*Algar, J. C. 'Posthumous Vicissitudes of James II', *Nineteenth-Century Review*, 1898
*Ashley, Maurice, 'Is there a case for James II?', *History Today*, 1963
Belloc, Hilaire, *James The Second*, 1928
Berwick, 1st Duke of, *Memoirs*, (2 vols.), 1779
*Brown, W. E. 'A Plea for James II', *Contemporary Review*, October 1925
Burnet, Bishop Gilbert, *History of My Own Time*, 1723–34
Clarendon, Henry Hyde, 2nd Earl of, *Diary for Years 1687–1690*, 1765
Clarendon, Henry Hyde, 2nd Earl of, *Correspondence*, Vol. 11, 1828
Clarke, J. S. (editor), *Life of James II*, (2 vols), 1816.
Dalrymple, Sir John, *Memoirs*, Vols. II and III, 1773
Dangeau, Philippe, Marquis de, *Journal de, 1684–1720* (19 Vols), 1817.
Davies, Godfrey (editor), *Papers of Devotion of James II*, Roxburghe Club, 1925
†Ellis, Henry J., *Correspondence* in MSS, B.M. Add. 36653, c. 1820
Evelyn, John, *Dairy, 1685–1689*
Fea, Allan, *James II and His Wives*, 1908
Gramont, Philibert Comte de, *Memoirs of the Court of Charles II*, (edited by Anthony Hamilton), 1846
Grew, E. and M., *The English Court in Exile; James II at St. Germain*, 1911
†*Inventory* of James II's goods taken in 1688, in MSS, Harleian MSS, 1890
James II, King, *Memoirs, or Life Writ with his own Hand, 1660–1698*, (see Clarke, J. S., editor)
Jesse, J. Heneage, *Court of England under the Stuarts*, Vol. III, 1856
King, Dr William, *Anecdotes of His Own Time*, 1818
La Fayette, Madame Marie-Madeleine de, *Mémoires de la Cour de France en 1688 et 1689*, 1890
Macaulay, T. B., *History of England*, 1849–61
Pepys, Samuel, *Diary, 1659–69*
Reresby, Sir John, *Travels and Memoirs (1685–1689)*, 1734

Saint-Simon, Louis, Duc de, *Mémoires*, Pléiade edition, Vols IX and XII, 1886
Sévigné, Marie, Marquise de, *Letters de*, Pléiade edition, 1881
Schimmelpenninck, Mary Anne, *A Tour to Alet and La Grande Chartreuse by Dom Claude Lancelot*, 2 Vols, 1816
Somers Tracts, Vols IX–XI, 1823
Turner, F. C., *James II*, 1948

QUEEN MARY BEATRICE

Bevan, Bryan, *I was James II's Queen*, 1963
Campana di Cavelli, Marchesa (Emily Rowles), *Les Derniers Stuarts à Saint-Germain-en-Laye*, 2 Vols., 1856
Fuller, William, Gent, *A Full Demonstration that the Pretended Prince of Wales was the Son of Mary Grey* (tract), 1702
Haile, Martin, *Mary of Modena*, 1905
Hopkirk, Mary, *Queen over the Water*, 1953
Jesse, J. Heneage, *Court of England under the Stuarts*, Vol. III, 1856
*Kenyon, J. P., 'Birth of the Old Pretender', *History Today*, June 1963
Kroll, Maria (editor and translator), *Letters from Liselotte* (Duchesse d'Orleans), 1970
Madan, Falconer (editor), *Stuart Papers, relating chiefly to Mary of Modena and the exiled court of James II*, 2 Vols., Roxburghe Club, 1889
Oman, Carola, *Mary of Modena*, 1962
Riva, Francesco, *Account of the Queen's Escape to France by the Keeper of her Wardrobe*, 1689
Strickland, Agnes, *Lives of the Queens of England*, 1846
Tracts (various) on the Pretender's Birth (bound together), 1702–14

PRINCE JAMES EDWARD

Bevan, Bryan, *King James III of England*, 1967
Brosses, Président Charles de, *Lettres sur l'Italie*, 1740
Calendar of Stuart Papers at Windsor Castle, Vols. I–VII, 1897–1923
Cowper, Mary, Countess, *Diary*, 1714–20
†*Carte MSS*, Bodleian Library, Oxford
Dennistoun, James, *Memoirs of Sir Robert Strange and Andrew Lumisden*, (2 Vols.), 1855
Dickson, W. K. (editor), *The Jacobite Attempt of 1719* from letters of the 2nd Duke of Ormonde, 1895
Doran, John, *'Mann' and Manners at the Court of Florence*, (2 Vols.), 1876
*Erskine, Hon. Stuart, 'The Earl of Mar's Legacies', *Scottish History Society*, Vol. XXVI, 1896
Haile, Martin, *The Old Chevalier*, 1907
Jesse, J. Heneage, *Memoirs of the Pretenders and their Adherents*, 1845
Lewis, Lesley, *Connoisseurs and Secret Agents in Eighteenth Century Rome*, 1961
Lockhart, George of Carnwath, *Memoirs Concerning the Affairs of Scotland*, 1714
Middleton, Dorothy, *Life of Charles 2nd Earl of Middleton (1650–1719)*, 1957

Miller, Peggy, *James Edward Stuart*, 1971
†Nairne, David, *Manuscripts of*, Bodleian Library, Oxford
*Petrie, Sir Charles, 'The Duke of Mar in Exile 1716–32', Royal Historical Society, Vol. 4, xx, 1937
Petrie, Sir Charles, *The Marshal Duke of Berwick*, 1953
Porcelli, Baron, *The White Cockade*, 1949
†*Rawlinson MSS*, Bodleian Library, Oxford
Shield, A. and Lang, Andrew, *The King Over the Water*, 1907
Sinclair, John, Master of, *Memoirs of the Insurrection in Scotland in 1715*, 1858
Sinclair-Stevenson, Christopher, *Inglorious Rebellion*, 1971
Spurr and Swift, *Several Declarations concerning the Birth of the Prince of Wales*, 1927
†*Stowe MSS*, British Museum
Steele, Richard, *Letter of the Earl of Mar*, 1715
Tayler, Alistair and Tayler, Henrietta, *The Old Chevalier*, 1934
*Tayler, Henrietta, *Jacobite Court at Rome in 1719*, Royal Historical Society, Vol. 4, xx, 1937
Terry, C. S., *The Chevalier de St. George*, 1901
Thornton, Percy, *Stuart Dynasty*, 1890
Vaughan, Herbert M., *The Last of the Royal Stuarts*, 1906
†'John Walton' (Baron Philip von Stosch), *Letters* in Public Record Office
Wolfe, Henry, 'Odd Bits of History (for residence in Bar-le-Duc), British Museum

PRINCESS MARIA CLEMENTINA

Gilbert, Sir J. T., *Narratives of the Detention, Liberation and Marriage of Maria Clementina Stuart*, 1894
*Law, Hugh, 'The Marriage of James III', *Dublin Review*, January and April 1928
Miller, Peggy, *A Wife for the Pretender*, 1965

PRINCE CHARLES EDWARD

Anon, *Istoria di S.A.R. Il Principe Carlo Odoardo Stuart di Galles*, 1760
Atholl, 7th Duke of, *Chronicles of the Atholl and Tullibardine Families*, Vol. III, 1908
d'Argenson, Marquis, *Journal et Mémoires, 1747–9*, 1859
Blaikie, W. B., *Itinerary of Prince Charles Edward Stuart from his landing in Scotland July 1745 to his departure in September 1746*, 1897
*Blaikie, W. B. 'Origins of the Forty-Five', *Scottish Historical Society*, 1909 and 1915
Cameron, Archibald, *Two Accounts of the Escape of Charles Edward* (with twelve letters from Lord George Murray to Andrew Lumisden), 1951
*Cordara, Padre G. C. (Conte di Calamandrana), 'Prince Charles's Escape from Rome to Paris in 1744', (written in 1751), Scottish Historical Society, 1926
Daiches, David, *Charles Edward Stuart*, 1973
Drummond, Norrie W., *Life and Adventures of Charles Edward*, 4 Vols., *c.* 1900
Duke, Winifred, *Lord George Murray and the Forty-Five*, 1927

Duke, Winifred, *Prince Charles Edward and the Forty-Five*, 1938

Eardley-Simpson, Llewellyn, *Derby and the Forty-Five*, 1935

Elcho, Lord, *A Short Account of Affairs in Scotland 1744–6*, (edited by E. Charteris), 1907

Ewald, A. C., *Life and Times of Prince Charles Stuart*, 2 Vols., 1875

Forbes, J. Macbeth, *Jacobite Gleanings*, 1903

*Forbes, Bishop Robert, *The Lyon in Mourning*, Scottish Historical Society, Vols. XX, XXI and XXII, 1895–6

Goyden, A. G., *Charles Prince Regent*, 1954

Griffiths, Ralph, *Ascanius or the Young Adventurer*, 1802

*Hamilton, Marion F. 'The Loch Arkaig Treasure', *Scottish Historical Society, Miscellany*, VII, 1941

Johnstone, Chevalier James, *Memoirs of the Rebellion in 1745 and 1746*, 1822

*Keith, George, 10th Earl Marischal, 'Two Fragments of Autobiography', (edited by J. Y. T. Greig), *Scottish Historical Society Miscellany* VI, 1933

Klose, C. L., *Memoirs of Prince Charles Stewart*, 2 Vols. 1846

Lang, Andrew, *Pickle the Spy*, 1897

Macdonald, Ranald of Clanranald, 'Account of Proceedings from Prince Charles's Landing to Prestonpans', *Scottish Historical Society Miscellany*, IX, (edited by Donald Nicholas), 1958

Mackenzie, Compton, *Prince Charlie*, 1932

Mackenzie, Compton, *Prince Charlie and his ladies*, 1934

Mahon, Viscount, 5th Earl Stanhope, *History of England*, 1936

Mahon, Viscount, 5th Earl Stanhope, (editor), *The Decline of the Last Stuarts; Extracts from Despatches*, Roxburghe Club, 1843

Maxwell, James of Kirkconnell, *Narrative of Prince Charles's Expedition to Scotland (c. 1760)*, for Maitland Club, 1841

Murray, John of Broughton, 'Memorials', (edited by Fitzroy Bell), *Scottish Historical Society*, XXVII, 1898

Nicholas, Donald, *The Young Adventurer*, 1949

†Nicholas, Donald, *Prince Charlie's Secretary, Sir John Murray of Broughton* (unpublished)

Nobili-Vitelleschi, Marchesa, *A Court in Exile*, (2 Vols.), 1903

Oman, Carola, *Prince Charles Edward*, 1935

O'Neil, Captain, *A Narrative of the Wanderings of Prince Charles Edward*, 1746

O'Sullivan, Sir John W., *Journal of the 1745 Campaign and After*, (edited by A. and H. Tayler), 1938

*Petrie, Sir Charles, 'The Elibank Plot 1752–3', Royal Historical Society, 4th Series, Vol. XIV, 1931

de Polnay, Peter, *Death of a Legend*, 1952

Scott, Sir Walter, *Introduction to 'Redgauntlet'*, 1832

*Seton, Sir Bruce, 'The Prisoners of the Forty-Five', Scottish Historical Society, 3rd Series.

Stewart, H. C. (editor), *The Exiled Stewarts in Italy 1717–1807*, Scottish Historical Society Miscellany, VII, 1941

Terry, C. S., *Life of the Young Pretender and the Rising of the Forty-Five*, 1900
Tayler, Henrietta (editor), *The History of the Rebellion in 1745–6*, Roxburghe Club, 1944
Tomasson, Katherine, *The Jacobite General*, 1958
Vestiarium Scoticum, etc., review in *The Quarterly Review*, Vol. 81, 1847
Wilkinson, Clennell, *Bonnie Prince Charles*, 1932
Wraxall, Sir William, *Historical and Posthumous Memoirs*, 1779

CHARLOTTE DUCHESS OF ALBANY

Albany, Charlotte Duchess of, *Mémoire addressed to King Louis XV*, 1774
Buchan, Susan, *Funeral March of a Marionette, Charlotte of Albany*, 1935
ᵗ Sherburn, George, *Roehenstart, A Late Stuart Pretender*, 1960
Skeet, F. A., *H.R.H. Charlotte Stuart Duchess of Albany*, 1932
Tayler, Henrietta, *Prince Charlie's Daughter*, 1950
Tayler, Henrietta, *Documents relating to Prince Charles Edward's Grandson*, Scottish Historical Society Miscellany, VIII, 1951

CARDINAL DUKE HENRY OF YORK

†*A Diary of the Sacred Functions and of the Illustrious Acts of His Royal Highness and Eminence the Lord Cardinal Duke of York, c. 1758–1805* (among the documents of Frascati now in the Vatican Library)
*Ademollo, A. 'Il Diario del Cardinale Duca di York', *Nuova Antologia XV*, 2nd series, 1 July 1880
Anon, 'The Stuarts in Italy', *Quarterly Review*, Vol. 107, December 1846
*Artaud, A. F. de Montor, 'Storia di Pio VII', *Pragmologia Cattolica*, Tom.29.30, Ch. 55 (for the Cardinal's published will in entirety), 1837
Boigne, Comtesse de, *Récits d'une Tante*, Vol. 1, 1907
†Borgia, Cardinal Stefano, *Letters from to Sir J. C. Hippisley, Bt.*, 1799–1800
Cloncurry, Lord, *Personal Recollections of Life and Times of*, 1850
Consalvi, Cardinal Ercole, *Mémoires de*, 1864
Diario per l'anno 1788 di Enrico Cardinale di Yorck, 1876
Enciclopedia Italiano, entry in
Forsyth, Joseph, *Remarks on Antiquities, etc. in Italy in the years 1802 and 1803*, 1825
Fothergill, Brian, *The Cardinal King*, 1958
Goranni, Giuseppe, *Mémoires Secrets et Critiques des Cours, etc, de l'Italie*, 1973
Haynes, Renée, *Philosopher King: Pope Benedict XIV*, 1970
Heeckeren, E de, *Lettres de Bênoit XIV au Cardinal de Tencin*, 1912
Historic Manuscripts Commission Report X, Part VI, p. 249 (Braye), 1887
Kelly, Bernard W., *Life of Henry Benedict Stuart*, 1899
Knight, Cornelia, *Autobiography*, Vol. 1, 1861
Montini, Renzo U., *Il Cardinale Duca di York*, 1955
*Munro, Ion, 'Books and Henry Stuart, Duke of York', *Book Handbook*, Vol. II, No. 4, 1951–2.

Perrero, A. D., 'Gli Ultimi Stuardi e V. Alfieri', *Rivista Europea*, Vol. XII, p. 683, 1881
*Seton, W. W. (editor), 'Some Unpublished Letters of the Cardinal Duke of York, 1767', *Scottish Historical Rev.*, XVI, April 1919
*Seton, W. W., 'Relations of Henry Cardinal York with the British Government', Royal Historical Society, Series 4, Vol. II, 1929
Shield, Alice, *Henry Stuart Cardinal of York and His Times*, 1908
Vaughan, Herbert M., *The Last of the Royal Stuarts*, 1906
Walpole, Horace, *Letters to the Countess of Upper Ossory*, publ 1903
Wiseman, Cardinal, *Recollections of the Last Four Popes*, 1858

PRINCESS LOUISE, COUNTESS OF ALBANY

†Albany, Countess of, *Souvenirs de Voyage en Angleterre*, 1791 (MSS, Fabre Museum, Montpellier)
Alfieri, Vittorio, *Vita di Vittorio Alfieri da Asti scritta da esso*, 1810
d'Azeglio, Massimo, *I Miei Ricordi*, Ch. IV, 1867
Bonstetten, Charles Victor de, *Souvenirs*, 1831
Charvet, G., *Une Correspondence Inédite de la Comtesse d'Albanie*, 1878
Chateaubriand, F. R., *Mémoires d'Outre Tombe*, 1849–50
Copping, Edward, *Alfieri*, 1857
Courier, P. L., *Conversations chez la Comtesse d'Albany à Naples le 2 Mars*, 1812
Crosland, Margaret, *Louise of Stolberg, Countess of Albany*, 1962
Herking, Marie-L, *Charles Victor de Bonstetten*, 1921
Holland, Elizabeth Lady, *Journals of, 1791–1811*, Vol. I, 1793–6
Lang, André, *Une Vie d'Orages: Germaine de Staël*, 1958
Lee, Vernon, *The Countess of Albany*, 1884
Matthews, Henry, *The Diary of an Invalid*, 1817
Maurois, André, *Trois Portraits de Femmes*, 1967
Mitchiner, Margaret, *No Crown for the Queen*, 1937
Morgan, Lady, *Memoirs*, 1819
Pélissier, Léon-G, *Lettres et Écrits divers de la Comtesse d'Albany*, 1901
Pélissier, Léon-G, *Le Portefeuille de la Comtesse d'Albany*, 1902
Pélissier, Léon-G, *Lettres Inédites de la Comtesse d'Albany à ses Amis de Sienne*, Vols. I and II, 1904
Pélissier, Léon-G, *Lettres Inédites de la Comtesse d'Albany à Alessandro Cerretani*, Vol. III, 1915
Pellegrini, Carlo, *La Contessa d'Albany e il Salotto del Lungarno*, 1951
Sainte-Beuve, C. A., 'Sismondi' from *Nouveaux Lundis*, VI, 1866
Sismondi, J. C. L. de, *Fragments de son Journal*, 1857
Taillandier, Saint-René (editor), *Lettres de Sismondi, Bonstetten, Madame de Staël, etc.*, 1863
*Taillandier, Saint-René, 'La Comtesse d'Albany', *Revue des Deux Mondes*, 1861
Thomas, Louis-J, *Une Femme, son Roi, son Poète et son Peintre*, 1928
Vaughan, Herbert M., *The Last Stuart Queen*, 1910
Nobili-Vitelleschi, Marchesa, *A Court in Exile*, (2 Vols.), 1903

INDEX

DATE DUE